Helen Edwards trained as a nurse, and worked in the NHS for several years, mainly in operating theatres. She then became a district nurse, before moving to Australia where she worked in operating theatres, casualty and a coronary care unit. On her return to the UK she was employed at the Nuffield Hospital in Newcastle, followed by a position in occupational health nursing. Forced to retire due to back problems, she qualified as a hypnotherapist and psychotherapist. She is married to Dennis Edwards and lives in Northumberland.

Jenny Lee Smith is perhaps best known for winning the very first Women's British Open Golf Championship in 1976. Internationally, she played for England in the 1975 European Team Championships, was a member of the British Curtis Cup team in 1974 and 1976, and played for Great Britain and Ireland in the Espirito Santo Trophy in 1976. She turned professional in 1977 and gained her player's card to compete on the American Ladies Professional Golf Association tour that year. In 1979 Jenny was a founder member of the European Women's Professional Golf Association going on to win twelve tour events. She was the highest-earning woman golfer on the European tour in 1981 and 1982 and was awarded the Order of Merit each time. Jenny now lives in Kent with her husband Sam Lucas, daughter Katie and sons Ben and Josh.

My Secret Sister

Helen Edwards
&
Jenny Lee Smith

With Jacquie Buttriss

PAN BOOKS

First published 2013 by Pan Books
an imprint of Pan Macmillan
20 New Wharf Road, London N1 9RR
Associated companies throughout the world
www.panmacmillan.com

ISBN 978-1-4472-2887-5

25 27 29 28 26 24

A CIP catalogue record for this book is available from
the British Library.

Typeset by Ellipsis Digital Limited, Glasgow
Printed and bound by CPI Group (UK) Ltd, Croydon, CR0 4YY

Visit **www.panmacmillan.com** to read more about all our books
and to buy them. You will also find features, author interviews and
news of any author events, and you can sign up for e-newsletters
so that you're always first to hear about our new releases.

Helen

for my very dear husband Dennis and my
much-loved son and daughter

Jenny

for my dearest husband Sam and my adored
daughter and sons, Katie, Ben and Josh

CONTENTS

PROLOGUE

Jenny

This could be the most important email I ever send. I go over it again, one last time. My finger hovers over the mouse. I hold my breath . . . Click!

'Haaa!' It's gone.

Immediately I panic. It's taken so many years to reach this point. So much heartache and rejection. I reread it once more. Oh no – I should have said I had a happy childhood. Why didn't I tell her that? I don't want her to think I'm jealous.

I check the time – 10.27 p.m. – still afternoon in Texas. I wonder when Helen will look at her emails?

From: jenlucas
To: helen
Sent: Wednesday 11 April 2007, 22:24 +0100
Subject: Mercia Lumsden

Dear Helen,

My name is Jenny Lucas and I was adopted at birth in 1948. After doing a lot of investigation, I believe you are my half-sister. Sorry for the complete shock, but there is no easy way of telling you.

I met Mercia in August 2003, when I was visiting the north-east for a family wedding. She was concerned that if anyone came I was not to say who I was. I have been looking for so very long to find the family that knows nothing about me.

I live in Kent. We moved back from Florida two years ago and now live in Tenterden. I would love to hear from you if you can come through the shock. My telephone number is ——————————.

Jenny

Helen

I open my laptop before I go to bed. In moments, the screen lights up. There is just one email from an unknown contact.

Who's Jen Lucas? Why does the subject line say my mother's name?

I click on the header and begin to read. The first two sentences explode in my head, blasting shrapnel through my past. My eyes widen and my jaw locks. Over and over I read the words: 'I believe you are my half-sister.'

I'm on the edge of the sofa in the semi-darkness; Dennis lies asleep in the bedroom. I begin to shake, slightly at first, and then great tremors start running through me. White noise deafens me as the blood charges through my brain.

I struggle to lower my shoulders and breathe slower, deeper. I read on, but I can't take it in. Is this a scam? I go back to the beginning and reread the whole message. How has this woman traced me? She claims to have visited Mercia, my mother. Can this be true? Why didn't my mother tell me?

I read the email through yet again, aloud this time, as calmly as I can. It sounds genuine. There is a hint of emotion, a deep feeling: 'I have been looking for so very long . . . ' That sounds authentic to me – I can identify with it in a way. This stranger thinks I'm her sister. I've always yearned for a sister. She wants me to call her, but what would I say? How could I begin to tell her?

CHAPTER 1

Helen

A Mystery Year

Fear is my earliest memory. Fear of being out there, alone. It was one of those dark winter evenings; the sleet slanted at me with a wind cold enough to sting my skin. I was sitting in my hand-me-down pram, strapped in with no blankets – just a loose waterproof cover on which a puddle had formed and was frosting over. I tried to lean forward and look out. The cover slipped and the icy water trickled down onto my bare legs. My damp clothes hung heavy around me and my bonnet's fur trim, bedraggled in the sleet, clung to my cheeks like icy fingers. I felt numb, abandoned.

I yearned for her to come. I whimpered and cried as loud as I could, my frozen cheeks smarting from the warmth of my tears. Shadows loomed. A lone tree bent and clattered in the wind, an ogre's arms stretching out to steal me away. I screamed. I don't know how long I cried for. I stared at the house and willed her to come, to rescue me. I craned forward as far as I could, my eyes fixed on the front door and the warm glow through the window. But no one looked out. No one came. I wailed. *Why doesn't she come and help me? Why doesn't she come?*

Finally, the door opened and yellow light spilled out across the wet path. But she just stood there, my mother, without even glancing in my direction. She stood on the front step, laughing and joking with my grandma inside, pulling her coat together in the arctic wind. They talked and talked until at last she shrugged, tied on her head scarf and ran down the path towards me. She took hold of the pram, her eyes fixed ahead, and pushed it at a run against the wind.

Why did she leave me outside for so long alone in the cold night? You don't leave a baby, a toddler, out like that uncovered at that time of year, do you? I don't think she even noticed what state I was in.

Years later, my husband said: 'You can't possibly remember all that! Nobody can remember before they were three.'

But I do. I must have been about eighteen months or so. I can still feel the fear now. My memory of that evening is indelible, locked inside. It's a feeling that echoed throughout my childhood. It has haunted me down all the years.

The first year of my life is missing – it's a mystery. Well, that's what an older cousin told me. Some time before my birth in April 1950, my mother, Mercia, left Seghill without a word – left the mining village, the bustle of the close-knit family and everything she knew.

'Mercia disappeared,' explained Alice. 'All of a sudden she wasn't there any more. She was gone. Nobody knew where she was. And then, a year or so later, she came back with you and married to Tommy. No explanation.' Of course, Alice was a child when that happened, so maybe she wasn't told the real story.

My mother had been married before, in 1939: 'A terrible

man, he was, mind,' she told me. 'He used to beat me and never gave me enough housekeeping money.'

Her husband had joined up and gone to war, so she had gone back to live with Grandma. My half-brother George was born in 1940. Not long after that his father was captured and spent the rest of the war in a German prison camp. My mother left George with Grandma while she went to work twelve-hour night-shifts doing war-work at Vickers munitions factory on Scotswood Road in Newcastle, by the river.

They were dangerous times, with nightly bombings as Luftwaffe pilots strafed the ship yards and factories along the banks of the Tyne. I recently found out that during this time she had an affair with an American airman, among others. It would be harsh to blame her, really. Her husband was a prisoner of war. Like many others, she risked her own life every night for the war effort – I suppose they all had to find some escape from the drudgery, fear and chaos of those years.

When I was a child I asked my mother how she had met Tommy. She paused for a moment.

'It was in Newcastle. I was working in Maynards, the tobacconist,' she told me. 'He came in for some cigarettes one day in his RAF uniform. He came back again the next day, and every day after that. He was a bonny lad, mind. Ciggies were rationed in those days, so I used to hide some extra under the counter for him.'

The address on my birth certificate is in Benwell, a notorious area of Newcastle. It's only twenty minutes' drive from Seghill, but in those days that was an hour-and-a-half's bus-ride away – another country. I drove there recently and found the street in the west of the city, near the Tyne. I looked at that house for a long time – an anonymous brick building divided into flats. I wanted to explore the area, but it was a forbidding place – one of the roughest parts of Newcastle, with the spectre of hoodied gangs round every corner and a high crime rate. I felt safer in the car, so I sat there and just stared.

I asked my mother about my birth once, when I was growing up.

'Tommy was at work when I went into labour. It was just me and George, so I sent him to call the midwife and gave him ninepence (4p) to go to the pictures. When he came back, there you were.' George was ten years old then. I never thought to ask him about it. 'What did I look like?' I asked her another time, hoping to provoke some sort of reaction, if only nostalgia. That would be something.

'You were little, six pounds, with blonde hair.' Her face was fixed in neutral and her gaze was turned away from me.

Sitting in the car, I tried to imagine my thirty-year-old mother seeing the newborn me for the first time, perhaps studying my face, gently stroking my fingers. Surely she would have held me then? Cradled me in her arms? Maybe there was a whisper of a smile on her lips? Wouldn't you think so? I craved a smile from my mother every day of my childhood, but I yearned in vain. I tried so hard to earn just one smile, but it was never any use. I shuddered as I sat gazing at my very first home, surrounded by seedy slums. I don't suppose it was such a bad area back in those days; perhaps even faintly respectable.

It was many years after my childhood before I began to discover some of what had happened in that missing year. My family guarded myriad secrets and lies; it was all a tangled web of deceit. Some of it I have recently unravelled; other strands I will never know – they are locked away for ever. My mother, the keeper of the keys, took them with her when she died, and her generation have all gone too, taking any remaining secrets with them to their graves.

What I do know is that when I was a year old or so, we moved back to Seghill, the Northumberland pit village where my mother had grown up in a large mining family. Most of the men in Seghill were miners, and all the women knew each other and helped one another. Everyone watched. You couldn't walk along the street in a new coat without the whole village knowing it.

We lived in a plain grey-rendered house with a slate roof on the corner of Barrass Avenue; two up, two down, stained with soot and next to the miners' social club. Downstairs we had the living room and kitchen, always called the scullery in our house. Next to that was a shivery-cold room with a basin and a bath – a luxury in Seghill. But the only toilet was outside at the back, freezing in winter, next to my father's shed. Upstairs were two bedrooms.

Seghill colliery, down the road, dominated the area with its vast buildings and giant machinery reaching to the sky. Wherever you stood in Seghill, the black pit-heaps rose up like mountains to blot out the morning and evening sunlight. They blocked our views of the surrounding farmland too. Some of the older boys used to lay planks up the sides of the heaps to climb up and slide down. Every now and then an accident happened and the horrified adults forbade us from going too close. But soon the planks came out again.

The shrill pit whistle sounded across the village to mark the end of each shift. It was the same whistle that was used to broadcast pit disasters, though I don't remember that happening while I lived there. I watched the men walk past with their long, weary strides, hands and faces as black as night from their day at the coalface. One or two would pause and wave at me in the window, their white teeth bright against the black.

Inside our house we had a huge coal fire, just as everyone had in Seghill, since coal came free from the mine. The wagon would come trundling along the street to unload the sacks of coal, drawn by a great big shire horse with blinkers and feathery ankles, his head hung low. I had to count the sacks as the coalman emptied them into our coal-hole. Sometimes I lost count because I was so busy watching the horse, willing him on. Finally he would oblige with the longest pee I have ever seen pouring endlessly onto the stony road and into the gutter, the steam rising in the winter's chill.

I remember the acrid smell of smoke and the air thick with the coal dust that shrouded the village. It made for a lot of dusting.

Grandma, aunties, uncles and cousins lived all around us. Some of them lived in the same street, others round the corner, but all within a hundred yards. My mother was the ninth of ten children. When she was little, everyone spoiled the baby that came after her, but she rarely had any attention. Even Grandma had little time or energy to lavish on Mercia. She had to fight to be noticed.

The house we lived in was Auntie Minnie's house. I don't know why. It had been rented out, but now it was empty. She lived in another house down that street, so when we unexpectedly turned up in Seghill, Auntie Minnie said, 'You can live in that house.'

My father resented this arrangement. He had to be king of his castle and couldn't bear having to take charity from his wife's family. 'It's all your fault,' he told me on many occasions. 'If it hadn't been for you, we wouldn't be in this mess. But, remember,' he would say, wagging his finger at me, his face reddening, 'I am master in this house. You will do as I say.'

I never dared move. I didn't know why it was my fault, but from my earliest memories I just accepted it.

I slept in with my parents for a long time when I was little. George slept in the other bedroom, the box room. When I was two or three, I remember the joy of tearing into his room early in the morning to jump on him while he was still asleep. He never moaned when I woke him up like that.

'Come on, tiger,' he'd say. Then we would do some tiger-wrestling – his tiger a great deal gentler than mine, of course. Having fun with George was my escape from the vagaries of life with my parents. He was my champion in that house. He always looked out for his 'kid' sister.

After our tussle, George liked to do his exercises, starting with push-ups. He'd lie on his back. 'Come on, kiddo.'

I would stand on the palms of his hands and try to keep my balance as he lifted me up by the strength of his arms and held me there. I felt I was touching the sky when he raised me right up towards the ceiling.

When I was still in my parents' room, I used to be out of bed sleepwalking every night. One day they woke up at three in the morning to find me on the window sill trying to climb out. I was taken off to the doctor.

'There's only one thing for it,' he advised them. 'You'll have to put bars over the window.'

They put bars on all the upstairs windows after that and moved me into George's room. I think my sleepwalking settled down once I was away from my parents. It was fun sharing with my big brother. We used to have riots in there.

George tried many times to protect me, which only made things worse for him as he became the brunt of my father's abuse on those occasions, But his bravery rescued me from some of Tommy's worse excesses. One of these was the cat-o'-nine-tails whip that my father kept hanging on a nail in the scullery. He would often take his anger out on me by thrashing my bare legs with it. That thing scared me rigid, hanging on the wall as an unspoken threat.

One day it disappeared.

As soon as Tommy noticed its absence, he turned on George. 'What have you done with it?' he shouted, the blood rushing to his face.

'What makes you think it's me?' George said, standing as tall as he could.

'I know it's you!' Tommy closed in on him. 'Where is it?'

'I don't know what you're talking about.'

'You stole it, didn't you?' Tommy shrieked, pushing his face up close to George's.

'No I didn't.'

'I know you did. And you'll suffer for it.'

So the interrogation unfolded in front of me. I put my hands over my ears, but I could still hear it all. I was torn between fear of my father and admiration for my big brother, but also anxiety for him, and for me too. They shouted at each other louder and louder, and Tommy dominated the argument.

'You bloody well will tell me!'

'I'm telling you – I didn't steal it.'

Tommy slapped George across the face. 'I'm the master of this house!'

It went on for what seemed like hours, and eventually I tried to get away, but my father saw me and barred my way.

'You needn't think you're going to escape!' He said. 'You're next. When I find that whip, I'll need to make sure it's working.'

I was quaking, but while Tommy tried everything he could to intimidate George, my brother refused to reveal where it was. I was surprised when Tommy finally gave up. Thanks to George, I never saw that instrument of torture again.

On the day of the Queen's coronation when I was three, several of us gathered round to watch it on Uncle Marcus's new TV. It was the first television I had ever seen. It had a tiny screen, but it seemed like magic to me. I think most of the family were there, and we squeezed in around the small room, with all the children sitting on the floor. To start with, I was sitting next to Patricia, who was some kind of second or third cousin (I never knew exactly). She was nearer George's age than mine but I always liked her. Auntie Dorrie beckoned to me. 'Come away, pet,' she said as she moved me across to the other side of the room. I was always being moved about; I never knew why.

George was there too that day, and with so many of us crammed into Uncle Marcus's little cottage, there was a lot of noise. All the adults talked and laughed together as we waited for the procession to begin. It was pouring with rain outside, so there was no parade or street party like some folks had, but we had sandwiches, and someone had made a special cake. I was looking forward to that.

But suddenly there was silence. Someone must have said something. My parents stood up, my father face-to-face with Uncle Marcus. My mother pulled me up and dragged me across the floor, trampling over my cousins, and as she propelled me towards the door, I saw the two men spitting sharp, angry words at each other, though I couldn't make out what they were saying, or perhaps I was too young to understand. As I was pulled out through the door, I caught George's eye and his rueful expression as he stayed on to watch the coronation.

As soon as we arrived home, my father grabbed me by the shoulders and shook me hard, then clipped my head. 'That's a warning to you,' he said. 'You will go straight upstairs and stay there. I don't want to hear another word out of you. Understand?'

'Yes, Daddy.' I answered. I always had to call him Daddy or Dad as he didn't like the Northumberland 'Da'. He was fanatical about using correct grammar and not swearing, though he didn't always stick to it himself.

Upstairs I went, while the whole of Seghill watched the coronation without me. I was upset to be missing the fun and the party, but I didn't understand its significance, and at least I seemed to be out of the danger zone now. I shut myself into my room and lay on my bed with a pillow round my head, trying to block out the angry voices downstairs, which rose to shouts and screams, then other frightening noises and the slamming of doors. I was frightened, alone, and disappointed that this exciting day had been spoilt.

I must have fallen asleep. I was too young to understand any of it, yet this sort of thing happened most days in our house. I was safely out of the way that day, but it wasn't always so. With George out with friends most evenings, I was often alone. My bedroom was not, for me, a safe haven.

CHAPTER 2

Jenny

Bumpy Down the Steps

'Why isn't there a photo of me as a newborn baby?' I asked my mother one day when I was a child. I was looking through my baby album.

'I don't know, pet.' She shrugged.

I turned over a page and found a picture of me at a few months old sitting on Auntie Dorothy's knee. We were all smiles. 'I like this photo, Mam.' I showed it to her. 'But where's Barbara?' Barbara was Auntie Dorothy's own baby, just a month older than me.

My mother looked at the photo. 'Oh, that's when Auntie Dorothy was feeding you. I had no milk,' she explained, 'so she breastfed you for a few weeks. She had plenty of milk, enough for two.'

I didn't realize as a child how unusual that must have been.

Born on 2 December 1948, I was the only child of older parents and the centre of their lives. Sid, aged forty-two, and Connie, forty-four, doted on me so much that they missed no opportunity to provide the very best they could for me. My mother used to tell me a story about the bonnet she crocheted for me when I was a baby to stop my ears from sticking out by holding them tight to my head. I had to wear that bonnet most of the time. One sunny day, my dad wanted to take me out for a walk in my pram.

'Don't forget to put her bonnet on, Sid,' said my mother.

When he brought me back, my dad made a great commotion about my bonnet.

'That thing doesn't fit our Jen at all,' he complained. 'I put it on and tied it like you said, but it kept flopping down over her face every few yards and I had to keep adjusting it. Hundreds of times it was.'

My mother came over to look at me in the pram. 'No wonder, Sid. The poor bairn has the bonnet on back to front!'

We were an ordinary hard-working family, full of love and laughter. Both my parents worked, Dad as a gas showroom manager in Newcastle and Mam as a hairdresser in our home in West Jesmond. It was a working-class area of terraced houses facing each other across cobbled streets with back lanes behind. Very few families had cars, but we had a black Austin 30. It was great, but whenever my dad wanted to turn right, I had to hit behind the place where the indicator hand flapped out. That always made me giggle.

Many of the flats and houses were rented, but most of them were kept clean and well-painted, and some of them had tiny manicured gardens in front. My mam was very proud of her annual display of roses, much admired by our neighbours. Her secret was that she used to dig her customers' hair cuttings into the soil around each rose bush together with the cold tealeaves from the bottom of the teapot.

For years before they had me, Sid and Connie shared a love of golf, so when I was six months old they bought a holiday hut on the edge of Dunstanburgh Castle golf links beside the beach at Embleton. My parents called the hut a bungalow from the start. It was a wooden-framed building perched in the lee of a low cliff, with steps down to the beach on one side and the third green on the other. There was no running water in the bungalow when we first had it, so we had to use a chemical toilet behind a partition. Mam cooked on Calor gas, which fuelled our lights as well. We went down every weekend through the spring and summer months, and on holidays too.

My dad was a practical man, skilled with his hands. He enjoyed woodwork, so he set to every weekend and improved the bungalow, turning the shack into a second home. He added two rooms, doing all the work himself. It was quite a little palace when he'd finished it.

Embleton was and still is an idyllic spot amongst the sand dunes of the North Sea coast. On National Trust land, it was peppered with pill-boxes and concrete bunkers, parts of the wartime defence systems. Landmines had been set at random into the beaches and dunes. When I was very young a band of army conscripts came to dig out all the mines they could find, but for several years we still used to see odd ones uncovered by the spring tides. We learned to walk carefully.

Ours was one of a cluster of bungalows right by the sea with Dunstanburgh Castle rising up eerily in the distance, high on the hill, at one end of the bay. Below us was the most beautiful stretch of sands with a shallow stream running through. Further along the beach towards Newton was a group of flat rocks, the Emblestones, from which the village of Embleton got its name. The golf course ran right round the bay, hugging the beach in its outstretched arms. In all these years it has barely changed – it remains unspoilt to this day.

The golf clubhouse was about half a mile back from the beach. At that time it was a corrugated-iron building, but it has since been replaced by a purpose-built brick bungalow complete with a terrace and bar, a far cry from the glorified shack I remember. This was the nearest access point. We had to park our car by the clubhouse every Friday evening and embark on the tricky walk with bags of shopping and possessions across half a mile of gorse-strewn dunes, up a steep hill and across the links to our bungalow. While I was a small child, my parents had a little wheelbarrow and I can recall my pleasure at being bumped along in the barrow, cushioned by clothing and buffeted by groceries, all the way from our car to the bungalow, my parents beaming at the thought of a relaxing weekend on the beach and a bracing game of golf.

It was a fantastic place – peace on earth – a natural playground and a great environment for children. The older ones looked after the little ones and everyone was friendly. We had a brilliant time, all of us together, carefree, living a healthy outdoors life in all weathers, safe and happy.

There was a little hill, almost a cliff, from our bungalow down about fifteen feet to the beach, with a flight of wooden steps from the top down to the sand. I can remember as a toddler, or perhaps my mother told me, that coming outside to find me one day she saw that I had disappeared from our bit of grass. She looked out and spotted me on the beach below.

'How did our Jen get there?' she asked an older child.

'She went bumpy down the steps.'

I was so determined to join the children playing on the

sand that I'd managed to bump down every step on my bottom.

My parents took turns to play their rounds of golf, so there was always one of them there to watch over me, usually from a distance, as I played with the others, and then to welcome me back with loving hugs and a hot meal of my favourite foods.

When I was three years old, my dad cut some old wooden golf clubs down to a size I could use and showed me how to hold them. I tried not to get my hands in a muddle. He taught me how to hit a ball and we practised together on the rough grass behind our bungalow. Obviously I couldn't play golf yet – I couldn't hit the ball very far – but my father would take me onto the course at night, after all the serious golfers had gone home and practise hitting golf balls while I watched. Then he'd let me hit them as well, with my special cut-down clubs. I was very proud of them. My dad loved having me with him, and I adored him.

From about this age, in our weekday home at West Jesmond, I started to develop some very chesty coughs in the wintertime. I can remember lying in bed at night listening to my own rasping breath. Every night my mother lit a vaporizer candle to moisten the air in my bedroom and soothe my breathing, but some nights I just coughed and coughed. She used to make little balls of butter rolled in sugar for me to suck on when the cough was really bad, but they didn't always help.

Eventually, Mam took me to the doctor's. 'There's a new drug called penicillin,' he said. 'I think we should give her some injections of it to stop any chest infections.'

So my godmother, Auntie Connie, who was a health visitor,

came along to give me these injections in my bottom every day. The trouble was that she wasn't at all gentle and they really hurt. After a few days of this, when she arrived and took down my pants I backed up into the corner of my room with my hands covering my bare bottom-cheeks and wailed, 'No, *Mammy. Not today, please.*' This happened every time amid floods of tears until eventually the deed was done.

It was only much later, when my mother herself had to have a series of injections given by Auntie Connie, that she turned to my dad and said, 'No wonder the bairn didn't like them!'

When I was three and a half I was taken by my mother to begin my first day at nursery school. It was a small, private nursery in Newcastle, part of Church High School for girls. Mam held my hand as we walked up the path that first morning – I remember feeling rather apprehensive, though I couldn't explain it. She gave my hand a squeeze as we got closer, which transferred a bit of her strength to me. I tried to look cheerful and keep the tears at bay.

'Be a good girl, pet,' my mother said to me as we approached the door. 'I want you to be a very good girl. You'll have a lovely time playing in the sandpit and with the little cookery things. Try not to be shy,' she advised.

'Yes, Mammy.'

'You have to be a good girl and not cry while you're here.'

I nodded and bit my lip.

'If you try hard and you're very good, mind, they will let you go on to the next class. Church High is a lovely school where they will teach you to have good manners and help you to gain confidence so that you'll not be frightened to speak to anybody. Your dad and I would like you to stay there, so do your best, pet.'

Miss Brewis, the nursery class teacher, was a lovely woman. A homely sort, but very correct. She wasn't married and had no children of her own, yet she was full of cuddles for us all. If a child cried or fell over, she would sit them on her ample knee and soothe them.

'Now, now, don't worry, pet. It will be all right,' she'd say, and it always was. She oozed sympathy and warmth. I'm sure she loved every one of us.

Obedient to my mother, I didn't let anyone see when a tear fell that first day. I remember even then feeling a quiet determination, a strong sense of working towards something. I was learning how to get on and succeed at what I set my mind to. Of course I couldn't foresee then how this attitude, along with the support of my parents, would open opportunities for me, nor the successes I would find in my future career. But there were a few obstacles to navigate along the way first.

CHAPTER 3

Helen

Grandma

In the early fifties, most of the men in Seghill worked down the mine, and most of the women and children walked everywhere – to school, to the shop, to church. In the summer, the whole of our extended family went for walks together down the country lanes on Sunday evenings, and occasionally in a straggly column down to Seaton Sluice beach for the whole day, where we children ran wild till it was dark and then all walked home together again.

The pit was easy to reach on foot or by bike. Most of the men would cycle around wearing caps, bicycle clips on their trousers, and pipes hanging out of their mouths. There were usually a lot of old pushbikes standing outside the working men's club of an evening, but hardly anyone had a car in those days.

My father Tommy had come from a self-made family who had earned plenty of money from their building business, and he had his own Bullnose Morris car before the war until his father's bankruptcy forced him to sell it. At that point Tommy split with his family and joined the RAF as a fitter. By now he worked as a brick-lorry driver, which was better paid and enabled him to save up enough to buy his own car again. I remember it well. It was a 1936 Singer Bantam. He polished it every Sunday and sometimes we would go out for a drive. It only had a small engine, so my mother and I had to get out at the bottom of a hill and walk all the way up while my father drove up and waited for us at the top.

One Sunday, my father came in from working in his shed. George and I were sitting at the table in the living room when we heard our parents talking in the scullery and then start an argument, their voices rising.

'You spend all your time in that shed!' shouted my mother. 'Can you not take me out for a drive?'

'Oh, stop your nagging! It's my day off and I don't feel like driving.'

'Tommy, I work my fingers to the bone for you. I've never worked so hard in my life till I met you.'

'I drive all day every day at work. I'm not driving today.'

'That's right, just think of yourself, as usual.'

The voices rose, punctuated by the sounds of pots and pans being crashed down on the gas stove. George and I looked at each other in silent beseeching, but we knew it had already escalated too far. Their noise boomed through the house and the familiar, sick feeling of fear gripped my stomach. We both knew we would be next in line.

'You're the selfish one,' yelled my father. 'All you want to do is to sit in my car and be driven around when you feel like it!'

'No chance of that, man!' Her shout was now a shriek. 'I'm just a skivvy as far as you're concerned.'

'That's all you're fit for. You're just a pit yacker!' he gloated.

She picked up a pan of potatoes from the stove. 'And this

is all you're fit for!' With a mighty heave, she threw it across the kitchen at him. It missed. The pan and its contents hit open the door to the living room and landed with a clatter all over the floor between the two rooms.

'Bloody hell, woman,' he bellowed. 'What on earth are you doing?' He stepped towards her. 'Clean that up *now*!'

She turned away. 'Go to hell!' she retorted and made a move to walk out of the room.

'Oh no you don't,' Tommy yelled, grabbing her arm and pushing his face into hers. He lowered his voice to a cold bark. 'I said *clean it up*!'

'I will not!' she shouted.

He gave her a hard slap across her face. She reeled backwards.

'*Get out of here,*' he bawled. '*NOW!* Or I will not be responsible for my actions.'

She spat at him as she stomped out of the room, marched past us and flew upstairs.

Now I was trembling, and George and I exchanged a fearful glance. We knew it was our turn. I tried to tidy away my colouring book and crayons, but it was no use.

Tommy stormed into the living room and with one swipe sent them flying. '*You!*' He pointed at me. 'Get in the scullery and clean up that mess!' He turned to George. 'You too!'

I shrunk back, frozen with fear. This angered him even more.

'I said, clean up that mess *now*, madam!'

I slid down from my chair and tried to squeeze past him, careful not to stray too close. As I passed, he turned and whacked a heavy blow across my back, so hard that it sent me to my knees.

'Don't hit her,' shouted George. 'She hasn't done anything!'

Tommy grabbed George by the shoulder and dragged him out to the scullery. 'Get it cleaned up, both of you. What I say goes in this house.' He turned. 'If it wasn't for *her*,' he pointed at me with a shaking fist, 'this wouldn't have happened.' He about-turned, marched through the living room and out of the front door, slamming it behind him.

George and I exchanged weary looks and set to. Well, he did most of it and I helped him, as much as a four-year-old could. We cleaned up the mess of the boiled potatoes all over the walls, the door and the floor, then mopped up the water. All the while, Mercia was upstairs, crying in great, noisy sobs.

With Tommy gone, our mother in a state upstairs and our lunch spoiled, George and I toasted some bread on the fire with a toasting fork and sat, the two of us, emotionally drained, to eat our toast in silence. It was just an ordinary winter Sunday in our house.

Mercia eventually came downstairs. By this time, George had gone out to see his friends and I was alone in the living room. She slumped down at the table, white-faced and red-eyed.

It seemed to be up to me to try to make her feel better. 'Are you all right, Mam?'

Silent at first, she then glared at me as if I were an alien. 'I suppose you think you're better than me because you cleaned up the kitchen?'

'No I don't. Dad told me I had to do it.'

'Aye,' she sneered. 'Everybody has to jump when the master speaks, don't they?'

I didn't reply.

'You have no idea what a terrible life I have with him.'

Her voice rose with anger. 'He's an *animal*!' She paused for effect. 'I wasn't brought up by a good family to have the life I've got with *him*. I hope he doesn't come back.'

I sat quietly, wanting to try and say something helpful, but afraid of making her worse; trying to understand what she was feeling, but unable to comprehend.

'*I'm leaving him*,' she shrieked as she stood up and took a couple of steps towards the stairs.

'What are you doing, Mam?'

'I'm going to pack ma case. I've had enough. When he comes back, I'll be gone for good.'

'No, please, Mammy. Don't go . . . What will I do?' I followed her upstairs and watched as she dragged an old suitcase down from the top of the wardrobe and opened it out on the bed. She yanked open the wardrobe doors and began to throw her clothes into her case.

'Please don't go, Mam.' I was distraught. 'Please, please . . .' My voice tailed away as she ignored me and carried on packing her case.

'You'll be all right,' she snapped. 'You can stay with *him*.'

Suddenly, I heard Tommy's car pull up outside. He stormed back into the house, slammed the front door and ran up the stairs two at a time, as he always did when he was angry. I shrank back against the wall, overcome with terror.

'*Where the hell are you going?*' he shouted at her.

'I'm leaving *you*.'

'Right, off you go, then. I'll get your coat for you. But remember, you're not taking her.' He pointed at me as I tried to make myself as small as possible.

'She's *mine*!' she snarled.

'Maybe so, but I'm her father, so she's staying here, and that's that!'

A few moments later I managed to escape and left them to it. My mother must have backed down eventually and decided to stay. But they didn't speak to each other for weeks.

I liked having the extended family around us – it gave me a feeling of warmth and safety. Our house was on a V-shaped corner overlooking the street behind, where Grandma and most of my aunties and uncles lived. I often used to play with my cousins in the road, with the aunties looking out every now and then to make sure we were all right – something my mother never did. The older cousins skipped and played ball. They taught us younger ones to play hopscotch, and sometimes they organized games we could all play together, like Grandmother's Footsteps or 'What's the time, Mr Wolf?'

One day, when I was about four, I remember falling over in the street and scraping my knee. I sat up and cradled it as I watched the blood rise to the surface of my skin and drip down onto my white sock. I tried to push my sock down because I knew my mother would be angry, but it was no use. The stain spread.

I cried out loud and tears ran down my cheeks. I think I was more upset and worried about my sock than about my knee, but my cousin Jean came and picked me up. 'Shush, don't cry,' she whispered to soothe me. 'Dry your tears.'

Several other cousins gathered round to see what all the fuss was about.

'That looks sore,' said nine-year-old Malcolm. 'I'll take

you to Grandma's house. She'll put a plaster on it for you.'
He held my hand and walked me across the road.

As we passed Auntie Dorrie's, she opened the window.
'What's the matter with the bairn?'

'She scraped her knee,' answered John.

Uncle James rode up the lane on his pushbike and stopped
near me. 'What's the matter, pet?'

'She fell down,' Malcolm explained.

'We're taking her to Grandma's,' added little Melanie,
tagging along behind.

'She'll put a plaster on Helen's knee,' agreed Gillian.

There were now several cousins following and we led the
procession to Grandma's front door. Malcolm knocked and
we all waited expectantly. Everyone loved going to Grandma's.

The door opened and there she stood, in a dark dress as
always, with one of her full-length flowery aprons stretched
over the top, a grey bun at the back of her neck, her thick
stockings wrinkling at her ankles, and a twinkle in her eyes.
She took one look at my knee and guided me indoors. 'Aahh,
haaway hinny. Let's put a plaster on that knee.'

She gave me a big hug as she set me down and carefully
cleaned the wound. I always loved Grandma's hugs. She radiated warmth. Hers were the only hugs I ever had from an
adult. Grandma took off my shoe, unrolled my blood-stained
sock and removed it. 'Don't you fret about that. I'll give it
a soak, shall I? It'll be right as rain in a jiffy.'

'Yes, please,' I said, wiping my eyes. I knew she understood. Grandma always understood.

'I made some shortbread today. Do you want to stay and
have a piece?' She always baked the best biscuits and cakes.
The shortbread was soft and still warm. It melted in my

mouth and cheered me up as she showed me the new pink bed-jacket she had made herself. 'I'll teach you to knit if you want, pet,' she smiled. 'But you'll have to grow your hands a bit first.'

I reached for another shortbread, but Grandma pulled the plate away. 'Oh no you don't!' she said with a mock-stern expression. 'You don't want to spoil your tea.'

When it was time to go home, Grandma put the damp sock back on my foot and did up my shoe. 'Look. White as snow,' she said. 'No one will know.'

She waved me off out of the door with some shortbread pieces wrapped in greaseproof. 'Give those to your Mam.'

I walked the short distance back to our house, my feet heavier with each step.

As soon as I opened the kitchen door, I could feel a chill in the atmosphere.

'You're late,' said my mother. 'Where have you been? I've been worried sick.' She had her back to me. 'Just you wait till your father comes home.' She clanged a frying pan onto the stove. Not a glance at me.

'I was at Grandma's house. She gave me this for you.' I put the greaseproof parcel on the table. 'I fell over and hurt my knee.'

'Well, you should have been more careful.' She still had her back to me.

The door opened and my father came in.

She turned towards him. 'Helen's been out all afternoon. She's only just come in. I told her she'd be in trouble.'

'Why are you late?' my father barked at me. 'Your mother's slaving away to make you some tea. If you can't be bothered to be on time, you can do without.' He pulled me by the arm through the door to the stairs, slapped the side of my head and pushed me up the first couple of steps, so that I landed on my bad knee. 'I am master of this house. You do as I say.'

I sat still on the step, not daring to move. He went back to get Grandma's shortbread and threw it at me. 'We don't take charity.' The paper fell apart and the treasured biscuits crumbled everywhere. 'Go up to your room. I won't have you treating this house like a hotel.'

I didn't know what he meant, but I scrambled up the stairs as fast as I could. Would he follow me? I ran into my room, the room I shared with George, but he wasn't there to protect me that evening. I sat behind the closed door and listened, breathing a sigh of relief as I heard Tommy go back to the kitchen. Now he and my mother were having a shouting match. I couldn't hear what it was about, but even at that age I was sure it was my fault. It was always my fault, whether I knew what I'd done or not.

I put myself to bed, but still they were raging at each other downstairs. I hid my face in the pillow, to block out the noise, but it didn't stop me hearing a scream, followed by silence. I wanted to go down and see if my mother was all right, but I feared he was still there, so I didn't dare. What would happen to me if . . .

Then I heard her voice again. 'You brute!' she yelled, and the row continued.

I was hungry and couldn't get to sleep. I curled up with my fingers in my ears and thought back to my happy afternoon with the cousins, playing games down the street. I think the only time I felt safe was when I was playing with them. I was a part of something out there. Something special. It wasn't something I felt in our house, but down the street I belonged. Especially with Grandma.

A real matriarch, Grandma was, despite her diminutive size. When she was married, very young, she had an eighteen-inch waist, but that was before she had ten babies. My grandfather was Deputy Overman at the pit and worked shifts. He was a tall man, over six foot, and stern but fair.

Whenever the children squabbled, Grandma would say to him, 'James, will you please speak to these bairns?'

'You're managing very well!' he would say to her. Then he'd turn to the children and raise his index finger. Apparently there was never another sound after that.

Grandma used to get up at three every morning and put an oil-lamp in the window to light his way home. He arrived to a cooked breakfast every day, while she boiled some hot water on the range to fill the tin bath in front of the fire. She washed the coal dust out of his hair and scrubbed his back as he rested his aching muscles. All this before the children woke.

One morning my grandfather came home with blood running down his face. 'I cracked my head on a beam,' he said. He was suffering from concussion, so a couple of his workmates had brought him home. Apart from a headache, he soon felt better and went back to work as usual.

Six weeks later, Grandma was woken early by a loud banging on the door. Her husband, who was only in his forties, had collapsed down the mine and died. He'd had a brain haemorrhage, caused by his head injury. Grandma screamed when they told her, a great piercing shriek. Devoted to her man, she never got over his death and wore mourning clothes for the rest of her days. The whole village turned out for his funeral and walked behind the hearse along the two-mile route to the church where he was buried.

It was 1932. There was no social security then, but the colliery provided a small pension to Grandma, and free coal for life. Somehow she managed to bring up her ten children, and her orphaned little brother too, keeping them all warm and fed. She was a great one for making do. Nothing was ever wasted. Clothes were hand-me-downs, with a lot of mending and alteration.

Once, when George needed some special shorts for a school boxing match the next day, Grandma sat up all night and hand-stitched him a brand new pair from one of her satin petticoats, bless her. She was always sewing. Old jumpers would be unpicked and the wool rewound to be used again. When the bed-sheets were threadbare from wear, she would cut them down the middle and stitch together the outside edges to make them last longer. Every old button and fastener went into the button jar for reuse. Leftover meals were fried up as pies. Old rags were made into clippy mats. Grandma threw nothing away.

When you think about it, she had a hard life, my Grandma. They all had a hard life in those days, didn't they? They had a lot of babies. I remember her telling me that she used to buy two stone of flour every week. Two stone! That would have taken some carrying. All that baking and cooking and doing all the laundry by hand. Every day she scrubbed the kitchen table white and blacked the grate.

Grandma carried on her thrifty ways all her life, but she adored her family and found a way to give us treats now and then.

Whenever I called round, if I hadn't seen her for a few days, she'd sweep me up in her arms and hug me tight. 'Ee, haaway hinny, it's been a long time since I've seen you.' Each of us cousins thought we were her favourite, but she was the same with everyone. She loved us dearly and spoiled us all in turn. She was the only adult who really loved me.

I stayed with her a few times when I was little, and enjoyed those sleepovers, except that she wouldn't let me eat the top of my boiled egg. She always took it.

'Let me have that.' She loved the top of a boiled egg.

'Grandma! I wanted to eat that.'

'There's one at the other end for you,' she'd say.

Grandma was a legend in our family. She would take to her bed and have a death scene whenever she had a cold or the flu. Of course she had witnessed the deaths of many in the 1918 flu epidemic. She had lost her husband young, and her first-born too. She had seen illness and death as a commonplace all around her throughout her life, since this was before penicillin and antibiotics. Serious chest conditions were the norm in Seghill, especially 'miner's lung', caused by the coal-dust that polluted the air we breathed. Superstitions surrounding illness were rife. I was always warned not to sit on the ground because 'The cold will strike through!' I didn't really understand that. 'It will strike your kidneys.' I was bundled into a vest and liberty bodice, even in warm weather. The spectre of illness lurked everywhere.

So whenever Grandma felt ill, she would call the whole family to the 'wake' before she died. One of the cousins would go round announcing, 'Grandma is very poorly', and all the family would dutifully appear at her house. We crammed in somehow, taking turns to sit with her in her bedroom, while the others would have a raucous time with tea and biscuits in her front room or on the stairs. My uncles Sam, Jack, Marcus and James were full of fun and quick-witted jokes. It was fast and furious when they got together, so they always brightened the mood, and Grandma would sit up in bed with tears of laughter rolling down her cheeks when it was their turn to sit with her. Even my father, if he was at home, didn't complain about going round to see Grandma. He was fond of her and teased her, which she loved. I was always surprised about this when I was little, but I suppose he recognized her seniority as the matriarch of this extended family.

I used to go too and see her lying in state, muffled up in a vest under her warm winceyette nightie with its elasticated cuffs and a high neck tied with satin ribbon. Over the top she would wear one of her hand-knitted bed-jackets in a pastel colour. She had a vast range of them in lemon, pink and powder blue. She kept her best bed-jacket for when the doctor came.

Her bed always had crisp white sheets and pillowslips, and was piled high with blankets, a bedspread and a matching quilt, which she straightened every now and then after one of us had sat on it and sent it askew. Her little wrinkled hand with its blue veins and the thin gold band of her wedding ring lying on the white turnover of the sheet fascinated me. I could almost see the blood pumping through those veins.

I was intrigued by the array of tablets and cough medicines on her bedside table. 'Don't touch those, hinny,' she would say. All those of us who could squeeze in would sit around her bed and take turns to hold her hand. I can feel now the stifling heat in that room with the roaring fire in the grate and the thick curtains closed 'to keep out the draughts'. The lamp, lit dimly on her bedside table, cast a warm glow over the proceedings.

Grandma brightened as each group dutifully trooped into her bedroom.

'How are you getting on, Mother?' Uncle Marcus would ask. 'Do you want a glass of water?'

'No thank you, pet. Nancy just brought this one. It's as fresh as can be.'

'Let's plump up your pillows,' Auntie Dorrie would say, leaning Grandma gently forward.

'That's champion,' she would say in a weak-but-trying-to-be-cheerful voice as she settled back again. 'Now, sit down and talk to me. How are the bairns?'

Even my mother would join in. She was always bright and witty in company, like a different person. She smiled at everyone . . . except me.

Grandma's wakes seemed like joyous occasions in some ways, but there was always an underlying fear – an anxiety amongst the aunts and uncles that this might be Grandma's last. But I don't think we children realized that at the time.

I always tried to sit near Grandma's dressing table, with its bowl of sparkly trinkets and her beloved dressing-table set. Overcome with curiosity, I would edge open her drawers and have a quiet rummage through her satin underwear or her pleated blouses, sniffing the mothballs. Going through Grandma's drawers was a treat. A ritual.

Eagle-eyed, she noticed everything. When she saw me open her drawers she would make a sudden recovery, sitting forward in bed, and waving her walking stick. 'Hey, out of there, you little monkey! Out of my drawers!' she would say, but with a grin. It was a great game between us.

There were many fun times at Grandma's. Her living room was dominated by a church organ. When we all went for tea on Sunday afternoons, my cousins and I were indignant that the adults ate first at the table while we were consigned to wait for the second sitting. We would peep over the edge of the table to see the sandwiches and cakes disappear, so that by the time it was our turn, most of the cake plates were empty and there were nothing but crumbs to share between us. We all thought that was grossly unfair! Sometimes we tried to sneak in and steal something before anybody got there and got a smack on the hand, but not too hard. It was because the family was so big that the best stuff was always gone. That was the way it was. We were just kids and we had to stand at the back of the line. We didn't know any different.

After tea, Grandma would say, 'Haaway James, let's have a tune, pet.'

The adults would stand around the organ, all smartly dressed in their Sunday best, while Uncle James played and the whole family sang rousing hymns and songs of the day. The one I remember best is 'Onward Christian Soldiers', a family favourite. Because I was one of the smallest, I often enjoyed the privilege of sitting on my uncle's lap while he played. I used to pull and tug at the organ stops, which earned me a cursory slap, but I couldn't resist. I remember the fascination of watching his huge hands as they lumbered across the keys, and feeling uplifted by the joyful singing of my uncles and aunts. Auntie Dorrie always led – she had the strongest voice. My grandma would look on with a sentimental smile as a tear or two escaped down her cheek.

Grandma always wore her best half-pinny tied around her waist on Sundays. Sometimes, while everyone was singing, I would get down from Uncle James's knee and join the younger cousins as we crept round behind Grandma and pulled at her apron strings until her pinny fell to the floor.

'You little devils,' she said each time in a mock-angry voice, with a twinkle in her eyes as she tied it back on again in a direct challenge to us to repeat our wicked ways.

There was a lot of laughter on Sunday afternoons. Something would start us off laughing and we'd have to begin all over again. But always, by the end of the afternoon, there would be a suffocating tension, a sense that the atmosphere could change in a heartbeat. An innocuous joke or thoughtless remark from a family member would cut the party dead as my father stiffened, his eyes flashed and his fists clenched. That was the moment things turned. Almost every Sunday. It was like some sort of secret I would never know or understand. I was aware that my father didn't like going to these afternoons and that he was uncomfortable with my mother's relations, all except for Grandma, so I assumed that was what the tension was about. It didn't matter much to me while I was surrounded by all the family. While we were there, I was OK.

Once an argument began, always started by my father, it would seem small at first, then get louder and fiercer. Then my mother would weigh in to make it worse. I was too young to work out whose argument it was, or why it had started, but it would always escalate. We'd often have to leave the party early, both my parents dark with anger, and that's when it started to matter. When we got home George was usually out, so there was nobody to protect me from their escalating rage. I was on my own.

CHAPTER 4

Helen

A Walking Heel

Hardly a day passed without a forceful reminder of my father's dominance. Without any reason that I could see, he would suddenly turn on my mother or me. We might be sitting at the table, eating our tea, when perhaps my mother would make some remark, or I'd drop my fork. He'd abruptly push his plate away with such force that food shot across the table and onto the floor, his face as dark as thunder and his eyes staring. A typical scene would be like this:

'Go on, then,' my mother would taunt him. 'Let's all see what a big man you are. What an animal, more like!'

'I am master of this house,' he would roar as he stood and pushed his chair back so hard it fell against the dresser. 'And don't you forget it. You will do what I say.' He stressed the 'I'. 'I will not allow . . .' Then he would turn on me and jab his finger into my chest. 'You'll never get away from me. Not if you want to stay alive.'

I would sit as still as I could, trying my hardest not to cry.

'Ee, yes,' my mother would say, adopting a sarcastic tone. 'Let's bow and scrape to the master.'

'Shut up, you slut!'

'What are you then? The big I am?'

I would shrink in my chair as he turned to hit out at her.

'Oh aye,' she would smirk. 'You are the big man now, aren't you?'

He would bend his face towards hers in a menacing pose. 'You will be quiet, *now*!'

'Ee, master, we're all so scared of you . . .'

Stepping back he would take a swipe at her again, harder this time, probably on the chin.

She would throw her cup at him. It would miss and shatter against the wall, and the tea would slowly drip in tracks down the wallpaper. I would slide quietly off my chair and creep towards the door.

He would catch me and pull me back. 'Where do you think you're going? This is all your fault.'

'Yes, Dad. Sorry, sorry . . .'

'You come back here and clear up this mess.'

'Yes, Dad.' I would try to gather the peas or whatever they were from where they'd rolled across the floor, and clear the plates away to the sink. I was only five years old and I had to clean up after them while they carried on with their sparring. It was always a battle-ground in our house.

My mother escorted me to school for my first few days at Seghill Infants. After that, I was on my own. It was a typical village school, just a short walk away. Most of my cousins had been there before me, so I soon settled in.

School became my refuge, until one lunchtime that winter when I slipped on an 'ice-slide' in the school yard. As I fell I heard the crack that set my ankle ablaze. I felt sick and faint as I lay on the snow, surrounded by gawping classmates.

I sobbed as older children helped me to hobble back past the outside toilets to the Victorian school building.

'Just sit down and keep it up on there!' My teacher scowled as she slammed my foot down on a spare chair to elevate it. The pain seared up my leg and I stuffed my fist in my mouth to stifle my scream. My ankle swelled quickly and throbbed so much it was hard not to cry out. The slow afternoon dragged on around me.

At home time I tried to walk, but was unable to put any weight on my ankle. Nobody came to fetch me and the other children had run off straight after school, including my cousins in other classes who knew nothing about it, so I had to make my way home alone in the dark. I hopped on one foot, glad of the support of garden walls along the way. I tried to hurry so that I wouldn't be in trouble for being late home, but my broken ankle jarred with every hop and it was the longest, slowest journey I'd ever made. By the time I got home my ankle was bulging and straining against the strap of my shoe.

When my mother pulled off my shoe, my ankle exploded like a suet pudding, and my mother took me for another agonizing hobble, this time with her reluctant support. She complained all the way to the village 'bone-setter'. At least, that's what they called him. He had no medical training and was more of a manipulator for aching muscles than anything to do with bones. But I didn't know that.

His look of shock alarmed me. 'There's nothing I can do with this,' he said. 'It's broken. You'll have to take her to the hospital.'

My mother was forced to carry me back home, grumbling all the way.

'If you hadn't been so clumsy, you wouldn't have hurt your ankle.'

'Sorry, Mammy,' I sobbed.

'You're much too heavy for me to carry. If you don't keep still, I'll have to put you down.' She knocked my ankle with her arm.

'Owww,' I yelped.

'Stop that noise . . . and stop fidgeting – you're making my arms hurt.'

We arrived back home and my mother plonked me down on a chair while she went out to the phone box on the corner to ring my father's workplace. Dad was out driving his lorry, so she left a message with his employers to let him know of my accident. I don't think she told them what kind of accident it was. I found out afterwards that he drove home like a demon.

'Your dad's on his way. He'll be home soon,' she said when she got back. She made me some toast, laden with butter and jam. Normally I would have loved that, but I felt sick, so I could only nibble a corner.

'Eat up your toast,' she said. 'You've got to eat something.'

I couldn't eat it, and I must have made a face, trying my hardest to quell the nausea.

'That's the last time I do anything for you, miss. You needn't think a broken ankle will get you any treats.'

'Sorry, Mam. I feel sick,' I said. I think the shock and the pain were all too much for me.

'Well, don't be sick in here. You'd better go up and get ready for your bed.'

I was five years old and had a broken ankle, but I had to crawl up the stairs and get undressed on my own with tears streaming down my face and pains like shards shooting through me with every movement. And on top of my pain, and the guilt I felt for upsetting my mother, I feared what my father would do. Mam had said he was coming home early. I thought it was because I had done something wrong. It was my fault I'd broken my ankle and I was sure I'd be in trouble. I realize now that probably wasn't the reason for him rushing home like that, but I was five and I already knew that everything was my fault.

When Dad got home he came straight up to my bedroom. My mother followed him up. 'She's broken her ankle,' she explained.

'Is that all it is?' he asked. 'I thought it was something serious. You mean you made me leave early and race home for this? Just a broken ankle?' They went downstairs and left me alone again.

That was it. Nobody did anything – there was no strapping, no support and no sympathy. I was left in the dark, crying through the pain. I remember how even the weight of the blankets was agony. The only thing that helped was stuffing my pillow down one side of the bed to raise them and take the weight off. I couldn't sleep. It would have been hard to feel more lonely in the slow, dark hours before dawn.

Finally, next morning, my mother came into my room. 'Come on, then,' she said. 'We've got to get ready to go to the hospital. We'd better get on with it.'

She must have heard me crying in the night, but she didn't say anything about it. Just her usual straight face, as cold as stone.

We took the bus to the General Hospital about eight miles

away. Of course I wasn't able to walk, so Mam carried me to the bus stop, and from the bus stop in Newcastle to the hospital. We were there all day.

She told everybody who would listen what a trial I had been to her.

'Ee, I've carried her all the way. I know she doesn't look much, but she's really heavy, and – look at me – I'm only slight.' Her put-upon look elicited some sympathetic nods.

'Poor you. What a shame your husband couldn't bring you,' said the receptionist.

'My arms really hurt from all that carrying. And it's all been such a shock. Do you think you could make me some tea, dear, good and strong?' She had deep, brown puppy eyes, my mother – capable of melting hearts wherever she went.

'Thank you. It's been awful for me. I don't know how I managed to carry her so far. But somehow I managed and got her here.'

'Ee, well done, pet,' said the orderly who made the tea.

'Very brave,' said the young doctor, smiling kindly at my mother, who was still a good-looking woman.

'I never slept a wink all last night, worrying about her.' She combed her hand through her waves of auburn hair.

'Well, young lady,' said the nurse, turning to me for the first time. 'I think you should thank your mother for being so devoted to you.'

'Thank you, Mammy,' I said, trying to hold back the tears. 'I'm really s-sorry.'

They put me in a knee-high plaster, with a small 'walking heel'. Then, joy of joys, I was given a ride home in an ambulance, which made me feel very important, especially at the end of our journey when it stopped in our road and all of the neighbours came out to look. For the first time all day, I was given some sympathy for myself.

'Ee, what a terrible time I've had,' complained my mother. 'I had to carry her all the way to the hospital this morning. Nobody offered us an ambulance then. I'm worn out.'

'I'm sorry, Mammy. Thank you for carrying me.'

This went on for weeks. She would tell everyone in Seghill, down the street, in the shops, and the family too. 'I had a terrible time of it, carrying her all the way to the hospital, you know. Exhausting it was. And little thanks I got!'

As children do, I made a quick recovery and soon forgot the pain. Before long I learned how to race around like any healthy five-year-old, plaster or not. In fact, my plaster was a positive bonus with my friends at school, especially the 'walking heel'. I found I could spin on the heel, 'ski' across wooden floors and perform all manner of tricks with this fantastic new 'toy'.

With the inevitability of hindsight, the day came when my boisterous antics broke the plaster and I had to go back to the hospital for a new one. My father was away on a long-haul trip then, so my mother had no one at home to moan to except me, but she made up for it a few days later, after my father had returned from his trip, when I broke my plaster again. This time the hospital gave up on the plaster and put my leg in a kind of splint made out of layers of two-inch elastoplast, right up to my knee.

My father was livid when he got home.

'Our Helen's broken her plaster again,' my mother told him 'We've been all the way back to the hospital to have a third new plaster fitted. We called for an ambulance this time, but it took all day and they decided not to put a plaster on again, so they bandaged it tightly instead.'

My father's face darkened as he took a look at my leg in its elastoplast binding. 'How did you do this?' He exploded with rage. 'What were you doing?'

I hesitated.

'You will answer me!' he shouted into my face.

'I was only playing, Daddy . . .'

'Don't you remember I told you *not* to walk on it?' The fact that it was a walking heel was lost on him.

'Y-yes,' I whispered.

Without another word, he picked me up roughly, put me across his knee and held me down with one hand pressing on my back, while he pounded me on my bottom with the other as hard as he could, on and on and on.

I cried out. I screamed. I bawled as the tears streamed down my face. My whole back was in pain as he pummelled me till I was black and blue. He took no notice of my protests, nor of the fragile binding on my leg, which was under pressure and throbbed throughout the beating.

Finally, when he was tired, he picked me up under the arms and threw me two or three feet into a fireside chair.

I yelped with pain.

'Now, perhaps that will help you to remember what you were told. You will *not* leave that chair without permission for two weeks.' He pushed his red, sweating face up close and his bulging eyes stared into mine. '*D'you hear me?*' he shouted.

'Yes,' I whispered again.

He banned me from walking for two weeks, forcing me to remain in the chair and sit still all day every day. I wasn't allowed to move for a fortnight – fourteen endless days. That's a long time for a small child, left alone with no television and nothing to do.

At least it was peaceful in the daytime. From the second he came through the front door, every moment became unpredictable and every word or movement a risk. But the beating Tommy gave me for breaking my plaster was slight compared with what was to come.

CHAPTER 5

Jenny

Barefoot Summers

As we drove away from our house in Jesmond to go to our bungalow, I would often look back at Newcastle, a grey city cowering under dark clouds and heavy rain, and then find, forty miles later when we got to Embleton, that the evening sunlight was spilling its golden glow across the dunes. In my memories, it was always sunny there. The fresh sea air infused us with energy and melted our stresses away as we crossed the links to reach our sanctuary. You could taste the salt on the air and smell the ozone. It was fantastic. 'There's more ozone in the air at Embleton, mind, than anywhere else in the British Isles,' my mother used to say. I don't know if it's true, but that's what she always said.

As soon as we arrived at the bungalow, it was off with the town clothes and on with our T-shirts and shorts, but no shoes. It was just grass and sand, so we were in bare feet all the time. The sea was close enough to our house that as I lay in bed at night I could listen to it breathing in and out. I imagined there were mermaids on the rocks, sea-gods on the sand and white horses prancing. Most nights I fell asleep to the ssshhh-shhhh of the waves running up and down the beach in the darkness.

I have a distinct memory of being woken one morning by sunbeams streaming through my window. I had learned to know from the sound of the sea on the sand whether the tide was in or out, so I knew it was a low tide that morning. I lay completely still, listening to the seals barking on the rocks below, a weird, eerie bark – 'oww-oww-oww' – echoing across the bay. The flat stones on the beach below our bungalow, where the seals basked, stretched to the water's edge. They gathered on the higher stones at the back, with gulls, terns and eider ducks nesting amongst them. Terns and kittiwakes skimmed over the dunes and swooped down to land on the stones. I could hear the rhythmic knock-knocking of the sea birds hammering snails on the stones, breaking their shells to extricate breakfast.

The whole bay was a playground, for the wildlife and for us. Some days we went looking for birds' eggs in the gorse, where thrushes and skylarks nested. We didn't touch them if we found some, just walked away to a safe distance where we could look through our heavy field glasses and watch the mother birds coming to and fro to feed their chicks. We watched frogs in ponds as they laid their spawn, and loved seeing the eggs hatch and the tadpoles stretch their legs as they darted about beneath the surface and gradually grew into frogs themselves. Nearby there was a nature reserve visited by cormorants and swans, and we often lie down in the gorse with our field glasses to watch them come and go.

Our bungalow was in the perfect spot for some daily golf practice as I got a bit older. As the light faded, I chipped balls from the long dune-grass onto the mowed lawn of the nearby green. The third was a difficult hole, a long green with two bunkers, one on either side, so from the bungalow I had to hit over a massive bunker to get onto the narrow part of the green. It was just a chip-shot – half a wedge; something like that. If I made it I knew it must have been a very good shot. Sometimes I practised till as late as eleven o'clock. I was still young, around six, but a perfectionist even then, and keen to improve.

All the children played golf. There were three holes on the top of the hill towards the sea, and we kids used to go out in our bare feet at night-time, carrying a few clubs in the darkness, and play these three holes round and round.

When I was old enough, maybe eight or nine, my dad started to take me round the course with him to be his caddy and carry his bag, which was great, because I enjoyed his company so much – I was happy to be anywhere with him. His joviality rubbed off on everyone, especially me. We used to talk about his golf as we were going round. He wasn't a fantastic player, but he loved the game and did well in our club competitions. It wasn't just golf he loved – he had so much enthusiasm for life. It bubbled out of him. It has stayed with me and inspired me in everything I've done.

Dad loved me coming around with him, caddying. We often used to practise shots together, and he was with me the first time I played round the whole course. Looking back now, I'm sure he was proud of me, especially the fact that I often chose to go round with him rather than play with my friends, though occasionally I would say, 'Oh no, Dad, I can't today. I said I'd go out in the canoe.' I'm sure he must have been disappointed on those occasions, though he never showed it. We were such wonderful companions. I don't suppose he could have realized at that stage that I would make a good golfer.

Sometimes a haar would come in across the bay and over the links. You get them a lot in that area, a kind of sea fog that blots out everything. We couldn't see our own hands held out in front of us one time when we were all coming across from the car park one night over the dunes. We managed to find our way up to the golf-course, then lost our bearings.

'Come on, pet, follow me,' said my mother as we inched along in single file. 'I know the waaaaaaaay.'

She disappeared. She'd missed her footing and had slid down the damp sand all the way to the bottom of a bunker about six feet below. I was alarmed until I realized, as she climbed out, that she was fine – covered in sand but unscathed.

'Oh yes, Mam.' I smiled. 'You know the way?' and we laughed together.

The contrast between Embleton and our home in West Jesmond was striking in almost every way. Where we used to live in West Jesmond is now a student area, by the Metro line that runs into Newcastle, but when I lived there as a child, in Ashleigh Grove, West Jesmond was a real community where everyone helped each other, and there were all sorts of shops just round the corner including a general dealer across the road from our house. The wife was Dutch, a lovely woman. I can still picture her cutting the bacon and shaping the butter with her ridged wooden paddles. (All the customers wanted to be served by her, as her husband drooled a little.) There was a dairy next to the dealer's, then the Co-op, where shoppers collected 'dividends', a bit like today's loyalty cards. My mother used to send me across for things she needed.

'Go for a loaf at the Co-op, Jen. What is the divi number?'

'65239.'

'OK, go quickly now, flower, and look each way before you cross the road. Don't forget to count the change, then come straight home.'

The old train station, next to the coal yard, was only a couple of streets away, and heavy steam trains rumbled through at regular intervals, blowing their whistles and blackening the buildings. I remember how much my mother had to clean. There was always a layer of coal dust lining our window sills that she could never get rid of, and it thickened the air and clogged our lungs so that we were always coughing. I had chronic bronchitis most winters, and was often sent to stand outside the classroom because I was coughing too much. One winter I fell so seriously ill with a more acute form of bronchitis that I missed a great deal of schooling and ended up having to stay down a year to catch up.

We lived in the house my mother had bought before she married, the last house in our street. When I was small, we lived downstairs and let out the upstairs flat. Everyone knew each other. It was 'Hello, Mrs Smith' – always Mrs so-and-so, never first names, even though they'd known each other twenty years.

I was six when my grandmother died and Grandpa Bill came to live with us. He was my dad's father, medium height and quite stocky, and still quite fit when he took up residence in our front bedroom. He always wore a felt beret edged with leather when he went out. He loved the football and went with Sid to watch Newcastle play nearly every weekend through the season. Because he wasn't very tall, he made himself a little wooden step that he took with him to stand on to get a better view.

I can still recall the aromatic smell of his pipe tobacco – sweet and fragrant. He used to go to bed every afternoon and take a nap. Although my mother didn't like him smoking in bed, he took no notice.

'Come on, Pa,' she would say. 'No smoking in bed.'

Grandpa would look suitably contrite until she'd left the room, then he'd turn and give me a wink.

Sometimes he fell asleep with the pipe in his mouth, and occasionally it fell out and the tobacco burnt a hole in the bedding. I won't ever forget the smell of singeing sheets.

'Sorry, Con,' he would say to my mother as she rushed in and poured a pan of water onto the smoking patch.

Grandpa had a little penknife with an ivory handle. One minute he was peeling a Cox's apple with it and the next he'd be clearing out his pipe. Sometimes he peeled apples for me, but I had to pick the bits of tobacco off them. When I got home from school, he read me stories sitting on his bed. We were very close and I loved him dearly. When he first came to stay and was well enough, he liked to meet me from school and walk me home with him.

I have lovely memories of Grandpa playing with me. He was always happy to join in my games. 'Ee, what's it to be today, Jen?'

One day when I came home from school, I devised a rather boisterous version of cowboys and Indians. He was lying down on his bed having a nap, so I ran in and jumped on him. It was meant to be part of the game and he, with his usual good humour, joined in. But when he got up he had a nosebleed.

'Oh dear me, Pa!' exclaimed my mother, raising her hand to her mouth. 'Look at your nose! It's bent.'

At some stage of the game I must have broken his nose. I felt awful about it, but nobody told me off. When my father got home, he had to take Grandpa to hospital to have it fixed.

After Miss Brewis's nursery school, I had moved on to the first class of Newcastle upon Tyne Church High School for Girls – Church High as it was known locally. Or 'The Green-Knicker Brigade', after the thick green knickers we had to wear. The teachers used to do a regular knicker-check, just to make sure we always wore them.

Church High was an all-through school for ages five to eighteen, and there I made friends with another girl called Jennifer. She was my only other close friend in Newcastle, besides my cousins and Joy McGill, who lived near me and walked to school with me.

One morning, as Joy and I were hurrying to school worrying about being late, a man in a long raincoat stepped out across the pavement in our way. As we approached, he opened his raincoat and flashed us. Joy, who was a little older than me, grabbed my hand and half-dragged me along for the last part of our journey. 'Don't look back,' she said.

On arrival at school, we reported this and then went to our lessons. Halfway through the day we were both called out of our classrooms to talk to the police and look through some photos to see if we could recognize the flasher. I don't remember whether we did or not, but this caused great excitement amongst our classmates and we were both very popular that day! Fortunately, it never happened again.

My main friends were the children I played with at Embleton, boys and girls of different ages. We all got on so well, but in my mind I was always an only child. Much loved, but very much the only child. I minded not having any sisters or brothers, but I didn't dwell on it much in my younger years. If Mam was working long hours, Dad and Grandpa were always there to play with and we had a lot of fun together, but there were moments when I missed a sibling's companionship.

One day, I spotted a dog tied up to the wrought-iron railings outside our school. When I bent down to stroke him, he turned round and bit me, which shocked me so badly that, for a long time after that, I was terrified of dogs. My father sensed my fear and spoke to my mother about it.

'I think we should have a dog. It would be good for Jennifer.'

'We are not having a dog in this house.'

'But a dog would be good company for her, pet.'

'I do not want a dog in this house. I have enough to do as it is, without dog hairs and worse to clean up. We are definitely not going to have a dog. That's my final word on the matter.'

She was so adamant about it that Dad didn't raise the subject again. But one day – I must have been about seven – he came home from work with a tiny bundle tucked under his jacket. It was a black and white cocker spaniel puppy he'd been given by one of his work colleagues.

'Oh, Sid. Not a puppy!' exclaimed my mother.

Dad put the puppy down gently on the floor and she scampered around, exploring her new home. As she watched, Mum's anguished scowl turned to an involuntary smile and she began to waver.

'Can we keep her, Mam?' I implored.

'We-e-ell . . .'

'Please, Mam. *Please!*'

'All right,' she surrendered. 'As long as you can train her properly. I don't want messes all over the house, mind.'

This dog took over the role of the sister I never had. I named her Janie and I talked to her all the time as we played together. She listened and sympathized if I had troubles at school, and was a loyal companion, always there for me – such a great friend.

'That dog is your shadow, Jen,' my dad used to say as she followed me about.

Much as I loved Janie, there were still times when I longed for a proper brother or sister. I got on very well with my cousins, some of whom were also only children, and with Barbara in particular, who was the same age as me, but she had sisters of her own, so for me it wasn't like having someone always there to play with and talk to, especially when difficult things happened. Sharing my feelings and worries with someone of my age would have helped so much.

CHAPTER 6

Helen

Ginger Wine

I thought it was normal for everybody to live with a constant feeling of tension. There was always the imminent threat of violence hanging over us, and the suspense that went with it. I spent my childhood with this voice inside saying, 'Don't put a foot wrong,' but somehow something always happened to set things off. George was the one person at home who cheered me up, when he wasn't out or staying over with his mates. He had left school as soon as he was fifteen and was now working down the mine, so he earned a bit of money, most of which he had to give my father.

One day he bought me a little grey rabbit and we built a hutch together. Well, he built it and I helped. I called my rabbit Smoky and he was a joy to me. George showed me how to look after him and I did everything I could to care for him every day.

It was winter time, I remember – a hard winter, bitterly cold. One Sunday morning I got up before anyone else and went outside to feed Smoky. To my horror, I found him lying on his straw . . . frozen completely stiff. I wailed, distraught. I so loved Smoky. I took him inside and cradled his rigid body gently in my arms, holding him close, trying to warm him up again. Of course it was no use.

When my parents came downstairs, first one, then the other, took one look at Smoky and broke into laughter, goading each other on into waves of hysteria. I couldn't believe it. He was my beloved pet and yet the more I cried, they more they laughed.

'Smoky's dead,' I blurted. 'Can't you see that he's dead?'

They couldn't speak for laughing. Couldn't they see how upset I was?

'Forget it,' spluttered my father between howls of laughter. 'It was just a rabbit. Plenty of them about.'

At that moment, George came in from his night shift. He straightaway took in this bizarre scene and understood. With a nod of his head in my direction, he acknowledged my grief, walked across and enveloped me in one of his big bear-hugs. He took me straight outside, found a spade in Tommy's workshop and somehow dug a hole in the frozen ground. When the grave was ready, we found a ragged old scarf, soft to the feel, and one of George's own handkerchiefs. With all the reverence we could muster, we gently wrapped Smoky in his shroud and lowered him into the ground, and I helped George to fill in the grave. Then we found two old lolly sticks and made them into a cross, which we stuck into a crack in the earth. Standing back together, our breath misting in the air, we said a prayer over his grave.

As we came back inside, George wiped a tear from my cheek. 'I'll take you to buy a new rabbit next Saturday. How would that be?'

All week I had to wait. On Friday night, I hardly slept, I was so excited about going with George to choose a new rabbit, and on Saturday morning, George strode and I skipped along beside him to the pet shop, pushed open the door and went straight over to the place where they kept the rabbits. My smile froze as I looked into the empty hutch. Not a rabbit in sight. But the shopkeeper pointed to a wooden box next to it, and when we peeped through its glass front, there was a litter of the sweetest, furriest guinea pigs I'd ever seen. We asked the pet-shop owner how to look after them and he explained what they ate, how to groom them and care for them and let me stroke them.

I chose the one I liked best, George paid, and I became the proud owner of Squeaky, named for the high-pitched noises he made. He was white with tricolours of dark brown and ginger – the most beautiful animal I had ever seen – and it was such joy caring for a cute little animal again. I loved the funny squeaks he made, especially when he heard my voice.

Everything was right again with the world until the day I came home from school and, running over to the hutch to greet him, didn't hear him squeak when I approached. I couldn't see him in the open part, so I checked inside the sleeping area. I couldn't believe it. He wasn't there. I checked again, in case he was hiding under a pile of straw, but the hutch was empty. Where was he? I ran to the scullery and asked my mother.

'Mam, where's Squeaky? He's not in his hutch.'

'Your guinea pig? It's dead,' she shrugged. 'Your dad put it in the bin.'

I gasped. I couldn't believe what she said. 'He was all right when I went to school this morning.'

'Well, it's not all right now!' she smirked.

It wasn't very cold, so I didn't understand what could have happened to him. I ran and looked in the bin.

'You won't find it in there. The bins were emptied today.'

I sat on the step and sobbed. How had this happened? He had been fine earlier. Now he was gone, with not even a body to bury and no explanation. It never occurred to me to question her any further. But I do wonder now.

It was one of those days of terrible rows. As usual, it began as they say on the news – 'scuffles broke out'. It always made me think of that phrase. Scuffles broke out in the kitchen . . . in the living room . . . On this day the scuffle started with our big old Hoover. My father would not allow the vacuum cleaner or the washing machine to be used when he was in the house. On this particular day, Mercia turned on the Hoover and started to swish it to and fro across the living-room floor.

Without a word, Tommy got up and switched it off, then sat down again.

My mother turned it back on.

He turned it off.

I could see the daring look on Mercia's face as she turned it on again.

This time, Tommy stomped over to the electric point and, with a triumphant glare, pulled the plug out, then back-handed my mother round the face, knocking her to the floor. He picked up the vacuum cleaner, marched it out of the door, lifted it to shoulder height and hurled it into the garden. I was amazed at his strength. But I was also frozen with fear. What would happen now?

When Tommy came back into the room, my mother had picked herself up. Now she faced up to him.

'That was clever, wasn't it?' she taunted. 'Now you'll have to buy me another vacuum cleaner.'

'I will not. I don't want that noisy thing in the house. It's *my* house. What I say, goes.'

'It's not your house. It's Minnie's.'

Even at my age, I had the feeling this wasn't a good thing to say to my father. I wondered if I could get out of the room without them noticing, but I was too far from the door. I made myself as small as I could and waited in stunned silence to see what would happen next.

I was surprised that my father, fuming inwardly, didn't answer immediately. Meanwhile, my mother calmly went to retrieve the Hoover from the garden, trundled it back into the living room and plugged it back in. She stood up with a smug expression on her face.

This was the moment Tommy erupted into one of his blind furies. His face turned first red, then white. He clenched and unclenched his fists several times and his eyes began to bulge. He pulled the vacuum cleaner away from her and away from the wall so violently that the plug flew through the air and caught me a stinging blow on the forehead. Then he stormed over to the door and smashed the Hoover with his full force into the concrete path, causing bits to come off it in all directions.

'*What do you think you're doing?*' screamed my mother.

'I told you, I will not have that thing on while I'm in the house, you stupid woman!' shouted Tommy. 'Did you not hear me?'

'Go on then, see what other insults you can think of. See if I care.' She picked up an ashtray and threw it at him.

He took hold of her wrists and shook her with great force,

so that she lost her footing again. 'You're just a stupid and ignorant pit-yacker!' He paused. 'Remember who's boss around here. You will do as I tell you.'

'Oh aye, there you go again. You reckon you're so scary? I'm terrified!' she taunted him, then pulled one hand free and lashed out at his face with her fingernails, drawing blood.

My father grabbed Mercia's arm, marched her into the hall, pulled her coat off the hook, then pushed her and the coat out of the front door, which sent her sprawling across the path. As she lay there moaning, he slammed the door and turned the key.

Now he switched his attention to me. At first I thought he would attack me in his rage, but he seemed to hesitate for a moment. Perhaps he saw the blood trickling down my face from the wound on my forehead. I don't know.

'Get out of here!' he roared. 'Get upstairs before I give you a hiding.'

I ran up as fast as I could, faster than my feet could keep up with, stumbling on the upper steps and nearly falling backwards. I had to get away before he attacked me. I knew I hadn't done anything wrong that day, but that wouldn't save me.

I was lucky on this particular day – Tommy stomped out of the chaos and left. I heard his car roar away and suddenly it was quiet again. I slumped, the tears poured down my cheeks, and my whole body was still shaking from the fear of witnessing yet another episode of domestic turmoil – almost a daily event.

I tiptoed downstairs to find George arriving home, opening the front door and helping Mercia limp through into the scullery. She sat down and he bathed her wounds. She gave him a weak smile; she often smiled at him. But she ignored me, as usual.

He looked over in my direction and we made silent eye contact. The warmth of that bond between us helped to gradually dispel the misery of our situation. I could read in George's face the anger he felt that his little sister should have to witness such things.

But it wasn't quite over. Mercia raged on in anger.

'That bloody man. He's a monster, an animal. He's a no-good loser. I wish I'd never met him. He makes ma life a nightmare.'

Next she turned to me. 'It's all your fault. I wouldn't have had to marry him if it wasn't for you. I shouldn't have kept you. You do all you can to ruin my life. I don't know why I ever had bairns. They're nothing but trouble. I could have been a model, you know. I could have had a glamorous life . . .'

'Sorry, Mammy,' I said as usual. I didn't know why. I suppose I thought it might soothe her, make her feel better. But it never did.

Unable to calm down yet, she carried on maligning Tommy, moaning at me, smiling at George. 'Thank goodness I've got you to look after me,' she said to him.

'Not for much longer. I'll be off to sea soon.'

'Must you go? I wish you wouldn't go and leave me. How can you leave me?'

'I have to go, Mam. It's part of my engineering apprenticeship. Remember? I start next Monday.'

'How could you leave me at the mercy of that brute?' she fawned and fumed by turns. 'If he kills me, it will be your fault. He'll murder me one of these days. Then he'll have to go to prison. He'll feel at home in there, with his own kind.' Mercia went on and on, like a terrier with a bone.

George sat at the table, solemn but seething, keeping his head down low. Suddenly, as if released from a catapult, he shot up straight in his chair and turned to our mother, his young face contorted with anger. 'Why don't you keep your mouth shut, Mam? You always make him worse. You know you needle him, but you still carry on. Helen and I are always the ones that suffer when you do that. Why do you have to be such a *martyr*?'

There it was – the word that epitomized my mother in every way. She was a martyr her whole life long, though few people could have been less deserving of the term.

We didn't have many visitors in our house; neither of my parents had friends. It was just the family who came, but only when Tommy was out – my mother made sure of that. Whenever we did have any of the aunties and uncles round, it was like a theatrical show. Mercia lit up, centre-stage, as soon as visitors arrived, and the lights didn't go down till they left again. She welcomed them in with a vivacity that mesmerized me. She was like a different person. A glamorous stranger.

On this particular visit, she hustled them in with her usual hospitality. 'Come in. Come out of the cold. I'm glad you came. It's lovely to see you all. Give your coats to Helen. She'll take them upstairs.' She turned to me. 'Put them on the bed carefully now.'

Then she led them all into the living room with a bounce in her step. 'I've put the kettle on. We'll have some tea and I've made a cake.'

I struggled upstairs with an enormous pile of coats and scarves, unable to see where I was going. As I laid them across my mother's pretty counterpane, I heard the uncles' laughter in the living room. Someone must have cracked a joke. I went down to join the party and watch the show.

'Dorrie, you're in the choir,' said my mother. 'Will you start us off with a sing-song?'

'Oh aye, let's sing some hymns,' suggested Uncle James.

'Or what about a good old-fashioned song?' added Auntie Gladys.

'"Daisy, Daisy"?' pleaded cousins Jean and Gillian.

'Right,' agreed Auntie Dorrie and started us off. Everyone joined in – the adults and the children. There were five of us cousins there that day: John, Jean, Gillian, Melanie and me. Halfway through the singing, some of the uncles put on funny voices, competing with each other to see who could sound the most absurd. All of us children had a fit of the giggles, which started the adults off too.

Then my mother stood up and pretended to be an opera singer, putting on all the prima-donna airs and graces, warbling at the top of her voice.

'Ee, our Mercia, you are a scream,' gasped Uncle Marcus, almost choking with laughter.

'You should have been on the stage,' shrieked Auntie Nancy.

My mother glowed with pleasure as she exaggerated her stage bows and blew kisses to her admiring audience. 'Thank you, dahlings,' she purred. 'I love you all.'

I watched this performance with amazement. Who was this? Was she really my mother, the same woman who did nothing but moan and argue when it was just us in the house? The woman who rarely smiled, and never at me?

After tea and cake, it was time to go home.

'Helen, go and get the coats.'

'Yes, Mam.'

I piled them up and struggled back down the stairs, stumbled on the bottom step and only just held on to them.

They all took their coats and turned to my mother to thank her before stepping out into the darkness, muffled up to their chins against the cold, still chuckling and joking in the night air as they went.

'Come again soon,' my mother called, waving after them, a broad smile on her face – till they disappeared round the corner. Then there was a sudden switch as she dropped her party mask and scowled at me, back to normal again. 'Clear the table and put the dishes in the scullery,' she said. 'And don't drop any of them. I need to put my feet up. I'm worn out.'

My father was almost as much an enigma as my mother. As a prisoner of war, he had suffered many ignominies that challenged his need to control everybody in his life. He talked about it very little, although he did tell me once that every morning for ten days the Japanese guards told him he was going to be shot.

'We shoot you. Ten days.'

They came up to his bamboo hut every morning, forced him to kneel, blindfolded him, cocked their pistols . . . and, as one day followed the next, backed out at the last moment, laughing at his fear. He was sure they would carry out the execution before the last day. The tenth morning came. They went through the same ritual, and this time he was certain it was his last breath. They paused for a long time. Then they told him to get up.

'You go. Go . . . go,' they laughed.

Can you imagine how that must have affected him?

On another occasion the guards ordered him to stand and watch as they said to a group of his fellow prisoners: 'OK. You can go. Just go. Run. We let you go. Run.' They made the men run away from them, though in their weakness they could hardly walk. They moved as best they could, and as they tried to run the guards shot them in the back, one by one.

My father never forgot that. Never forgave them. He burned with that flame of fury all his life. Maybe that's what made him the tyrant he became in our house. He couldn't be in control when he was a prisoner of war, but he could now. And he was going to make sure it would stay that way.

I remember Tommy's husky voice – deep and rough from being such a heavy smoker, I suppose. His voice was a danger signal because when he was angry it rose in pitch. Rage shook his whole body – it was like an illness that overtook him. Perhaps it was an illness. The only way he could respond, his only remedy, was physical aggression towards anyone who happened to be there, me included. If I couldn't get out of the way of their fights, as so often when I was little, I was knocked to the floor. They never seemed to realize I was there. I tried to make myself as small as I could, curling up into a ball in the corner and protecting my head. They moved about so much, I used to call it the dance of anger. It was a macabre ballet of the furies.

I'm sure my grandma and the others knew. But it was that old custom – what goes on behind the front door, or in a marriage, or what a parent does to a child . . . you can't interfere. So they knew, but they did nothing.

*

When my mother wasn't there I saw my father in a different light. Dad drove a huge brick wagon in those days. The bricks were loaded by hand onto the lorry, and after a lengthy journey, he then had to unload them by hand again at the other end. Sometimes he took me on long-distance trips with him. I rode all day on top of the engine cowling in between the seats in the cab. I liked the warm hum of the engine beneath my tummy as I lay across it, holding my head up to watch the road through the windscreen. Dad used to steer one-handed as he went round a corner, reaching out to put his free arm over my back to stop me from sliding off down to the floor.

Once we arrived at the building site, Dad would share his lunch with me – usually jam sandwiches packed in an old Oxo tin. He called it bait. The sandwiches were always dry and stiff from being made the night before, but they tasted good to me. We washed the crusts down with a plastic cup of hot tea from his Thermos flask. Dad used the big cup and he gave me the little one. I can still taste that tea – hot and sweet, with the tang of plastic. It seemed to me the best tea in the world.

After our lunch, I watched Dad unload the wagon four or five bricks at a time. It seemed to take for ever. As he worked, he laughed and joked with the men on the site, and sometimes they came over to help him. Occasionally one of them would come and give me a couple of toffees, softened by the warmth of their pocket. Half-melted, it would take all of my concentration to extricate them from their wax papers. But they were worth it.

On the long journey home, the rhythmic heartbeat of the Leyland engine and the flapping of the windscreen wipers to and fro, to and fro would soothe me off to sleep, wrapped in the old tartan rug that my dad kept in the cab of the wagon, with its delicious aroma of petrol and engine oil.

As we neared home in the dark of the evening, my dad would stop the empty wagon outside a certain confectionery shop. It was always open. I woke up, excited to go inside this magical grotto with him. He would buy me a tube of Smarties, or some Fry's Chocolate Cream chocolate, which we ate together on the last leg of the journey. Finally we would arrive home and the wagon seemed to heave a sigh of relief as my dad picked me up and carried me inside on his shoulder.

I have always remembered those trips in the big wagon, the togetherness of me and my dad, and his deep voice singing 'Onward Christian Soldiers' to me as my eyelids drooped and I dozed off into a peaceful sleep. I think having me on the truck with him, sharing that time with me, was the closest he was capable of being.

Even my mother had her lighter moments. At Christmas time every year she made a lot of ginger wine, which she loved. My big treat was when she filled the miniature ginger essence bottle with some ginger wine for me. This was a great excitement, like having something forbidden, but with permission. It was delicious.

The Christmas Eve when I was five, I raced into the kitchen from the bathroom, wearing my new pyjamas, their Christmas present to me, to have my coveted bottle of ginger wine. I found it on the dresser, unscrewed the top and drank it all down. What I didn't know was that my father had been varnishing something in his garage, had poured the leftover varnish into an empty bottle, just the right size, and left it where he found it in the kitchen. As soon as I'd taken in the golden fluid, I started to choke and retch by turns. In panic I tried to catch my breath.

My mother sent the neighbour to call the doctor, who rushed over. I remember he poured copious amounts of salt water down my throat to make me vomit. It worked, with dramatic speed – up came all the varnish, along with my tea. The only other thing I remember is the misery of being sick, continually, throughout Christmas Day, while my parents danced from room to room to the music of Glenn Miller, giggling like teenagers.

I don't think I ever did get my ginger wine that Christmas. My parents carried on in their usual way, frivolity and combat, turn by turn. Maybe it didn't seem like an important incident to them. 'Ah well, Mercia, wrong train again,' my mother smirked. 'Better go and have a bit more shuggy on the grate.' It's what she always said when something didn't turn out right.

It might have been trivial to her, but the memory still shocks me now. It's an example of their carelessness, isn't it? Their indifference to the dangers they exposed me to every day.

I do remember the doctor giving my mother a very strong telling off. 'Helen could have died, you know.'

But she shrugged it off when he'd gone. It was Christmas. She wanted to be pampered and enjoy herself. She wasn't going to let me spoil it.

CHAPTER 7

Helen

Talking to the Cows

When I was six, my parents had to move. Either my father's job changed, or they fell out with the family, or maybe Auntie Minnie needed the house for someone else. I suppose they had nowhere to go, nowhere that they could afford, anyway. My mother took a job as part-time domestic help in a farm-house, working every morning, because it came with a tied cottage, rent-free, in Murton Village. I don't remember the day of the move, but I do recall how far that five miles seemed from all I knew in Seghill and the sanctuary of my extended family. There seemed to be a chasm between us now.

There was no easy bus ride between the two places and we rarely saw the aunties, uncles and cousins. Or Grandma. We went over to her house for tea a couple of times when we first lived at Murton, and I remember the lovely baking smell as we went in and saw the table laid for tea with scones, jam and her delicious Victoria sandwich – my favourite. My father also picked her up to bring her to tea at our house two or three times. I was so surprised when she took her coat off and I saw she wasn't wearing a pinny! I'd never seen her without one. On one visit my father persuaded her to sing some old Northumbrian songs and recorded them with his Grundig tape recorder. I have no idea what happened to that tape. I wish I had it now.

Though we rarely saw her, Grandma used to write a letter every week to my mother, asking when she was going to come and see her, and giving her the family news. I don't think my mother often wrote back and I don't remember her going over to Seghill on her own, though she might have done. In with her weekly letter, Grandma always put a silver sixpence for me. That was the only pocket money I ever had as a child. Thanks to my Grandma, I could buy sweets and other treats at a shop near the school.

At least we had a nice house. It was in a tiny hamlet, which was made up of just the farm and a few cottages and was surrounded by fields and hedgerows, not a pit or a slag-heap in sight. The view was clear to the horizon, the air clean and bright. I can still picture the farmer, Mr Potts, and his wife – both large, jovial bodies with rosy cheeks and friendly, smiling faces, in contrast to my parents.

There was friction from the beginning. My mother did not want this job, but she had no choice. She railed against it every day.

'This is no life. I've been put out to work so that we can have a house to live in. I'm nothing but a skivvy here. Work, work, work! Just when I've finished at the farmhouse, I have to come home and start all over again. It's all your fault!'

I wasn't sure if she was talking to my father or to me. She seemed to blame us both.

'It's your fault I have to work to earn this house.' She looked at me, then she looked at him. 'Where would you live if it weren't for me? I work my fingers to the bone for you. No thanks I get for it.'

'Oh shut up, woman!' barked my father. 'Do you think I wanted to come here? It was your bloody idea.'

'Well, you didn't come up with a better one.'

'Pit-yacker. Pit-yacker,' he taunted.

'Up yours,' she snarled. 'When I married you, I didn't think I'd end up being put into service.'

So it went on, day after day. We dwelt once again in the shrine of my mother's martyrdom. Worse still, my father didn't want to live here either. The man who needed to be in sole control felt forced to move from one house belonging to his wife's family to another secured entirely by his wife. Only this time, as the ultimate blow, it was by dint of her work, rather than his. He was now a tipper-truck driver on the pit heaps at Wallsend. No house came with that job. Tommy was a man fuelled by pride in his superiority as the master of the house, and this was an open wound that ate away at him day by day. He had to reinforce his position in this family somehow, and there was only one way he knew how to do that.

If I closed a door too noisily, he would shout, 'Get back here. You did that just to annoy me, didn't you?'

I always said nothing. I had already learned it was safer that way.

'You will open and close that door silently – not a sound – twenty times. I shall count, mind.' He sat down to look at the paper.

'Yes, Daddy.' I started my penance. Twenty times I opened and closed the door, trying my hardest not to make a sound. If I did, he would make me start all over again.

After a meal, he would point at me. 'You – dishes, now.'

So at six years old I washed the dishes after every family meal. If he wasn't happy with the way I did them, I would have to start all over again . . . and maybe again. I had to jump to every command. Total obedience. I knew that to argue or protest would lead to something worse.

Every time my father ordered me to do something, my mother chimed in with her sarcasm. 'Let's bow and scrape to the master! He has to be the big man, bossing a little girl around.'

There were no other children at Murton and I had to get used to playing on my own. I became a 'country kid', and I soon got to know every burrow hole in Murton village. I knew the feral cats in the farmer's barn and played with their kittens. I counted the newts in the village pond and investigated their markings. I found a weasel colony and watched them foraging for food. I revelled in the freedom of endless sunny summer days as I wandered alone through fields of wheat between meadows of sweet buttercups and cowslips. I made friends with the hedgerow animals and enjoyed many a conversation with the farmer's cows.

My new school was more than a mile away across the fields, at Monkseaton. I dawdled on the way home, spinning out the time before I would have to enter the house again and its aura of menace. Halfway I stopped to pick handfuls of the juiciest green grass before climbing a stile. As I strolled through the field, grazing cattle put up their curious heads to look at me. I offered them the new grass and a few of them snatched it, their velvet lips brushing my skin. Gradually they became used to me feeding them by hand with such tasty morsels from the other side of the fence.

Before long the cows came to meet me at the same time every afternoon. This loving herd of raven-black cattle nodded their heads when I arrived and followed me back to the farm. 'What's it like to live in this big field, with all your brothers and sisters?' I would ask. They listened, their wise eyes focused on me. 'Where are your mammy and daddy?' I used to talk to them as if they were people. They accepted all this with earnest contentment. I thought myself the Pied Piper of Hamelin on those carefree afternoons.

'I wonder if I'm going to be in trouble when I get home tonight,' I confided to them. 'I expect it will be my fault. It always is.' I used to talk to the cows about everything, and they listened with great reverence, it seemed to me, their soulful expressions responding to every word of the small human who poured out her heart to them, sharing her woes, day after day. I always felt, with a nod of their heads, that they understood. In this way we walked in a solemn procession together across the field.

I grew to recognize individual cows and love them. Eventually, some of them let me climb from the stile onto their backs. I used to ride them. You know, it never occurred to me that this could be dangerous. I don't think anybody saw me, or I would certainly have been in trouble. I've always loved animals. To me they are to be respected and adored. They were. They listened to all my problems and I knew they wouldn't tell anybody. That was quite powerful for a troubled six-year-old.

I loved the summertime, especially on Saturday mornings when George came over. Although he didn't formally move out, George hardly ever stayed at our house any more. He was now well into his engineering apprenticeship at the Wallsend Slipway on the river Tyne. This was a busy ship-building yard and he loved his work there.

'You should have seen the thrill on ma face, pet, the first time I helped to start up a huge ship engine,' he said, his face shining with enthusiasm. 'The noise it made – it was like the music of a grand orchestra with an enormous percussion section.'

When a new ship was built, George was one of those who took it to sea on its trials, up the coast of Scotland, or across the North Sea, for days, sometimes weeks at a time. When he wasn't at sea, he mostly stayed with friends, and he had a succession of girlfriends, so I didn't see him much, except on these Saturday mornings. During the term time, he took me to my ballet classes and sat watching while I cavorted around the ballroom floor trying to be a ballerina. Thinking about it now, that must have been a chore for a sixteen-year-old boy, but he always made it a very special time for me.

'That was good,' he'd say after I'd demonstrated a new move. 'Do it again, pet.' He was the one person who gave me confidence and made me feel valued.

After ballet, we walked past the bus stop and on towards home together through woods and meadows, talking, playing, happy in each other's company. I used to show him my 'secret places', where I knew there were animals living. Once I showed him the nest a stoat had made for her babies. When we got there, the babies were out of the nest and I sat down on the parched ground to play with them.

George was cross. 'Don't do that, pet. The mother could attack you. They always go for the neck. They can really hurt you.'

'She won't hurt me,' I said. I felt confident about that because I played with these stoat babies most days after school. The mother stoat always sat and watched me. She never tried to attack. It almost felt like we shared a language, that we understood each other.

We had some hard winters at Murton. I remember one particularly harsh spell when the whole village was snowed in so that no one could get on with their work or go to the shops. I recall getting ready for school one dark morning, aged seven, bundled up in my coat, scarf, mittens and Wellington boots. I was sent out to walk more than a mile through thick, deep snowdrifts. I tried my best to keep plodding on, though it was difficult to walk. In places the drifts were up to my chin, and flakes kept falling down the back of my neck. I trudged on, one slow, sinking step at a time. I could see nothing but white as the snow whirled into my eyes, nose and mouth. I was frightened that I wouldn't make it, but afraid that if I didn't I would be in big trouble for not going to school.

Halfway along the journey there was another farm where I called for my friend every day to walk the rest of the way together. It was hard to find it in this unfamiliar landscape, but somehow I made it. My friend's mother opened the door and stared at me, her mouth wide open, horrified.

'What on earth are you doing here, Helen?'

'I'm on my way to school,' I said, my voice thin with cold and weak with the struggle.

'You can't get through. We are completely snowed in. You cannot possibly have got here all that way by yourself!'

'Yes I did.'

'Ee well, you'll have to go straight back home again. Don't

even try to go any further than here, pet. Go home and get warm.'

I tried to hold back the tears as I turned and trudged the first steps homeward.

'I cannot imagine what your mam was thinking, mind, sending you out this morning, alone, in this weather. It's too dangerous.'

This parting shot muffled in the blizzard was barely audible just a few feet away. It didn't occur to me that maybe this woman should have told me to stay there.

I battled all the way back, planting my feet in my earlier footsteps where I could, but the fresh snow had obliterated many of them. I finally reached our house, ice-cold and exhausted. My mother was still at work next door and I was locked out, so I had to go to the farmhouse to find her. She hurried me back and let me into the freezing house, then left me to change my clothes and sort myself out. She was gone with hardly a word. It didn't appear to cross her mind that she'd sent me out into a blizzard in which I could have got lost and died of exposure. It took me all day to warm up.

The years we lived at this house saw an escalation of the rows, the fights and the misery they caused. Every Sunday morning my parents' battle flared up. They shouted and screamed, objects flew and doors slammed. If George was there, he would sit and practise on his guitar upstairs.

My parents hurt each other more with every word and gesture. Looking back, I can see they were two immature adults, unable to resolve the issues between them. Now, of course, I know most of those issues were about me. He must have known some of her history, and didn't like it. If he'd known it all . . .

But Mercia guarded most of her secrets. What he did know would have been difficult enough for any man in those days. They simply took it out on each other, both of them hitting out against their demons on a daily basis. On one occasion I was sitting in a chair when they started rowing. They went on and on and on, trading insults and worse. I sat still, my hands over my ears, hoping to keep out of the way. I didn't want to hear all this. Finally, something snapped. I held out my hand to signal a ceasefire. 'Stop it! Stop it! Please stop it!'

I was amazed to see them both click out of their fury as they turned to look at me.

'Stop it!' I pleaded.

In an instant, Tommy's hand shot out and slapped me across the head. 'Get to your bedroom!'

What was I thinking of? I ran for safety as they resumed their fight.

Most Sundays at Murton I sat on the stairs, too frightened to venture all the way down. I had nothing else to do but listen to my parents as they charged around the house, spat hateful words at each other, crashed dishes, threw things and slammed doors. I quaked with fear. I knew I couldn't escape. At some point I would be dragged into it, usually by my father.

'This is all your fault,' he'd snarl at me. 'You've caused trouble again.'

I didn't have to do anything to cause trouble. But I was always to blame. It was many years later that I found out what he meant.

Then he'd turn to Mercia. 'If it wasn't for that bloody kid, I would walk out of here.' A tirade of malicious insults would ensue.

The worst thing was when my mother screamed, 'Just you wait. One of these days you will come home and I'll be gone. I'll just put my coat on and walk out of here. I'll walk into the sea and you'll never ever see me again.'

This consumed my thoughts. I was terrified. I couldn't get the image of her walking into the sea out of my mind. I think I went into shock. How could she leave me? What would I do?

One Sunday I was downstairs when they started. I was in the way, so Tommy picked me up and slammed me into the kitchen wall. Flattened, the breath knocked out of me, flaming darts of pain shot through my spine. As I collapsed onto the floor, my back on fire, they battled on, oblivious, wrapped up in their mutual rage. I struggled to subdue the pain and looked for an opportunity to escape.

Relieved to find a moment at last, I stumbled upstairs and shut my door. The pain subsided to a deep throb as I lay still on my bed. It didn't occur to me then that it might be anything serious. It was weeks before the pain faded to a dull ache, but I tried to hide it, and my parents never noticed. I'd have been in more trouble if they had.

From a very young age, I understood that my mother was overstepping the boundaries with relish. She aggravated Tommy beyond reason. If she would only be quiet for a minute. I willed her to stop, but no – every time, it came to a point where he suddenly snapped. He lost control and punched her in the face or pushed her to the ground.

One day, when George was there, he tried to intervene at

the early stages of a row. Each of them was pushing and jabbing at the other in the chest, backwards and forwards, Tommy more strongly than Mercia, doing their dance of anger. Nose to nose they spat out scathing insults.

'You're such a big man, aren't you, pushing a little woman like me around?' she goaded.

'And you're such a bitch, always trying to find ways to annoy me. You bloody well do it on purpose!' he shouted. Then he hit out at her.

George was seventeen now, a strapping lad, as tall as Tommy. He stepped forward and tried to push himself between them. 'Please calm down, Dad,' he said. 'You're not doing any good, hitting out at Mam. Stop this now!'

But in his anger, my father gained superhuman strength. 'Who are you to tell *me* what to do in my *own* house? I'm the boss here,' he said furiously, and then manhandled George all the way through the house and out of the front door. 'Get out . . . and don't come back!'

As Tommy turned towards the kitchen he spotted me at the bottom of the stairs. 'You see? You've caused this again. It's all your fault. Come here!'

I ran upstairs as fast as I could towards the sanctuary of my bedroom with Tommy, now a purple-faced ogre, chasing me two stairs at a time. I tried not to fall, to get to the top before he caught me, but it was too late. The blows started, his fists flailed. As he hit me repeatedly, I cried and cried. What had I done? Why was it my fault? When would he stop?

Once it was over, between my sobs, I heard Tommy storm out of the house. Mercia bashed things about, ranting and raving to an invisible audience. Finally the air fell silent. A bruised peace enveloped us and the house heaved another sigh of relief. My whole body smarted from my father's blows. I curled up in the corner, hot tears streaming down my face. What had I done? Whatever it was, it must have been very, very bad.

I had learned early on to try and be the peacemaker. Bruised and sobbing, I tiptoed downstairs. My mother was slumped in a chair, exhausted. I put on the kettle and made her a cup of tea. I climbed up on a chair and reached down the prettiest plate from the top cupboard, arranged some biscuits on it and took it through on a tray.

'I'm sorry, Mammy. I'm sorry . . .' I tried to soothe her.

She remained silent. No acknowledgement of me or the tea I'd brought her. She sat and stared out of the window, her face white with anger, Tommy gone who knows where.

'Can I do anything, Mammy?' No reply. The long silence had begun again. I was used to it by now. I knew she probably wouldn't talk to me for days.

I trailed with weary steps back upstairs to my room and sat in the corner. I made myself as small as possible and hugged my one-eared teddy bear, my only friend. I began to think back. What had I done to upset my parents? Why did they always blame me for everything? I didn't know what I'd done wrong, but it must have been something bad. It must all be my fault. I always said sorry, but it was never enough. All I wanted was for them to love me. If I tried as hard as I could, maybe I could make them love me. But whatever I did, it never seemed to make any difference.

Mercia had a black eye the next day, but she told our neighbours she had walked into a door. They looked like they understood. I had to stay at home for a few days till my bruising went down.

My father did come back, but he and Mercia were not speaking again. Not speaking to me, either. That was nothing unusual. Indeed, for me as a child, these were the good times. They ignored each other for days, sometimes weeks on end. My father went off to work each day with barely a word. My mother got me up for school and silently dragged the wire brush through my long auburn hair, hitting me on the head when I cried out as she yanked on the tangles, and then propelled me out of the door without a word. When nobody was speaking, there were no rows, just heavy silences. I would be safe for a while.

George came round rarely after this, and only when he knew Tommy wouldn't be there. It was always great for me when he came, but I didn't see much of him now. I didn't blame him for steering clear of this nightmare family. I was so much younger than him anyway that I was used to feeling like an only child. I was glad he was living his own life, but I often wished I had a brother or sister, especially a sister, close in age to me. Someone at home to commiserate with.

I felt safe when everyone was out and I was alone in my bedroom, but that didn't mean I wasn't lonely. And whenever there were problems in the house, there was nobody to turn to. I yearned for a sister to share things with. I suppose that's why, at about this time, I developed an imaginary one. I used to talk to her when I was on my own. She didn't have a name, I just called her 'Sister', and she was always there for me. She was a good listener. She walked to school with me and I talked to her about everything.

*

My parents never came to school, not even for parents' evenings, but my mother did once turn up to a 'Parents' Day'. We had Scottish dancing lessons at school and the whole class practised a display. I loved Scottish dancing. As I didn't have a kilt to wear, a teacher lent me one, and dancing in it as it swirled was the most exciting moment of my life. I was so proud of myself and I couldn't wait for the performance. My mother sat with the other parents and watched me dance, then she met my teachers, and it was all going well until a teacher asked her about my little sister. Her face froze into a granite mask. 'Helen does not have a sister,' she sniped, and pushed me out of the door.

It is incredible how a day, a moment, can change in a heartbeat. That special day suddenly crumbled to dust. The dark clouds of my mother's anger threatened the promise of what was to come. She dragged me with such force all the long walk home my arm nearly came out of its socket. I begged her not to tell my father about my imaginary sister, but I knew she would. I was sent up to my room to wait.

I started to tremble when I heard Dad's car pull up outside. The angry crescendo of voices downstairs. His footsteps approaching.

My door burst open.

'What is this about a sister? What do you think that makes *me*?'

I didn't know what he meant. I didn't understand. I must have done something very bad.

'I didn't mean it, Daddy, I didn't mean it,' I cried again and again.

He slowly removed his two-inch belt from the waist of his trousers and wound it round his hand. He stepped closer and bellowed at me like a warrior as he held back his arm and began the onslaught. I squeezed into the corner of the room and made myself as small and as safe as I could, but the thrashing went on and on, lash after lash. I couldn't turn away enough. My back and my bare legs were cut and bleeding. I buried my face for protection, and because I didn't want to see his evil expression. At first, the pain burned me more with each stroke of his belt, but after about ten or twelve lashes, I seemed to become more distant from the physical sensations, almost as if it was happening to somebody else. He attacked without pause as I wailed and pleaded for him to stop, which seemed only to goad him all the more. He threatened me, as he did so often: 'If you tell anybody about this . . . you will never live to see another day.' I believed it and lived in fear. Finally, suddenly, he was gone. I did not move. I didn't dare.

Downstairs I heard the angry feud, the raised voices, but I felt so distant now from the present, as if in some sort of cocoon, that I couldn't hear what they screamed at each other, and I didn't care.

However, to my horror, he ran back up the stairs, flung open my bedroom door and slammed it against the wall. The dent in the plaster stayed there for years. I peeked out from underneath my arms. His eyes were bulging.

'You see. It's all your fault again. If it wasn't for you, this wouldn't have happened. You have always been trouble and you always will be!' He turned abruptly and raced down the stairs. The front door creaked open, then smashed against the jamb.

Curled up in the corner, blood oozing from my wounds, I heard his car engine start, rev up and roar away. I remember the relief as the sound faded into the distance; the silence that followed. I remained for quite some time without moving. No one came to comfort me, to tell me it would be all right, or to give me a hug. I knew I would be left alone now.

Cold, stiff and sore, I could feel the caked blood pull and tighten over my wounded skin. I tiptoed silently to the bathroom, ran the tap and used my flannel to clean my injuries. The water ran red.

That night, I sobbed myself to sleep. How long would it be before my father returned? And what would happen to me then?

CHAPTER 8

Jenny
The Water Baby

My father was tall and slightly built, always happy and full of jokes. I don't know how he was so slim – he ate for Newcastle. And he smoked almost non-stop. I don't think I have a single photo of him without a cigarette hanging out of his mouth. Dad loved doing magic and card tricks for me, and he was always telling me stories. I especially remember his tales about the fairies who lived in the basement of Woolworths.

He worked hard – always a full day. When I was old enough, I used to meet him at the station every night with my cocker spaniel, Janie. I loved my dad – he had a smile for everyone he met and was a friend to them all. He adored me. Absolutely adored me.

In fact my cousin and now my very close friend Wendy said to me one day when we were grown-up, 'I wondered sometimes if your mother resented the close relationship you had with your father.'

'You could be right,' I had to agree. 'She never showed it, mind.'

'You were very much a daddy's girl.'

'Yes, that's true.'

I was a daddy's girl and we all knew it. If I had a lot of homework and didn't meet him at the station, he came home and said, 'Where's my love?'

'Well,' my mother replied. 'I know it's not me he wants. It's either Jennifer or the dog!' She adopted an offended expression for a moment, then broke into a smile. She didn't mind really. We all shared the joke.

Mam was a happy person too, most of the time. She was always busy working in the house or going out to do clients' hair in their own homes. A natural redhead, with a vivid mop of orange hair, she always stood out in a crowd. My hair is red too, but a darker shade than hers – more auburn, like in Titian paintings. Mam was as short as my dad was tall – there was more than a foot in height between them, so they made a striking couple. But her small stature belied the strength of her character.

Dad had his own workshop at work and he often used to stay on there to make things for us. One Christmas he gave me a fabulous dolls' house he'd made. To keep it secret, he'd been working on it all year in the kitchen at Wendy's house in the next street to us. It was a wonderful surprise. Dad really loved designing and making things, and he was a talented artist too. I have kept one of his sketch books – a possession I treasure.

My father was an only child, but my mother came from quite a big family, one of six children. We all lived in the same area, most of us only a street or two apart, and we saw each other a lot, always getting together at Christmas, New Year and on family occasions. I had cousins a street away on each side. Wendy was the nearest – her house was only fifty yards away from ours, across the back lane between our yards. Most of the cousins came to stay with us at Embleton at one time or another in the summer. We once had ten people sleeping in our two-bedroom bungalow, all top-to-tail in bed. That was fun.

Because one of Mam's sisters, Gladys, was seriously ill and bed-bound all her life, and Mam's mother had to look after her, Mam worked all the hours she could, sometimes in two or three jobs at the same time, helping to provide for her extended family. They were all very close-knit, always helping one another, and it felt good to have a happy family around us.

As well as hairdressing, sometimes door-to-door to gain new customers, my mother had a part-time job at the Tote, working on a race-track nearby. But her most unusual job was selling Pul-front corsets. She took them round all the pit villages, selling them where she could. She had quite a few customers in Seghill and around that area. Sometimes, clients would come to her, and other times she would fit the corsets in customers' own homes.

She told me a story once about a phone call from a new customer who made an appointment to be measured up for a corset. As soon as the customer arrived, Mam suspected the 'lady' was in fact a man – the stubble on 'her' chin was a big clue – so she made an excuse that she had to go into another room to get something and ran out of the back door to a neighbour and asked her to come and knock on our front door saying there was an emergency at my school and she had to go. Our neighbour saved the day, Mam reported the man to the police, and he never did get his Pul-front corset!

Mam had never played golf before she married dad at the age of thirty-six in 1940, when he was on leave. After the war, he took her along to an exhibition match where Henry Cotton was playing. Henry won his first British Open Championship in the year I was born and Mam was hooked on golf from that day onwards. She learned to play on the Dunstanburgh Castle course at Embleton and became quite a good club player.

Although golf was a keen pastime at Embleton, we children spent much of our time on the beach or in the water, though I did skip off to play golf with my dad quite a bit. I learned to swim very young, without being taught. I remember the day – there was a mother with two daughters, a posh family, watching over us and she called up to my mother.

'Connie. You have to come down. Jennifer is swimming. She is actually swimming!'

My mother looked down. 'She can't possibly be swimming. She's probably just walking along the bottom, you know, just pretending she's swimming.'

'No, Connie. She is swimming!'

Mam came down the steps and was amazed to see this was true.

'So she is.'

'Yes,' replied the other lady. 'She's a natural.'

I was probably about seven or eight. I'd just picked it up by watching the others. I do remember the North Sea water was freezing that day, absolutely freezing!

Soon I was swimming so confidently, I could join in all the swimming games with the older children. I became a strong and competent swimmer after my summers at Embleton, and back home at Jesmond I started spending a lot of my spare time at the Jesmond Baths, which were within walking distance of our house. Seeing how well I was doing, my parents sent me for extra swimming lessons two days a week, which I loved, and very soon I was entered for competitions in various locations. Mum and Dad drove me to all the galas and gave me huge support – I think they enjoyed watching my progress. I just loved swimming.

I was a born competitor, but I didn't realize it then. That carefree summer, all I was doing was having fun with my friends.

When I was a little older, several of us had canoes, and I often went out canoeing with others across the bay, usually taking the dog with me. Sometimes the boys tipped me and Janie out on the other side of the Emblestones. Occasionally, on a calm summer's day, some of us ventured further out to sea and tipped each other out in the deeper water, but always with our life-jackets on, of course, and we always made sure we were all safe. In the bay, seals swam around our canoes, playing with us, barking with excitement. It was all great fun and we often had the bay more or less to ourselves.

On the sunniest days, visitors from a wide area around us would drive up to the clubhouse and make the trek across the dunes and the golf course to our beach. It was sufficiently remote that it never got crowded, but I have a memory, aged seven or eight, of standing at the top of the steps and looking down on strangers, small family groups settling in for the day with their picnics and their striped wind-breaks, carefully arranging them to shelter their deckchairs on the warm sands. Some of them were building sandcastles, some were playing bat and ball as it was a calm day. One girl, about the same age as me, maybe a bit younger, was sitting alone in the shallow water playing with a spade, poking at worm holes on the rippling sand. A man, presumably her father, was trying to persuade a woman to stand near the child. She took a lot of coaxing. I watched with curiosity and a mild sense of discomfort. The girl ignored the woman, who seemed very reluctant to go near her, though eventually the woman came close enough for a photo, but it struck me as strange that she didn't smile or hug the girl or play with her in the water, like my parents would have done.

At that point, my dad called and I went off to caddy for him on the course. When I got back I looked out for them, but they had gone.

When I was ten, my dear grandpa died. It was the first time I lost someone close to me. He had become gradually more poorly, and of course I knew he was old, so I think it was expected, but I'm not sure what he died of. I just remember how sad I felt and how much I missed his warm smile whenever I came in from school. Now his room was empty, which was how I felt inside without him. I don't remember a funeral, so it must have been on a school day, when I couldn't go. Or perhaps they didn't want me to go.

The winters were always icy cold in our house at West Jesmond. There was no heating other than the coal fire in the lounge, and I used to sleep in my clothes on the coldest nights. I made a game of breathing out long warm breaths and watching them freeze in the chilly air. In the mornings I scraped ice off the windows in my bedroom and the bathroom, which was the coldest room in the house. Thank goodness we now had an inside toilet, which Dad had put in, so we didn't have to brave the low temperatures outside.

It was a particularly bleak winter's day when Auntie Edna lost Bobby, her budgie. He flew out of the open window, and Auntie Edna was inconsolable because Bobby wasn't just any old budgie. He could say a lot of words. He could even say his name and address. She was so upset that all the family had to rally round, regardless of the weather – the snowdrift on our front doorstep was so deep that we had to dig our way out of the house. Local kids were sledging in the street and throwing snowballs at each other and I wanted to join in, but all the family were detailed to go out and hunt for Bobby the budgie. We went down all the local streets, calling out his name, but there was no sign of him. We asked around, but nobody had seen him. We all trudged home that night through a blizzard, tired, freezing and disappointed that we hadn't found him.

Auntie Edna put a lost budgie notice in the *Evening Chronicle* the next day, but had no calls. She was devastated. It seemed hopeless. But a week later, somebody rang her doorbell. It was a family from the other side of the Town Moor, several miles away, with Bobby the budgie in a box. They had found the bedraggled bird in their garden, thin and cold, but alive and relatively well, considering his ordeal.

'When we saw him,' the man told Auntie Edna, 'the budgie just kept saying, "Bobby Scott. 28 Fairfield Road".'

CHAPTER 9

Helen

Home Alone

Schooldays were the best because I was out of the house and with other people. I loved school and made lots of friends, but they would never come back to my house. Later I discovered why – they were all terrified of my father. School holidays, therefore, were lonely. Each day Mum left early, telling me, 'Stay in bed till I get back.' She went off to work in the farmhouse, where she did all their domestic chores, including their laundry, hating it. She never let us forget how much she hated it.

Those mornings were long in the empty house, sitting in bed with only colouring books to keep me company till her return at lunchtime, when I was allowed to get up. I wasn't even allowed to go down and watch the television that my father had bought when we moved to Murton village, but I suppose there would only have been black and white westerns to watch in those days.

My bedroom was an empty space. I was never allowed pictures or posters. I had no furniture, except a cardboard box for a night-table. Even my light bulb lacked a shade. I slept on an old pipe-framed hospital bed my dad had found in a scrapyard and painted white to hide the rust. It was a spring-base with a hospital mattress, full of lumps the size of tennis balls. Fortunately, it didn't occur to me then to wonder how many people had died or were incontinent on that mattress. I was aware of the contrast between my barren bedroom with its cold lino floor and my parents' elegant boudoir, carpeted and decked out with a 'Swedish design' suite and frilled soft furnishings.

Mercia never lit a fire in our house till lunchtime when she got home, so it was often bitterly cold while I waited. I spent long hours wrapped in a blanket with my nose pressed up against my bedroom window, drawing pictures in the condensation, watching the farm workers drive their tractors to and fro in the farmyard opposite our house. At least with my parents both at work there was no friction during those times. Alone was always the safest place for me.

During this period, when I was about seven or eight, my father's practical jokes, always bizarre, developed a cruel quality. Indeed, the worse they were, the more he enjoyed them. One day, after he came home from work, he called me into the kitchen. He had a matchbox in his hand which he held up towards me.

'Look, I cut my finger off at work today. Here it is.' He slid open the matchbox, into which of course he had pushed his finger, covered in red paint to look like blood. I flinched in horror at the sight of it and a terrible wave of nausea welled up inside me. He collapsed with laughter – it put him in a good mood all evening. I had nightmares for weeks.

Another day, when I was sitting on the floor in the living room with my sketch-pad and pencils, drawing, my father leaned across to look. 'Give that to me,' he said. 'I'm going to draw your portrait, so sit still.'

I sat as still as I could for a long time. I knew I'd be in trouble if I didn't. I hardly dared to breathe. It seemed like for ever.

Finally he stopped, triumphant. 'There you are. That's you!' He passed the sketch-pad over to me and I took it and looked, unable to hide my dismay. The drawing that was meant to be me was a picture of a monster with huge buck teeth and protruding eyes, a fat, spot-strewn face and hair like wild string. I stared at this horrific image.

'Can't you take a joke?' he guffawed.

Much as he expected to be in absolute control of everything and everyone, my father met his match from an unexpected source one afternoon. He always had unreliable cars, and his latest one needed a lot of work, so he spent all his spare time on it. Every time we looked out of the window, all we could see was his feet sticking out from underneath the car.

The nearby pig farm had a huge and vicious boar that often escaped and rampaged through the village. Tommy was working under the car as usual when this boar broke free and came down our street. It stopped still and stared when it noticed my father's feet. Oblivious, Tommy slid out and to his surprise came face to jowls with this slobbering monster. The boar snorted and pawed the ground, then squared up to charge. My father squealed and shot back under the car. The boar stood there waiting for him to emerge again, while my mother and I watched from the window, too scared to do anything. We didn't have a phone, so couldn't raise the alarm, and it happened to be a quiet day in the village when nobody came by, so Tommy was trapped under the car for several hours until the boar was recaptured and returned to the piggery.

It was quite a revelation to me to see my father dominated by a mere animal.

At about this time, my parents received a letter to say polio vaccinations were now available and would be carried out in my school. All parents received the note, requesting a signature of consent for their child to have the vaccine. This started a huge row in our house. Predictably, my parents disagreed. My mother wanted me to be vaccinated. My father was adamant that I should not be.

'It's a government plot,' he said. 'Children's lives are cheap to experiment on. It's never been done before, so it's bound to be dangerous.' There was an angry exchange, their voices rising in turn.

'She's mine,' protested my mother. 'I want her to have it.'

'And I don't.'

This accelerated throughout the evening, until Tommy tired of it and my mother eventually got her own way.

'Well, just do as you like,' he snapped. 'I don't care.'

With the consent form signed, I returned it to school and was vaccinated as arranged.

The next day I woke up with a temperature of 104 and the doctor was called out. He checked me over with a puzzled expression. He prodded and poked me, then stood back and scratched his head. 'She's clearly ill . . . from an indeterminate cause.' I didn't understand that. He gave instructions and said he would come back the next morning.

My mother, for once, followed his orders and put a wet

cloth across my forehead in a vain attempt to cool me down. However, muffled up with layers of blankets, I sank into a delirium. I was in the midst of a weird scenario of green and brown snakes that crawled up my walls and across the ceiling to the light fitting, right above my bed. As the snakes coiled down the light fitting and reached out their snapping fangs towards me, monsters broke through my wallpaper and spoke in distant, hushed voices, words I couldn't quite hear.

When I came to later in the day, confused, my parents were in the middle of a row, trading insults downstairs. Through the fog of my illness I could hear them arguing. It was obviously my fault and I feared another thrashing.

'You see,' taunted my father, shouting loud enough for me to hear. 'I told you! It's the polio vaccination that has done this! She is probably going to die,' He was triumphant because I had proved him right.

I lay in my darkened room and pondered those words, repeating them in my head over and over again: 'She's probably going to die . . . going to die.'

Next morning the doctor returned. 'It's measles,' he said. 'The worst case I have ever seen.' He stood over the bed with a gleeful smile and peered at my eyes. 'Keep the curtains drawn at all times. Do not expose her to any light as her eyes are badly affected. You will need to bathe them three or four times a day. This little girl is gravely ill.'

So that's it, I thought. I will surely die and go to my grave. Then I must have lost consciousness.

In and out of delirium, I was not aware of days merging into nights over the next ten days. Every morning Mercia went to work as usual. I was left alone, 'gravely ill', at home. I don't know how carefully my mother followed the doctor's instructions – I was too ill to notice. Gradually I improved a little. Soon I was allowed downstairs for lunch and spent the afternoons wrapped up in a blanket on the sofa, the coal fire roaring up the chimney, dozing in the warmth, with nothing else to do. Sometimes, when my father came in, he would bring me a packet of Maltesers or a tube of Smarties, but I had no appetite for them yet.

I recovered from the measles, but I felt weak and couldn't regain my usual energy. I developed another high temperature and the doctor was called for. This time it was chicken pox. Once again, my life was 'Stay in bed until I get back.' I sat for hours on end, itching and scratching as I watched the world outside my window. When my spots went I was allowed downstairs. A few days later, I was hit by another fever – mumps.

This period of childhood illness created a lifelong memory of isolation and loneliness. For a large part of each day I could only sleep, go to the bathroom, look longingly out of the window and try to entertain myself. Nobody was there to see if I was all right, whether I needed anything. With no exercise and little food I weakened further for a time. There was no human warmth, not even a sympathetic smile. They attended to my physical needs, but did not in any way *care* for me. I just accepted this. I don't think I realized then that other parents hugged their children.

All in all I was at home for three months, which was a big chunk out of my learning. Finally the day came for me to return to school and I skipped through the fields till my pulse raced. I missed my friends, as none of them had dared to come and find out how I was, so I couldn't wait to see them all.

When I arrived, they all gathered round, curious about my absence and pleased to see me again. We went into the classroom and started the day's lessons.

Then I realized that something was wrong. Everyone else had their heads down, doing their sums or answering questions in their books, but I couldn't do it. I had always been quick at schoolwork before. Now I didn't know how to do it – it was too hard for me. I felt adrift, frightened. I'd had no teaching or tutoring for three months and my peers had leapt ahead of me. The previous year I had been top of my class in English and mental arithmetic. I was a class monitor and excelled at PE. Now I was bottom of the class, not yet strong enough to do well at PE, and I couldn't do the work. I had always enjoyed school – it had been a happy place for me; but not now.

One day, the teacher announced to the class, including me, that I was being transferred to the 'B' stream. I was horrified. Nobody had warned me. I shrank in my seat and prayed to disappear, while the teacher gave a long talk to the children explaining that not every child could manage the 'A' stream. 'I want you all to understand and be kind to Helen.'

They all turned to look at me. I closed my eyes and turned away to hide my embarrassment.

At the end of the lesson I joined the 'B' stream class. I didn't know anyone there. I began to hate the school I'd once loved, and the 'friends' who now shunned me because I was no longer one of them. While I was away I had become a stranger to them. With my demotion, that was how they wanted to keep it.

Then another problem arose. I was tall for my age, quiet

and well-behaved, so I was put at the back of the class. I didn't mind, but something about it worried me.

One day the teacher asked me to read a sentence out from the blackboard. I had been dreading this. I was an excellent reader and I loved reading, but I couldn't read what the teacher had written on the board. All the other children turned around to look at me, some of them sniggering and some laughing aloud, and when the teacher asked me to come to the front of the class, I flinched because I thought I was in trouble.

But it was all right. She asked me again to read what was on the board, and this time I read it out loud without a problem. I was so grateful to that teacher. She understood that I couldn't see the writing clearly from the back, and sent a note to my mother: 'Helen needs an eyesight test.' My mother read the note and gave her martyr sigh.

I was taken to the optician. 'I'm afraid your daughter's vision has been affected by the measles,' he said. 'She needs to wear spectacles.'

Six weeks later, my glasses arrived, with thick Buddy Holly frames – hardly feminine! For a nine-year-old girl, at this difficult time in her school life, this was another hurdle to face. Several of the children laughed at me and my spectacles and called me names, so I avoided wearing them whenever possible, but in time everyone got used to them, and they came into fashion soon after that, so I didn't mind any more.

My grades began to improve dramatically. I was moved back to the 'A' stream where I regained my place in the top three of the class – thanks to my pop-star glasses.

A few months later, while walking home from school one day, a man with a bike stopped and approached me.

'Hello. I'm a police detective,' he said. 'Your teacher sent me to take you back to school because you stole some money from her purse.'

I burst into tears. 'No I didn't.'

'Well, I'll need to search you. Your teacher said you'd put the money in your knickers.' He lunged forward and grabbed me, and before I could get away he pulled down my knickers and started to touch me.

I screamed and screamed as loud as I could – fortunately very loud, which made him hesitate and look around. I think I had unnerved him. Then he picked me up and threw me high into the air to the side of the road and into a pile of nettles, got on his bike and rode away.

I sat on my bare bottom in the nettles, stung all over, hurting like hell, then scrambled up and ran home, crying hysterically. My father was home early from work that day, so he took me to the police station and a very kind policeman sat me on the counter.

'Can you tell me what happened?'

I answered his questions – very shy because of what the man had done. I was nervous about mentioning my knickers to a strange man, or even to my own father, but the policeman wrote it all down in a statement and Tommy signed it. There was no doctor, and no medical examination. That was the end of it, and I never heard any more about it. I don't even know whether they caught the man.

After this, my parents bought me a bike to ride to school. I suppose they thought I would be safer that way. I was thrilled, of course, to have my own bike. It was two-tone blue. I polished it every day until it sparkled.

Every summer we went out at weekends with Uncle James, Auntie Gladys and my cousin Malcolm. Uncle James was always my mother's favourite brother, and the only one my father got on with. He and Uncle James both had old cars which constantly broke down. Once when we were on the way somewhere, following each other, my father changed gear and the lever came off in his hand. He stuck it out of the sunroof and waved it about, Uncle James stopped behind us and we all dissolved into fits of giggles. On another trip, my uncle put out his indicator flap to turn right but drove straight on. My father followed him as he slowed down and stopped.

'What are you playing at?' said Tommy. 'Why didn't you turn right?'

Uncle James wound down the window. 'That's why,' he laughed as he handed my father the steering wheel.

We used to picnic wherever one of the cars broke down, and the men would spend the rest of the day fixing the cars so that we could get home again. Those were fun days – the rare occasions when my parents were almost normal and there was little threat of a row because the others were with us. The greatest joy was the occasional rides in my uncle's car, surrounded by laughter, singing and sandwiches.

Sometimes we drove up the coast of Northumberland to a windswept beach at Embleton, where the seals played and the kittiwakes wheeled over the sand dunes. We had to walk across the golf links to reach the beach. I sat and built sand-castles or paddled in the rippling stream, beneath a low cliff.

At the top there was a higgledy-piggledy group of little wooden houses where people came to stay.

There was always a group of children playing games behind the houses, or on the beach nearby. Sometimes I watched them swimming out in the bay and wished I could join them. They were mostly older than me, and strong swimmers.

I have a photo of me with a wide smile, sitting in the shallow water at Embleton. To the right of the picture stands my mother, detached. She didn't want to be in the picture with me – she always preferred to do her model pose on her own – but my father insisted on snapping the two of us together that day. She wasn't happy about it.

When it was done, I saw a girl standing on top of the dunes looking down at us. I caught her gaze, then she ran off.

George was now progressing well in his engineering apprenticeship at Wallsend ship yards. We didn't know at the time, but he had met his future wife, Joan. They were both seventeen and very much in love.

Soon George brought Joan over to meet us. He didn't have a car and there was no bus back to Wallsend, or to Whitley Bay, where she lived, so if they came on a Saturday evening, they used to stay overnight and go home the next day.

When Joan and George stayed, I had to move into the spare room and share a bed with Joan, while George slept in my room. I didn't mind – it was fun because I liked Joan. She was always kind to me and easy to talk to. She used to talk about her family.

'My dad's a ship's captain,' she told me with a wide grin

and a sparkle in her eyes. 'He's away at sea a lot, and we all miss him, so it's lovely when he's home for a while.'

Joan was a typist at Tyne Brand Foods. She used to tell me stories about things that happened at work, or about her two younger sisters and the mischief they got up to. To me, their lives sounded so much more interesting than mine.

The thing that fascinated me most about Joan in those early days was her hair. I never knew what colour it would be – every time she came it was different. She kept it short and I used to watch her back-comb it every morning. There wasn't a mirror in the bedroom, so she'd say, 'What do you think?'

I'd put both thumbs up. 'Champion!'

Then I'd watch her, mesmerized, as she put on her eye make-up and lipstick, and giggle as she did up the suspenders to keep up her stockings. Her clothes were amazing – full dirndl skirts over layers of stiff lacy petticoats, with little bolero tops over broderie-Anglaise blouses. Or sometimes flouncy satin or chiffon dresses with stripes or swirly patterns. For a child with very few clothes, this was heaven, but I couldn't help feeling a little jealous.

The atmosphere in the house was tricky on those weekends, with George and Tommy resentful of each other and a cold disdain hanging between them. But Joan was such good company that even Tommy tolerated George's presence.

In fact, Joan and George sometimes used to listen to their fifties music on our radio. My father hated Elvis's 'Jailhouse Rock'. 'I won't have that screeching rant in my house.' But he didn't mind some of the ballads, like the Everley Brothers' 'All I Have to Do Is Dream'.

My parents' favourites were the big band productions of

the thirties and forties, especially Glenn Miller, which they danced to all over the house on their good days. I think their favourite fifties singer was David Whitfield, who sang with Mantovani's orchestra. We all used to sing along to his 'On the Street Where You Live'.

After a few months, George and Joan split up for a time and George had a series of different girlfriends. Every Saturday night I was uprooted from my own room to share a bed with another girl who was a complete stranger to me. I hated this. I didn't know any of them and dreaded the weekends. Why couldn't he go back to Joan? She was always my favourite.

When his wages as an apprentice went up, George bought himself a sleek black overcoat with a black velvet collar. Very trendy at the time. When he came round one day wearing it, my father went ballistic.

'Get that bloody coat off,' he yelled at George. 'I will not allow you to wear that coat.'

George refused. 'No. I bought it with my own money. I'm going to wear it.'

I sat at the top of the stairs in a state of consternation, watching this altercation in the hall.

My father picked George up by his new coat collar and slammed him back against the wall. He pushed his face into George's. 'You look like a hooligan. Take that coat off.'

'No.'

Tommy slammed him against the wall again and punched George hard in the face, making his nose bleed. With that, my father released his grip a little and George took the opportunity to wrestle himself free. He walked straight out of the front door and slammed it behind him. To his credit, he did not fight back or retaliate in any way. But I think if he had it would not have gone well. When Tommy was in a rage, he acquired a physical strength that conquered all.

George never came round again. If only I could have left with him.

CHAPTER 10

Helen

The Madhouse

When I was about ten, my father became a bus driver and we moved to a two-bedroom flat on the top floor of a Victorian terraced house in Whitley Bay, which I later found was about three miles from Murton.

My mother packed the boxes and Tommy ordered the removal van, the day came and we were ready to go. I had mixed feelings about it. I thought it seemed like a bit of an adventure, but I was apprehensive about having to start at another junior school and being the 'new girl' again. They loaded up the car to its roof. It was so full that I wondered how I would squeeze in.

Then I noticed something.

'What about my bike?' I didn't want to leave that behind.

'You can ride your bike to the new house.' This was an order. I could see from my father's set expression that I had no choice. 'You'll have to follow the car.'

They didn't give me the address or tell me the way.

'Make sure you keep up with us,' added Tommy as they climbed in and started up the engine.

I loved my bike and enjoyed riding it the mile to school,

but I had never gone any further than that. I had no idea that day how far we were going and had no time to hesitate. They were off.

I got on and pedalled furiously as they pulled away at some speed. With each bend or turning, panic set in as I felt sure I would lose them – I couldn't turn my legs fast enough. I'd only cycled on country lanes before and the open roads and urban streets were packed with traffic that morning. I was especially afraid of the buses and lorries, whose lumbering wake nearly blasted me into the gutter. I suppose my father must have slowed down when I fell back, because I never entirely lost their trail, but I was petrified I would. Then what would I do? Somehow I managed to stay on and keep up until we reached our destination.

Exploring the new place didn't take long. We had two bedrooms, a living room, dining room and kitchen, plus the eighteen stairs down to the hall and the front door. We also had the divided half of a stone staircase down to the back door and the back yard. This kind of arrangement was known as a Tyne flat. We had a tin bath under the kitchen counter, but the toilet was down the back stairs and outside in the yard. My father used to hang an oil lamp in there in a vain attempt to prevent it from freezing in the winter.

Although our new flat was fairly cramped, I did have my own bedroom. My window overlooked life in Eskdale Terrace, a busy side road, just off the seafront. No cows or tractors, but plenty going on – people bustled by or paused to chat, seagulls squawked on roof-tops, and when I opened my window I sucked in the tang of salt in the air. We were near the middle of town, with a roundabout at one end of the street and the sea at the other. Great excitement!

My parents crammed in their furniture as best they could and my father set about redecorating the whole flat. His first job was to knock out a huge black range along one wall in the dining room. It was so big and heavy that it took him a week to get it out. He replaced it with a neat modern fireplace. Next he wallpapered the dingy walls of the main rooms with floral wallpaper, which came untrimmed, so it was my job to sit for hours trimming the wallpaper on both edges, as straight as I could.

Later Tommy divided the kitchen up to make a small bathroom, just big enough to squeeze in a proper bath, but nothing else. He put up washable wallpaper in what was left of the kitchen – a pale blue background with red teapots and vegetables all over it, and bought a cheap kitchen table and chairs at the auction rooms, painting them bright red to match, though my mother always covered the table with an oilcloth. Against one wall was the only other piece of furniture – a wooden kitchen cabinet with glass sliding doors and a drop-down flap which doubled as a worktop.

Once we'd settled in, my mother, released at last from doing housework at the farm, took a new job in the local laundry, five minutes' walk away. I quickly made friends at my new school and everything began well. I felt strangely optimistic, but I think I knew this couldn't last.

The move coincided with George finishing his apprenticeship, and going off to sea in his new job as ship's engineer. He would be travelling the world on long trips often lasting a year or more. George had always been my champion and I missed him terribly. but I loved the excitement of receiving his postcards, addressed only to me, from every port of call. I read and reread them and collected them in a scrapbook.

I was amazed that these flimsy postcards reached me across the seas from so many countries. I tracked his journeys on a globe at school and looked up the places in our classroom atlas.

I remember one postcard in particular, sent from Japan. This was the early sixties, and transistor radios had just become available in England. I was desperate to have one, but I knew my parents wouldn't give in. George wrote: 'I've got you a little transistor radio. It's very small and I'm going to bring it back for you to have.' Well, you can imagine how excited I was about that, but there were six months of this trip to go and it was hard to wait all that time.

In another card from the Suez Canal he told me he'd bought me a pair of red satin curly-toed slippers, embroidered with gold thread. I was thrilled as they were really fashionable then. In most of his cards he wrote things like: 'I'm missing you and I hope you do well at school.' I always rushed to look when the postman came.

When he got back from his first long trip away, he and Joan got back together again, which was a great excitement for me, and when George went off again, Joan missed him terribly and came to visit us every Sunday for tea. I loved it when she came, because I always felt safe when she was there. Joan knew how things were in our home, and many years later we talked about those visits.

'I loved teatime at the madhouse,' she said with a giggle. 'It was like a horror movie. I never knew what was going to happen next.'

How true.

Soon the arguments, the shouts and screams began in our new home. My father found out that our flat was next door to the sister of my mother's first husband. This was a disaster!

Mercia's former sister-in-law was quite a lot older and a bit of a terror, not afraid to speak her mind. But she was nice to us at first.

'Haaway, Mercia, pet,' she said when she came and knocked on our door. 'Fancy us being neighbours. What a coincidence. And the family too. Well I never!'

'Hello, Annie. I haven't seen you in years.'

'And how old is your bonny lassie?'

'Helen is ten.'

'Well, but. Where have the years gone? She's big for her age, isn't she?' She paused and turned to look at Tommy with a sneer. 'And this is your new man?'

He bridled at her tone, clearly taken aback.

As soon as the door closed, he turned on my mother. 'Did you know about this? Did you know she lived here?'

'No.'

'You should have told me. I'd never have agreed to move here if I'd known.'

'I didn't know,' she smirked.

'Don't you lie to me!' His face reddened with rage as he grasped her shoulders and slammed her back against the wall. 'I won't have her in this house. You will have nothing to do with her. Is that clear?' This was no question.

Mercia stayed silent, which angered Tommy all the more.

'Pit-yacker,' he shouted in her face. 'You'll always be a bloody pit-yacker, wherever you live. I've had enough of your insolence. I *forbid* that woman to come into our house. There will be hell to pay if I ever see her here again.'

In those days, nobody used to lock their doors, so only

the next day Annie came up the stairs and straight into our living room without being asked. 'I've come to see how you're getting on.' She cast a scathing glance round the half-wallpapered room and the rubble from the range through the dining-room door. 'Eee, pet. It looks like a bombsite up here.'

'Let's go down to your place,' suggested Mercia. Then she turned to me. 'Don't you tell your father, mind,' she warned.

I nodded. There was no way I would tell him anything I didn't have to. But over the next few days Annie continued to come up whenever it suited her. It seemed that, being senior to my mother in age and status in that family, she was fearless. She took no notice of Mercia's requests not to come up to our flat. Of course, she didn't know what Tommy could be like.

I suppose it was inevitable that he would find out. One Saturday morning, Annie walked straight in without any warning. Tommy leapt to his feet and stamped over to her.

'Stop right there,' he ordered. 'Who gave you permission to come into this flat?'

She stood her ground. 'I'll come when I like, man. I'll have you know that, as Mercia's older sister-in-law, I should have the right to enter her home whenever I like.'

Tommy clenched his fists and puffed out his chest as he pushed himself forward, bodily propelling her towards the door. 'You have *no* rights in my house,' he bellowed. 'I am master here and no one can come in without *my* permission.'

'Is that so, Mr High-and-Mighty? Well, she's my sister-in-law.'

'You're nothing to me. What I say goes. Get out of my house, *now*.' As he said that, he manhandled her, protesting, out of the door and to the top of the stairs. 'Good riddance to bad rubbish.'

It seems this scene didn't deter Annie from coming round again, but it was always when Tommy was out. She and my mother slipped into an uneasy sort of friendship. Mercia had no friends really, so I thought this was a good thing until one day when my mother made the mistake of blurting it out to Tommy when he came home.

'Annie was round here for tea,' she began.

'I *told* you she must never come round again,' he shouted.

'I didn't want her to,' said Mercia. 'When she'd gone, I found out what she's really like. She found some dust on the sideboard and wrote in it.'

'What did she write?'

'Slut.'

'Well, she's not wrong there.'

'You brute,' said Mercia. 'I thought you'd stick up for me.'

'I'll stick up for you, all right,' he taunted. 'Like this.' He slapped her across the face. 'That's for being a slut.' He did it again on the other side, with even greater force. 'And that's for disobeying my orders.' Then he gave her a punch in the eye. As Mercia reeled and fell to her knees, her hands to her face, he had one last outburst. 'I'm master of this house and that bloody women is not coming back over my threshold. She's just a useless fishwife. That's all she is. She's as bad as her brother, that bastard you married before me. Scum. They're all scum, the lot of them.'

He stormed out of the flat, down the stairs and round to Annie's next door. I didn't hear much of the raucous alter-cation that followed, but that was the last time we ever spoke to her or any of her family.

My father worked shifts on the buses, while my mother worked shifts in the laundry. I came home from school each day to an empty flat. It was my job to clean the grate and light the fire, and I became proficient at this, aged ten. Next I peeled the vegetables and cooked the dinner. By the time my mother came home, the flat was always warm and tea was nearly ready. When Tommy came home I put the meal out on the table.

As we ate, he watched the six o'clock news on the BBC. No talking was allowed. When we had finished, my father clicked his fingers at me, pointed towards the kitchen and said, 'Dishes. Now!' While they relaxed in the living room and watched television, I washed up and put away in the kitchen, in silence. This was the routine every day. Finally, I was allowed to sit down for an hour to do my homework, then it was off to bed.

It was always the same. Whatever Tommy said, I had to jump to attention. There was one day, when I was sitting at the dining table doing a jigsaw puzzle, when I was just a moment too slow.

'Get a bucket of coal for the fire.'

Engrossed in my jigsaw, I hesitated for a second.

'*NOW!*' he bellowed.

I ran down the back stairs and out to the yard behind the house, where I filled a bucket with coal as quickly as I could. I dragged it to the back door and up the step, then struggled up the concrete stairs with it, one by one, trying not to spill any on the way. When I got back to the living room and went to put some coal on the fire, I was horrified to see my jigsaw in pieces burning brightly on the embers in the grate.

'When I tell you to do something, madam, you will do it immediately.'

I had to hide my tears and bite my lips shut. I knew any emotion would fuel his anger.

At around this time, things really started to fall apart. I arrived home from school one day to find my mother sitting in the lounge with a padded bandage swathed round her leg.

'Something happened at work,' she said. 'It was an accident. I gashed my leg on a machine.' She paused for effect. She never missed an opportunity to build up the drama. 'They took me to hospital to have my wound stitched.'

'Is it bad?'

'Quite bad,' she pouted. 'The doctor said it was a soft-tissue wound.'

When my father came in, he flew into a temper. After a great deal of bluster, he decided to make the most of the situation. 'I'm going to sue that laundry for negligence.'

I don't know how long this case took to be scheduled for the court, but eventually the laundry settled for £200 compensation, which was a great deal of money in 1961. My mother was delighted. My father was triumphant.

The next day they took the day off and went on a spending spree. They both bought themselves new clothes and shoes, together with a few other things for the flat. I remember that day so well. I arrived home from school to a C&A bag lying on a chair.

My mother pointed at it. 'Look what we bought for you.'

With a feeling of dread, I opened the bag. I could not believe what I saw. It was a coat, a beige coat. Beige of all colours! It had a knitted collar and cuffs. This was already bad enough, but the real shock hit me when I lifted it out. It was lined with *foam-rubber*. *This coat was so stiff it was capable of standing up on its own!*

Total humiliation. 'Thank you,' I mumbled, and turned away to hide my tears. I was nearly eleven years old . . . I thought: my world will surely end if my friends see me in this monstrosity. I will die of shame. I can't wear this coat. I just can't.

They made me wear it, of course.

The final surprise was what they spent the rest of the money on. A huge, black beast – a Rover 90 car with the softest blue leather upholstery. Its previous owner was a famous singer – David Whitfield, the crooner whose songs we had heard on the radio at Murton. The whole of Eskdale Terrace, all our neighbours, gasped and called each other to come and look when my father drove it home the first time.

'David Whitfield used to own this car, you know,' announced my father.

Amazement spread like an infection. The car was indeed a wonder.

Tommy took us over to Grandma's one afternoon. He wanted to show it to her – he knew she would be impressed – so we drove over to her house and took her out for a drive in it. She was all dressed up in her Sunday best, with her scarf, coat, matching shoes and bag, topped off with her favourite straw hat, flowers strewn around the brim. She sat next to my father in the front, a permanent smile on her face.

'Eee, lad. It's a grand car. I feel like a grand lady.'

'You are a grand lady,' smiled Tommy with a mischievous look. 'Most of the time!'

'Haaway!' she chuckled.

I loved the way Grandma laughed, with that twinkle in her eyes.

Tommy drove the Rover to work every day, even though he was allowed to jump on a passing bus for free. It was immediately clear to my mother that this car required a lot of petrol. It was too expensive to run. Then my father started getting home later and later. He was always on different shifts, so I didn't really notice, but my mother did. I was often woken in the early hours by their rows – I heard the fights, the violence. One night they raged at each other right outside my bedroom door, trading insults and accusations as usual. But this night was different. I sat up. My mother seemed to be accusing Tommy of something. I couldn't quite make it out, but it was something to do with a female bus conductor he worked with. Mercia had mentioned her name before, with disastrous results. She couldn't stop herself. But this time she had gone too far.

'*I'm leaving,*' shouted my mother.

'Go on, then,' said Tommy.

'You can have your trollope, for all I care.'

I heard the tussle as they bumped against my door and screeched at each other. Then there was an almighty heave as he pushed her over the top step. 'I won't have you accusing me, do you hear?'

She let out a piercing scream.

'NO!' I yelled as I jumped out of bed.

I heard her roll, thud, thud, thud, one stair at a time, all the way to the bottom. Then silence. I rushed to open my bedroom door – I knew she'd need help – and in his fury, my father picked me up and threw me down after her. I tumbled and bumped by turns, all the way to the bottom, where I landed on top of my mother.

At the head of the stairs stood my father, his eyes bulging. '*Get out! Get out!*' he bellowed.

We both lay still. We couldn't move.

After a few seconds, he raced down the stairs, jumped over us and ran out of the door to the street. As it slammed behind him, I slumped into a faint. It must have been only moments because I was roused by the sound of his thirsty Rover as it revved away into the night.

Somehow, we picked ourselves up, bruised and shaken.

'Are you all right?' I said.

'Aye.'

'Me too.'

We both picked our way gingerly upstairs and went to bed. It was the start of another long silence between us.

I don't know where my father went. He didn't come back for weeks. My mother didn't speak to me – she ignored me in every way. Nothing unusual, maybe, but she frightened me this time. Tommy was gone who knows where? Would he ever come back?

It was eerily quiet. With Tommy gone and my mother almost in a trance, I was walking on shaky ground. We were in limbo. The prolonged silence and uncertainty disturbed my thoughts, especially in bed at night. I couldn't get to sleep for worrying about it all. What would happen if Tommy didn't come back? Would my mother ever speak to me again? How would we manage? I worried that somehow I'd caused this to happen and that now we would all suffer for it.

One night I woke up in a cold sweat in the middle of the night. I couldn't breathe properly – I gasped for air. The more I tried to breathe, the less I seemed to take in. I could only take short breaths and my heart was pounding, very fast and shallow. I was terrified. What was the matter with me? When I tried to slow down and breathe deeper, I rasped, and a desperate panic rose up and blocked my throat. My lungs hurt so much I was afraid they would burst. I knew I must be very ill. I tried to sit up. A draught of fresh air from the window blew across my bare arms and shocked me into taking a breath. Would this be my last? My head spun and I fell back on the pillow, staring at the ceiling, terrified. Was I about to die? I wanted to call for help, but I couldn't. I didn't dare wake my mother and cause more trouble, but I might die with no one to help me. I felt abandoned in my own home and the most frightened I've ever been.

It seemed as if I was awake in this state for a long time, but I must have fallen asleep eventually. I woke up in the morning exhausted, but I got up as if everything was normal. I felt weak and faint when I went to school, but somehow I kept going without anyone realizing.

That night was the worst, but I continued to have these attacks for quite some time – perhaps a few months – whenever there was conflict in the house. I think I learned to deal with the attacks better, and gradually they receded.

Finally Tommy turned up again. They didn't speak to each other, or me, for a couple of months. I was confused – relieved he was back, but scared about what might happen. At least we had money coming in again – we wouldn't lose our home. But I found it surreal that nobody spoke for so long. If my mother made a meal at the weekend, she didn't say it was ready. It was just plonked on the table. It went cold if I didn't see it was there. Nobody woke me up for school in the mornings. I got myself ready and went, with no goodbyes. It was a solitary time, but at least I wasn't in trouble for a while.

I'm not sure exactly when it happened, but at some stage my mother took to her bed. I didn't realize at first, with us all living so separately, but at some point I noticed that she had simply stopped getting up at all. When I arrived home from school each day, she was lying down, covers up to her chin. I cooked some tea for my father to eat when he came home from work, and tried to prepare something tempting for her too. But it was no use. She refused everything.

My eleventh birthday passed by with no recognition. I did all of the laundry, I shopped, lit the fires, cleaned the house and ironed – all those bus-driver shirts! My mother didn't speak to me, whatever I did for her. If she looked at me at all, it was with distaste, sometimes hatred. Especially when I tried to persuade her to talk, or to eat. She weakened day by day.

Eventually it struck me this was serious. I garnered the courage to speak to my father. 'I think Mam is really ill. Can we call the doctor?'

He gave me a long look. 'Really?'

I nodded.

'All right. Maybe we should.'

The doctor came and examined her. I remember so well the words he uttered when he came out of the room.

'She has malnutrition.'

'Malnutrition?' exclaimed my father, incredulous. 'That's impossible. Surely not?'

'It really is, I'm afraid. Malnutrition. You'll have to feed her up. You must feed her round the clock. Otherwise . . .'

Otherwise . . . That was the last word I heard. It was enough. I didn't want to hear what followed.

They carried on talking, oblivious of me, while I crept

downstairs and out of the front door. Safely outside, I strode down the road and along the seafront. It was a bracing day – the sky, the sea, everything shades of steel. The wind blustered, and the sea roared. I walked along the promenade and down the steps to a spot where nobody could see me from the road, sat on the concrete ledge, as cold as stone, and looked out across the waves. I couldn't stop shivering. Was it the chill in the air or the turmoil in my brain?

Malnutrition? What did this mean? Surely it was a third-world condition. How could she have it? I knew, of course, that my mother had eaten hardly anything for weeks. That she'd lost a lot of weight – she was thin and gaunt. But malnutrition? It was like being hit by a pile-driver. 'Otherwise . . .' Did he think she would die?

How could we make her eat? I was really afraid we couldn't help her, and that she wouldn't recover.

The cold seeped into my bones and my world held its breath for a time. I pictured the anguish on Tommy's face when he heard those words, the doctor's diagnosis. For the first time in my life, my father and I were allies in a common cause. It was an uncomfortable thought, and an even more daunting prospect, but the doctor had made it clear we would have to work together. I shuddered.

The wind whispered ghostly taunts. 'She never loved you . . . let her die . . . live your own life.'

'*No!*' I shouted, my hands over my ears to block them out. I needed her to stay alive, to get better. I had always been at fault. Here was my chance to redeem myself. I needed to help her, to earn her love, so I resolved to do everything I could to make her better.

I gazed out across the rolling waves, dark and powerful,

to the horizon. There is so much beyond, I thought. Where is George? If only he was here. He could help. He could support me and share the burden. I needed him badly, and I felt sure he would want to be here, but he was far away, and not due back for months.

When I returned home, the sun had set and the house was quiet. Tommy heard me come in and, as I slipped my coat off, he came out to the hall.

'We'll have to get stuck in and do this,' he said.

His face was pale and drawn. I had never seen him look anxious before – almost vulnerable. We both knew it was a critical situation.

Over the next few weeks, I nursed my mother night and day. I bed-bathed her, emptied her bedpans, mixed up protein drinks for her and fed her with a spoon, like a baby . . . when she would take it. Mostly she didn't. She always tried to stop me.

'I don't want it. Take it away. I don't want it.' At least she was speaking now.

'Come on, Mam. You've got to have something. Have it for me. Just try a little bit for me,' I coaxed her.

Often, she refused to open her mouth. Just looked at me as if I was an insect crawling out of a hole. 'No, I don't want it.'

Then I had to get my father to come upstairs. He always managed to get something down her, somehow.

It was a stressful time – there was always the threat of that word 'otherwise' – and it was such hard work, physically as well as emotionally. I was soon exhausted. My whole body felt heavy as I dragged myself about, day after day, but this was my duty – I had to keep going. There were times when I resented my mother's cold recalcitrance, but I was too anxious about her to dwell on my feelings. I just focused on coping, on doing what needed to be done. I did not want my mother to die. For some reason, it was my fault that she was so ill, and it would be my fault if she died. I might be only a child, but I had to help her through this.

I realize now that she was in a severe depression, a serious psychological crisis, coupled with anorexia. I realized then that she needed me, even though she repeatedly shunned me for being a constant reminder of whatever it was she didn't want to think about. She depended on me to look after her and keep everything going, but hated me for it. Her resentment and her refusal to cooperate made me all the more determined to help her. I even stayed up during the night sometimes if my father was out, as I knew I alone was responsible for her feeding and toileting if he wasn't there. Yet every day she gave me those ice-cold looks that made me squirm.

The day approached when I would take my eleven-plus at school, the exam to decide whether I went to grammar school or secondary modern. I knew I was bright enough to pass and that this was my big chance, so I struggled with what school work I could manage in between nursing my mother round the clock. I rarely had the time or energy to complete my homework, and if I got stuck with something there was no one to ask for help, but I did the best I could. I don't think my teachers realized what I was having to cope with. Lack of sleep was the worst deprivation. I felt woolly and lethargic, but I managed to keep going.

On the day of the eleven-plus I woke up with a huge sty, which swelled up and closed my eye completely. I sat in the exam room staring at the paper, unable to see it properly, my eye was so sore. I read the questions again and again, but I couldn't take them in. I looked at the clock. The black hands stood still. A wave of fatigue engulfed me. I just wanted to lay my head down and go to sleep on the desk. I don't recall much else about that day.

When the results letter came, my father left it unopened. I knew I was capable of passing the eleven-plus and I desperately wanted to go to the grammar school. Though I realized I probably hadn't done enough on the day, a brave flame of hope still burned inside me. Maybe, just maybe . . . I kept looking at the plain brown envelope and its embossed lettering: 'Education Department'. I took the letter up to my mother, but she pushed it away. I placed it on my father's plate that evening. He threw it away.

Later that evening I retrieved it from the bin and opened it. I held my breath as I unfolded the stiff white paper . . . then let it go with a heavy sigh. The letter said what I feared. I had failed the exam. The disappointment was a silent wound that didn't heal for a long time.

CHAPTER 11

Jenny

Six Terrible Weeks

When I was eleven, the people who had rented our upstairs flat in West Jesmond for years moved out, leaving it in a dreadful state. My father gutted it and started to do up the whole house. The plan was for us to live mainly upstairs, which was more spacious as it spanned part of another property, and to convert two of the downstairs rooms into a larger hairdressing salon for my mother. That way she could serve her customers better and at the same time earn a bigger income to help pay my school fees.

Dad worked very hard in his day job, came home, had a meal and spent every evening renovating the house. He was determined to do all of the work himself, so it took him a long time, making a little progress every day. He got increasingly tired, and developed a tickly cough which he put down to all the dust generated from dismantling the brickwork and drilling the woodwork.

I remember the day he came back from the doctor's. My mother was concerned.

'What did the doc say, Sid?'

'Don't worry. He said I was fine.'

'What about the weight you've lost?'

'Oh, I told him that was because I've been working so hard on the house.'

'But you don't eat enough . . .'

They suddenly realized I was there and sent me off to bed, so I didn't hear the rest of the conversation, or all the other conversations that followed subsequent visits to the doctor. I later discovered that each time Dad was told he was 'fine'.

Finally, the doctor sent him to see a specialist, who took X-rays and did some tests. I was very worried when I heard about this, but neither of my parents would tell me anything more. My mother shielded me as much as she could from her own anxiety, and my dad somehow managed to stay cheerful whenever I was around.

I suppose I presumed that all the hard work and stress had affected his health and he just needed a good rest. I don't think I wanted to consider any other explanation, even if I'd been given it.

Then my Dad took so ill that he had to stop work altogether, leaving the whole house in a state of chaos.

He was admitted to the local hospital, where they did more tests, and while they waited for the results he grew worse every day. It was clear that Dad would not be able to continue with the house, so my mother managed to get some money together and gathered the help of various friends who gave their time for free. Meanwhile, before the results were back, Dad was transferred to the hospital at Shotley Bridge. Mam was in a terrible state, trying to get me to school, keep her hairdressing business going, oversee the renovation work and visit my father as often as she could. Even I could see she wouldn't be able to keep that up for long. I was secretly frightened about him going into Shotley Bridge, as I'd heard somebody say in a shop once, 'They don't come out of there alive, you know.' I thought she must have got that wrong. Surely there was some mistake. My dad couldn't die. He was such a positive man. I was sure he would recover. He'd probably just gone in there for a rest.

Mam took me to see him a couple of times at the beginning, before he was too ill. I was shocked to see him so thin and gaunt, yet he made a huge effort to be cheerful for me. As he saw me enter the ward, he pulled himself up a little and gave me the best smile he could. I remember that smile – always a smile for me. I remember too the pain in his eyes and the sallow skin stretched taut across his hollow cheeks. As I sat by his bed and held his hand, he spoke to my mother in a hoarse whisper.

'They did a test today. They tried to look down my throat, to see the blockage.'

She made some soothing, tutting sounds, as if to say 'not in front of Jen'.

But he seemed oblivious and carried on as if afraid he would run out of time. 'They gave me an anaesthetic, mind. It was supposed to knock me out, but it didn't quite work and I could feel it – very painful.'

'Shh, shh,' continued my mother as she stroked his forehead. 'It's over now. Lie back and rest.'

'They said I have a tumour.'

'What's a tumour?' I asked.

'Oh, nothing for you to worry about, pet,' said Mam with a look that said the opposite.

I couldn't believe what was happening. My mother refused to believe it too. She came home from the hospital one day and bounced in to pick me up from my cousin's house. As we walked home, she told me that the test results had come back. 'They've made a big mistake and they've got all the results mixed up,' she said, smiling. 'They've given me the wrong results, so, you see, it's going to be all right.'

This was wonderful news, and we rejoiced together that we would soon have him back with us, on the mend.

But the next day she came back even more despondent than before.

'They muddled up the tests,' she muttered.

I didn't understand. What was going on? I thought it was all going to be all right? Now I was in fear again.

I had no time to find out from Mam what she meant about the muddled tests. It was the beginning of the holidays and Mrs Dwerryhouse, a school-friend's mother, came to take me to stay with them at our Embleton bungalow, so for the next two weeks I was separated from both of my parents and any news.

The first night away I lay in bed sleepless, praying and crying. I prayed and prayed to God through my tears to make my dad better. I prayed every day and night we were there. I realized it made life easier for my mam for me to be away and know that I was well cared for, but why couldn't I visit my dad? I was desperate to see him, but nobody would take me.

'Why can't I go and see my dad?' I asked in anguish, trying not to show it.

'They don't let bairns into the hospital,' replied Mrs Dwerryhouse. But I knew this wasn't true, as I'd been there when my dad was first admitted.

My mother had told me nothing, and she didn't contact

me at all during those two weeks. I didn't like being shuffled away sideways with people I didn't know very well and kept in the dark. With no news about what was going on, I was frantic with worry and fear, mostly for my dad, but also for myself. He was my best friend. How would I cope if he didn't get better?

I couldn't talk to Mr and Mrs Dwerryhouse, and although I went to school with Sheena, I didn't know her very well. They were nice people, but quite detached. There wasn't anyone I could turn to; no one who would understand. I tried to go on as normal, unable to tell anybody how I really felt. If only I had a sister or brother to share all of this with, I thought. We could cope together.

It was a Saturday. I gazed out of the window across the plateau of grass. There were no phones in the bungalows, so it was a surprise to see my mother plodding round the green with her sister, Auntie Edna. I couldn't believe how much weight my mother had lost as she approached the bungalow. She had turned into a thin woman in such a short time. She was a wreck, an empty version of herself, her eyes red and puffy, her shoulders stooped.

As I watched them approach and saw the look on her face, I went cold. I just knew they were coming to give me the news I didn't want to hear, the news that would change our lives for ever.

I ran outside and she wrapped her arms around me, sobbing.

'*No, no!*' I cried out. I didn't want to hear her say the words that would make it true.

'He's gone, Jen,' she whispered.

'*NO!*' I slammed my hands over my ears.

She led me inside the bungalow and we sat down together, holding each other with a frightening ferocity. With the tears pouring down her face and wracked with grief, she tried to tell me. 'I'm sorry, pet. He died this morning. Now there's no more pain and he's at rest.'

I refused to hear. The words came out of her, but I couldn't take them in and didn't want to believe what she was trying to tell me, over and over.

Finally she stood up. 'Come on now, pet. Pack your things, we're going home.'

Mam drove our little A30 car all the way back to West Jesmond, with Aunt Edna in the passenger seat at the front and me on my own at the back. For the whole of that hour-and-a-half drive I sat in desolate silence, with only the sound of their sniffling in the front as they tried to contain their sobs.

I lost my faith in God on that journey. All those days and nights of fervent prayers, praying that it was all be a mistake, or a nightmare I would wake up from, pleading with God to cure my father so that we could all live happily together again had been for nothing. I felt God had abandoned me. I wanted to be angry with him, or with the whole of religion, but gradually came to the conclusion that it was all a lie, that he didn't exist, that my prayers had been for nothing. It would be twenty-one years before I would believe in God again.

I don't remember the rest of that day, till bedtime, when Mam came into my room, sat down next to me and told me all over again. She put her arm around me, but this time I couldn't respond. I felt numb. Empty. Yet I couldn't cry. Why couldn't I cry? I felt so guilty about that.

It was a long time before I fell asleep that night. Not because of my dad – I still hadn't accepted the news, so that wasn't the reason. It was because of my guilt at not having reacted as my mother expected, or as I expected. What was wrong with me? Then I felt worse because I was being selfish and only thinking of my own reactions.

Several days went by before I finally recognized the reality of my father's death, and at the point of realization, I broke down and couldn't stop crying. Now the tears of all those anxious days and weeks poured out. I had to accept that I had lost my father. But how could I accept it?

I began to resent more and more that I hadn't been allowed to be there for him when he most needed me, that he had died and left me without saying goodbye, and that it was just my mother and me now.

Dad's death seemed to separate me from Mam at first. But I couldn't sleep – I cried alone in my bed night after night – so she took me into her big bed to sleep with her. I became clingy for a while. Very clingy. I had nobody else to comfort me now.

When Mam was arranging things for Dad's funeral, I just assumed I would be going to the funeral with her.

'You can't come, pet,' she told me when I mentioned it.

'Why not?' I protested. Everything was being pulled away from me.

'Bairns don't go to funerals,' she said, her face blank of emotion.

'But it's Dad's funeral. I want to go. He would want me to go.'

'No, Jen. You can't go.' There was a finality in her voice. No emotion or explanation.

Much later, when I thought about it more rationally, I realized that she was probably trying to protect me. It's what adults did in those days, wasn't it? Children weren't allowed to go to funerals. That's the way it was. But not being there to see my father buried left me with a strange feeling, a doubt that I couldn't shake off. Maybe he hadn't really died. I felt that for months afterwards, though I kept it to myself. Did he die? Are they telling me lies? They're keeping him hidden from me, but where is he? I went over and over it in my mind.

There was nobody who could understand how I felt. No one to help me come to terms with it all – we didn't have counsellors in those days. Nobody to talk to except my dog Janie, who listened with endless patience. She kept me going. And of course it was my Dad who had given her to me, so she was a precious link to him, to all the happy memories.

My mother withdrew into herself for a while. Perhaps I did too. Finally I realized that nothing would ever be the same again.

CHAPTER 12

Helen

A Sunbeam for Jesus

One day I came home from school to find my mother shivering in front of the unlit fire. It was the first time I'd seen her up and dressed since she'd fallen ill. She was still thin and her cheeks were hollow, but she was eating a little now. I should have been happy to see her up, but I gasped at the shock in her face, her red-rimmed eyes and the dried tracks of tears down her cheeks. Something dreadful must have happened.

She looked up at me, straight at me, startled as a fawn. The silence was as loud as thunder. She gave me a slight nod, as if relieved I was home, then gazed back at the empty grate.

The suspense was frightening. 'What's the matter?'

'Grandma is dead.' Her tears began anew – great uncontrolled sobs that wracked her frail body.

The shock stabbed me deep inside. I shook with grief, with fear. '*No!*' I shrieked. 'She can't be.'

My first instinct was to console my mother, to have her console me. I wanted to hug her, but she had turned her back to me and showed no sign of wanting any solace from me, so I didn't dare.

I was twelve years old and I didn't know what to do. I had lost my wonderful grandma. For several minutes I was too stunned to really believe it, except that my mother's misery made me think it must be true. My tears welled up, and immediately I felt guilty – I hadn't seen Grandma for ages. The last time had been at least a year ago, when my father had bought the big Rover car and we'd taken her out for a drive. A vivid memory of her laughter popped into my mind – she loved that afternoon. It was my last memory of her, and it made me smile for a moment . . . before the tears began to flow. Why hadn't we seen her since? I knew it was beyond my control, but I felt guilty all the same. She would have missed us. We should have been there for her, with her.

I went to the kitchen and made my mother a cup of tea. I knew sweet tea was good for shock, so I put an extra spoonful of sugar in it. I lit the fire to keep her warm and made her something nourishing to eat. Instead of her usual protests, she ate in a trance, then I led her up to bed. Still she paid no attention to my presence, said not a word. I tried at first to stroke her hand, but she flinched. Why couldn't she let me comfort her? And who would comfort me? I sat with her until my father got back from work at ten o'clock. I heard him come in and close the front door below, so I slipped out to the top of the stairs.

'Why aren't you in bed?' he grumbled as he started up the steps.

'Grandma has died,' I sobbed. 'Mam's in the bedroom. She's very upset.'

He looked at me, expressionless, then pointed to my bedroom. 'You – get to bed.'

He ran up the rest of the stairs, two at a time. The last

thing I saw as I closed my door was Tommy sitting down on their candlewick counterpane with his arm round my mother as she talked to him, spilling out her grief.

I went to bed, alone with my sorrow. My beloved Grandma had been a mother to me in my early years, and all the years of sixpences since then proved she had never stopped loving me. Her unconditional love would be no more. If only I had been able to spend more time with her.

No one thought how I might feel. It was all about her, my mother, just as it was always about her.

I cried long into the night. I thought back to all those 'wakes' we had at her house. Now it had finally come true. All those happy times – the family gatherings, the Sunday teas, the sing-songs – would be consigned to the memory-box. Who would ever love me like Grandma did? Yes, of course I had George – I'm sure he loved me – but it wasn't the same. He was always far away and he had his own life to lead. At least he had a life. With Grandma gone, I felt more alone than ever. I sobbed myself to sleep.

The day before the funeral, all the family gathered at Grandma's house, including Patricia and her parents, who lived further away from Seghill than we did so I hadn't seen them for years.

The aunts and uncles sat around with their endless cups of tea, discussing and sharing their memories of Grandma. My mother sent me out of the room with my cousins, until it was time for us to go upstairs one at a time to see Grandma in her open coffin, lain on top of her bed. When it was my turn, I walked nervously into the bedroom. I had never seen a dead body before and I was apprehensive about this being her body, but no longer her. I understood, but I wasn't sure I wanted to look.

'Eee, come on, Helen. It's your turn, hinny,' whispered Auntie Nancy. 'Come and say goodbye to your grandma.'

I stepped forward to look into the coffin. She was lying with her head on a satin pillow. Serene. Her grey hair brushed back neatly. I could have imagined her to be asleep, had I not known.

Auntie Dorrie came into the room behind me. She put a gentle hand on my shoulder. 'Give your Grandma a kiss, pet.' She gently eased me forward till I could lean over the side. 'Go on, then.'

I bent my head down towards hers and gave her a gentle kiss on the cheek. I was not afraid any more. As I straightened up, I noticed the smoothness of her skin, as if all her wrinkles had been ironed out. I took one last lingering look.

'Goodbye, Grandma,' I breathed.

After that I was ushered outside to play with my cousins, but we didn't feel much like playing. We stood around and talked about when we were little.

On the following day, my father drove us back to Seghill again. Everyone was gathered once more, and Auntie Dorrie was in charge, welcoming my parents into the house. As we stood in the living room, she turned to me and said, 'You go off with the younger cousins, Helen. You're too young to go to the funeral.'

I was shocked, incensed. Why shouldn't I go to my own grandma's funeral? Normally obedient, I suddenly became defiant.

'She was my Grandma. I'm twelve years old and I am

going to the funeral, even if I have to walk there myself!'
I burst out.

Silence suddenly shrouded the room. My mother frowned
and my father clenched his fists. All the adults exchanged
surprised glances. I stood my ground and set my face. I was
inwardly determined, and I think they must have realized I
meant what I said.

Uncle James was the first to break the silence. 'Let her
come with us if she wants to.'

'All right, pet,' nodded Auntie Dorrie, and nothing more
was said about it.

It was a bitterly cold winter's day, with a thick carpet of
snow on the ground. We all travelled in a long, slow line of
cars behind the hearse to Seghill's Trinity Church. I don't
remember much about the funeral service, but I do recall that
we had to crunch, slip and slide our way across the lovely
old churchyard to the graveside. It was where my grandfather had been buried all those years before I was born,
when my mother was a child. His grave had been opened up
and now the men lowered Grandma's coffin into the cavity
to join her beloved husband. The aunties, uncles and older
cousins stood solemnly around the grave with my parents
and me. They were all sniffing and crying and holding each
other, while Tommy and Mercia stood back. Nobody held
me, so I just thought back to the times when as a small child
I'd sat on my grandma's knee, and a warm glow spread
through me. I looked around at this large family, my family,
which I still felt part of, always surrounded by comfort and
love – if you excluded my parents.

After the service, we all went back to the house, each
silent, deep in our thoughts, remembering her in our own

ways. Later that day, the will was read. Because I had been at the funeral, I was allowed to stay for that, too, but I can't remember any of the details.

It was a sad day for us all, but I had the feeling she knew I was there with her. I would miss her every day for the rest of my life.

I had been at 'Park Pen', my new secondary school, for more than a year by now and had settled in well. I liked the school. It was just a short walk from the house where our flat was in Whitley Bay, across the road from the famous local funfair – very lively then, but since demolished – and I made lots of good friends. We met up outside school in the evenings, did our homework together, and saw each other at weekends. My mother never seemed to notice that I wasn't at home. I think Tommy was glad to have the place to themselves. Perhaps they rowed less when I was out.

Some of these friends invited me to go to their houses, meet their parents and have meals with them. The first time I went, I was greeted with 'Come in. Would you like a cold drink? Or a cup of tea? Would you like a biscuit?' It took me by surprise.

I had realized early on in my life that there was always a happier, kinder feeling at Grandma's or my aunties and uncles' houses, but then my parents were nicer people too when they were in company – it was only when we went home that they changed. I thought the other cousins' parents changed as well when nobody else was there. I hadn't ever really questioned it.

But when I went to another friend's house and her parents were the same, it was a bit of a wake-up moment for me. I realized it was *my* parents who were strange. It wasn't like that for other kids. These adults were welcoming and *kind* to me. There was fun and laughter, a happy atmosphere, not like my home. Having thought until now that my life was like everybody else's, then discovering that it wasn't, was quite a shock.

I suppose I realized all this now because I was old enough to look around me and make direct comparisons and consider differences more perceptively. I was so unused to the welcome I received from these strangers that it made me feel ill at ease, but my friends' parents recognized my shyness, gaucheness even, when I first visited and showered me with kindness. It was not only the people, the love and affection, the warmth and fun that struck me; I noticed too their comfortable homes, which were well furnished, my friends' bedrooms, painted in pastel colours, with proper beds and mirrors, pictures, lampshades and nick-nacks. All things I didn't have. They showed me the colourful clothes in their wardrobes, their toys and books. It was a revelation to me.

The most important difference for me, the starkest contrast, was that I knew my parents would never welcome my friends into our home. Indeed, my friends wouldn't even come and call for me. I asked them why.

'I don't like your dad,' said one.

'We're frightened of him,' said another.

So instead I had to call on them or meet up somewhere. I remember those friends and classmates with great affection. We were just normal kids, having fun – a new experience for me. I loved those carefree times together – life away from home. It was a very happy contrast.

Another place I found kindness was the Cullercoats

Fisherman's Mission, a Methodist church at the end of our street. Neither of my parents ever went to church – my father was an atheist – but I was curious, so when a girl in my class who lived near me asked if I'd like to go with her to church, I went. It was the Sunshine Corner bible study class, and here I became a 'Sunbeam for Jesus'. I started going to church services twice every Sunday, and suddenly I was part of something. Something that included people who were friendly and caring, who were interested in me and welcomed me. I loved the time I spent there. I involved myself in all the activities, the religious life of the church, and got to know many members of the congregation. It felt as if I had a new, kinder family. I felt I belonged to something. I believed I really was a sunbeam for Jesus. My parents never visited the church with me or came to see what I was learning. This helped me to feel that my being there was a special time doing something that was mine only, something my parents couldn't touch.

One of the church's big occasions was Easter. All the children learned a piece from the Bible, a few verses which we recited in front of the congregation on Easter Sunday. I learned my piece by heart – I could have recited it in my sleep! When the big day came, my mother said she would come and watch me do my recital. We sat in the choir stalls, which were raised above the rest of the congregation, and each child in turn stood up to recite their verse. I was excited beyond belief, especially as my mother was sitting there, watching. Then my turn came, and I stood up to do my recital . . . and passed out.

When I revived only moments later, to find myself lying on the floor, the ladies who taught us were gathered around me. They were so kind to me, and concerned in case I had hurt myself, but I was flushed with embarrassment. I wasn't used to this kind of attention, especially in front of so many people. Then I looked over towards my mother's seat. It was empty. Apparently, she had just walked out and gone home. She never mentioned this incident. She didn't even ask me what had happened and whether I was all right. She just ignored the whole thing, but I knew only too well the look of disdain she would have worn on her way back home.

Some weeks later, after fainting or blacking out several more times in various places, my mother took me to the doctor's. He gave me a quick check-over.

'Sorry to waste your time,' said my mother. 'She keeps doing it. She's probably just putting it on.'

'Well, Mrs Lumsden, I don't think she is putting it on. It may not be anything to worry about, but I'd like to send her to the Royal Infirmary at Newcastle for some tests, just to rule out any possibility of a brain tumour.'

I'd never heard of a brain tumour, but it sounded serious.

'So I've got to take her all the way into the city? Can't you tell she's fine really?'

'We'd better just make sure,' insisted the doctor, beaming a smile in my direction. 'I'm hopeful they will be able to give you the all-clear. If that's the case, you can just put it down to growing pains – part of a girl's natural development, though she seems a little on the young side for that.'

My mother gave a loud sigh at the inconvenience and off we went. Fortunately the doctor was right and the brain specialist told us there was nothing amiss.

'A whole day sitting in the hospital again for nothing,' she moaned on the bus when we travelled home from the hospital. 'I've been worried sick about all this. It's making me ill.'

'Sorry, Mammy.'

I continued to be a regular member of the congregation at the Methodist church. I believed in God, and it helped me during the lonely times. I still spent a lot of time alone in my bedroom, but now I always had someone to talk to, someone to ask for help, someone who understood how I felt – all of those things. He gave me strength. How else would I have survived? I needed something, someone, to support me through all my troubles.

I know some people would say it was my character, my ability to be strong, that helped me through all this, and I think I did have strength, but it was more than that – it was the strength that came with faith. Of course there have been times when I haven't believed any more, when things have gone wrong, when times have been bad and I have felt abandoned again, but those times have always passed and I have always come back to the realization that He is there for me. It was a good day when that young girl, that Sunbeam for Jesus in search of meaning, found God's love.

Meanwhile, a strange new tension loomed at home. I sensed there was something wrong, but I didn't know what it was. My parents see-sawed between hushed conversations, tight-lipped arguments and blazing rows. I listened in when I could, and gradually pieced together what the new problem was. My father had sparked off an altercation at work, at the bus garage. The other man was a driver whose wife was a bus conductor – the same female bus-conductor my mother had mentioned the night Tommy threw us both down the stairs and disappeared. In the course of this confrontation, my father had lost his temper, punched the man and slammed his head against a brick wall. The man lost consciousness and was taken to hospital, to intensive care, where he lay in a coma, hovering between life and death.

The police took my father in and interviewed him. They told him that if the man died, they intended to charge him with manslaughter or murder. I was terrified – I felt sure he would go to prison for murder. He and my mother were subdued all the time the man's condition was so critical. It was a tough few days, but fortunately the driver survived, regained consciousness and recovered with no permanent damage. I believe no charges were made, but I'm not certain. It was never mentioned again.

One day, when I was at home on my own and very bored, I started to look through some family photos I found in the desk in the living room. I wasn't allowed to open the desk – it was forbidden territory – so I was curious. I only hesitated for a moment, because I felt sure I could return them all in the right order well before either of my parents came home. They would never know.

I got all the photos out and sorted through them with some amusement. In amongst the photos I found lots of birth, marriage and death certificates for grandparents, great-grandparents and some whose names I didn't even recognize.

Finally, I came across my parents' marriage certificate. I unfolded it and read what it said. No, surely not. I read it again and again, just to make sure I'd got it right. The date on the certificate was 31 March 1951. I was stunned. Even at twelve I recognized what this meant. I was born a year before they were married. Exactly one year. It was a terrible thing in those days. I was illegitimate. I could hardly say the word. My hands shook and my breathing quickened.

My first thought, once I'd taken it all in, was that obviously I wasn't planned or wanted. This was an important piece in the jigsaw – it explained a lot. It was my fault that they were unhappy. If it hadn't been for me, life would have been wonderful. They were always telling me it was my fault, whatever 'it' was, and here was the proof. That's why my father was the way he was. If I hadn't been born . . . I had always felt guilty, though I rarely knew why. Now I understood.

Suddenly I realized what the time was. I'd spent so long looking at everything that I'd forgotten that my mother would be home soon. I put all the papers and photos away as quickly as possible. I couldn't be caught looking at them, and I could never ask her about it because I couldn't admit I'd disobeyed her. Even when I was grown-up I never dared ask. This was a secret I carried in my heart for fifty years.

The marriage certificate in my mother's desk was proof that my mother resented me. It was a fact and I could finally accept it. I had always felt I shouldn't be there, that I was in the way. She acted, every day, as if I owed her something just for being my mother.

It seems pitiful to me now, knowing what other people's childhoods were like, that from the age of about nine I had never come home from school to a hot meal, to any meal, only to a cold and empty house. Except for one single day when I was twelve. It stands out in my memory. I got back from school to find my mother already home. Perhaps she had been off work and was bored. The fire was lit and glowed with warmth, the table was laid, and in the middle stood a big bowl of steaming soup. It was tinned soup, of course, but it was hot, and it was for me. I had never experienced this before – and I could hardly believe it. In fact I was so shocked, I burst into tears.

My mother didn't say anything. She just turned round and walked back into the kitchen. It never happened again.

CHAPTER 13

Jenny

Swimming Along

The winter after my dad died, my mam had to drive me, every Saturday, nearly sixty miles each way to Stockton-on-Tees for Northumberland Swimming Club coaching. The swimming helped me to have something else to focus on, and I believe it helped her too, as it was something she and Dad had both been keen to support me in.

Mam was very dedicated and never complained at the early mornings and late evenings, no matter how hard she worked to pay for all this on top of my school fees. She was amazing. She just worked and worked, often from eight in the morning till ten at night. She always made sure I was able to enjoy these opportunities to shine.

But Mam's long hours after Dad died meant I was alone a great deal of the time when I was at home. She was consumed by work and hardly stopped to eat. I was so worried about her that I used to come home from school in the middle of the day to make her some lunch. Whenever she did have time to cook a meal for us, she used to set three places at the table. When she brought in the food and realized, she would burst into tears. After a while I learned to remove the extra place before she noticed.

Left alone at home so much, I was a very lonely child, living a solitary life. I felt like a single sapling on a vast plain, all alone as I grieved for my dad. On those solitary evenings I wished again and again that I had a sister or brother to share the grief with, to banter with, to tease me, to help lift me out of the void.

Every Sunday I was taken to the communion service at church in preparation for my confirmation. I didn't want to be there and felt uncomfortable with the situation, but I had no choice. My school was quite high-church, and it was expected of us, so it was just something I had to do. I often wonder whether that discomfort and lack of belief caused what happened the first time I went. A short way into the service, I keeled over and passed out onto the cold stone floor. My class-mates gawped as they craned their necks to try and see what the drama was, while several of the staff and congregation gathered round to revive me.

Unfortunately it happened again the next time, and the next. I now dreaded the embarrassment of fainting every week. It became such a regular event, always at the same part of the service, that the lady who lived across the road from the church would put her kettle on when she saw me go into the church. Sure enough, twenty minutes later I would be carried out and across to her house for a reviving cup of tea.

On one particular occasion, I remember that I was sitting on an old oak chair with struts of wood underneath. At the beginning of the service, I must have tucked my legs under the chair, and entwined my feet around these wooden stretchers, so that when the inevitable happened and I passed out, my body fell forward and took the whole chair with it. It took four men to free me from my seat and carry me out, oblivious of all the trouble I'd caused.

My confirmation day loomed. The Bishop of Newcastle, who was the chairman of Church High School, would be leading the service. It was planned with great care, so that we all knew where to stand and what we were meant to do. Of course, when it came to my turn to kneel down in front him and he put his hands on my head, I fainted right there in front of him, flat onto a marble memorial plaque. Without hesitation, he moved across to the next person and carried on, while I was revived sufficiently by the churchwardens to have another try at the end, and finally I was confirmed. My abiding memory of that day is one of total embarrassment – I couldn't get out of that church quickly enough.

It wasn't just at church that this happened, though. I began to feel there must be something awful wrong with me, because I kept on fainting and having blackouts, feeling woozy for a while afterwards each time. I couldn't understand it and became quite anxious when I was with other people that I might collapse or something. Then one day I fainted in front of my mam at home and she got the doctor round.

'I don't want you to worry, Mrs Smith,' he said in a grave voice. 'But I think we ought to investigate whether Jennifer could possibly have a heart condition.'

Of course that worried my mother greatly. 'What sort of heart condition?' she asked in a quavering voice. 'How will they find out? What could it mean?'

'Now, now, Mrs. Smith. It may be nothing, but I just want to make sure, so I'll send her for some tests.'

I was sent to the Newcastle Royal Infirmary for some investigations, but fortunately it was a false alarm and there was nothing wrong with me.

'It's probably just a phase,' said the kindly consultant to my mother. 'Although it's unusual, fainting fits can be a symptom of growing up.'

I think I was even more relieved than my mother that I wasn't going to die. Soon after that the fainting stopped completely.

The swimming training continued. I went to a swimming class every Thursday evening with Jeff Knowles, who was a selector for the England rugby team, and I had another class on Friday nights. The Friday coach used to scare the breath out of me. He had a voice like a foghorn, and as I was quite a shy child – I didn't speak a lot in those days – his shouting made me cower. One occasion I remember was when there were five of us swimming in a line, with the fastest at the front to set the pace. For some reason I was swimming at the back that day, behind the others, and kept bumping into the next one's feet and continually having to slow down.

'Jennifer – get to the bloody front!' he shouted, his voice echoing around the pool.

I had to swim past the others, trembling to be picked out like that and sworn at in front of everyone. Fortunately I swam to the front of the line quite easily, because I swam so fast.

Although I had great opportunities in both my favourite sports, I preferred swimming to golf in my early teens because I enjoyed the competitive side of it. As well as the outside classes and coaching sessions, I joined the school swimming team. When our sports teacher became pregnant and had to take maternity leave, she asked my mother to take over coaching us mainly, I think, because Mam was always so encouraging and so involved with all my swimming activities. Perhaps she was the only one willing to take it on. And she had a stopwatch of her own, so that sealed it!

Mam took on this new role as our school swimming coach with her usual energy and determination. She was always a competitive woman, and it rubbed off on me in the years to come, driving me on to scale surprising heights. Thanks to her training, our school team won the Inter-Schools Championship in the Newcastle district for the first time ever.

Friday nights continued to be swimming club nights, when we trained for matches with other clubs. One of our trainers was the man who coached Brian Phelps, the Olympic medalist.

Every year we competed in a match against Hawick and Galashiels in the Borders. This was a major event for us. One year we would travel there to swim, and the next they would come down to us. On one occasion when we travelled north to Hawick, we had a very smartly turned-out swimming coach with us on our rickety old bus. When the bus broke down about ten miles short of our destination, our coach, Verna Watson, in her impeccable navy blazer and white skirt, walked to a nearby house and asked to use the phone.

'Where are you all going?' asked the elderly resident.

'We're from Newcastle, on our way to compete in a swimming match against Hawick and Galashiels.'

The elderly lady paused for a moment, then replied in her tuneful Borders accent, 'I hope you lose!'

When we finally reached the pool and started the competition, we gave Mrs Watson our watches to look after and she wore them all in a row up one arm. It was an old-fashioned pool with rounded corners and the coaches stood at one end to shout us on. The whole competition was very close in every race. The women's relay the final race and guess who was swimming last? So it all depended on me whether we won the trophy that year or not. When it came to my turn, I dived in about two yards behind their last swimmer. Gradually I pulled back the distance, and on the second leg managed to pass her just in time to touch ahead of her and win. The whole team, watching along the side, erupted with joy. I looked around to see Mrs Watson no longer on the edge but in the water, looking bedraggled but jubilant, with her arm straight up in the air, gallantly keeping the watches dry!

Despite all the coaching and the tournaments, we still went to Embleton, Mam and I, whenever we could. It always felt good to be out in the fresh air and the sea breezes, and I loved relaxing with the odd round of golf there.

I missed my dad terribly when we were there. I suppose I never had time to think about it when I was training for swimming events, but here I could reminisce. Memories of our companionable happiness came flying back on the salty breeze, all those times when I had caddied for him across the links. I stood on the third green one day, next to our bungalow, and watched the kittiwakes gliding low over the gorse-strewn dunes. It was as if he was there, close by, watching them with me. I felt his encouragement, his infectious enthusiasm, his special pride in me as I played on around the course with renewed energy.

Golf was my relaxation from the main focus of my life, swimming. Strange that I didn't realize then the direction my future would take.

When I was thirteen, my mother decided I really ought to have some proper golf lessons, and took me to the Foxton Hall Golf Club at Alnmouth, about ten miles south of Embleton. I've got a photo somewhere of me having my first golf lesson. I can remember wearing golden corduroy trousers with an awful jumper that I think my mother had knitted. It was a Fair-Isle jumper, quite fashionable then I suppose, but thick and itchy. It was the first time I had worn it and it brought me out in a rash. I had to wear it as my mother was watching and I didn't want to offend her. Now, of course, I realize that I'm allergic to wool, but we didn't know about allergies in those days, so I just tried to ignore the itching as much as I could.

Mam paid over five shillings for my first lesson – a lot of money in those days. Eddie Fernie, a brusque Scot, was the golf professional at the club, renowned as an excellent golf teacher. 'Now then, Jennifer. Let's see what you've got.'

As I stood on the lush green grass, teeing up, a man walked past the practice ground towards the first tee. I hit my first ball and as I watched it whistle through the air I heard a voice nearby.

'Now, Eddie. That wee laddie has got a lovely swing.'

Eddie laughed. 'That wee laddie happens to be a lassie!'

At the end of the lesson, he walked with me over to where my mother was waiting.

'How did Jennifer get on?' she asked.

'I don't want any more money from you,' he said with a

broad smile. 'It will give me great pleasure to turn this wee lassie into a champion.'

I was astonished. I think Mam was rather surprised too. She tried to protest, but he was resolute, so I went for free lessons with him every week after that, and she used to bake him a cake, or take him a dozen eggs, to thank him for his generosity.

I was fourteen the first time I entered the ladies' tournament at Dunstanburgh Golf Club. I had always gone barefoot there, and I wasn't worried about how I would play but about the fact that it was the first time I'd ever had to wear shoes when playing golf.

'You have to wear shoes in the tournament, mind,' the captain said.

I didn't know if I could play in shoes. I was sure it would affect my game. I was wrong. I was runner-up to my mother.

Coming that close to victory in an adult tournament surprised me. I hadn't realized I could do so well at the game I loved, and it made me determined to win the next year – to beat my mam – so in between my swimming commitments, I carried on with the golf lessons and practised whenever I could, barefoot, just as I'd always done.

However, a few words said in anger were to change everything for me.

CHAPTER 14

Helen

My Hero

My discovery of my parents' marriage certificate simmered beneath the surface, but I was happy at school at this time, and, in spite of everything, I did well. One day we were all given the opportunity to go on a school cruise, but we had to have parental consent. The cost of the cruise was £28, which doesn't sound much now, but in those pre-decimal days, when houses could still be bought for less than a thousand pounds, £28 was a lot of money. The school arranged for weekly payments of £1.

In trepidation, I took home my consent form. I didn't believe I would be allowed to go, but I had to hope some miracle would make it possible. To my complete amazement, my parents agreed to let me go. They knew it was six months away, so they didn't seem too worried about finding the money to pay for it. I was astonished when they signed the form and my place was booked. I wanted to dance, sing, shout with joy. Every day when I woke up I felt it must have been a dream, but it was real. My parents made the weekly £1 payments and I got a paper delivery round after school to earn some pocket money for the trip.

It was all going so well. But then they stopped the payments. I never knew why and they didn't say anything. My earnings were five shillings (25p) a week, so it would take me four weeks to save up each £1. I took on Saturday and Sunday morning deliveries as well to earn another five shillings, and this meant it took two weeks to earn £1. Gradually I began to make up the deficit.

The date came when the final payment was due. I was still in quite a lot of arrears as I simply couldn't earn enough to pay for it, and my parents refused to pay any more.

At this point George came home from sea. When I told him what had happened, he was furious. During his trip he had saved some of his wages to spend with Joan. Now, without a murmur of complaint, he gave me enough money to cover the arrears. Of course I always loved him coming home, but this time more than ever he was my saviour.

So the cruise was paid for. It was really going to happen. My first holiday, my first time abroad – I was in heaven just thinking about it. My parents didn't seem to care whether I went on the cruise or not. Nor did they care that George had paid off the rest of the money when it should have been them. There was just one shadow. Having used most of my earnings to make the back-payments, I had the grand total of £1 pocket money for my big adventure. It would have to be enough.

George took me to the meeting place to board the bus for the docks, and I shall never forget what happened next.

'Goodbye, George. And thanks for paying for the trip.' I stretched up and gave him a kiss. 'You're my hero.'

He blushed. 'Have a great time, kiddo.' He reached into

his pocket, pulled out all the money he had with him, and gave it to me.

I was flustered and overwhelmed. I hadn't told him about my pocket money problem, yet he had worked it out. I didn't know what to say. I felt I should give it back to him, but he waved it away.

'Keep it, pet,' he said. 'And spend it on yourself.'

He stepped back as I climbed onto the bus to sit with my friends, relieved and excited. He beamed a wide smile at me and waved as the bus pulled away. I kept waving until I couldn't see him any more.

The whole trip was one long thrill, a happy, carefree interlude with my friends. Being away from home is often a great experience for children at that age, but for me it was wonderful to be free to enjoy each day without threats or worries to spoil my fun.

Too soon we were back home again and everything was back to normal. But for me, after the cruise, it was all in sharper relief than ever before.

Having just become a teenager and conscious of fashion, it was a great humiliation that my mother would not buy me any clothes. She didn't buy herself a great many clothes that I remember, and there were times when she was in such a depressed state that she didn't pay attention to her appearance. But when she went out she was always smartly dressed, and she had some pretty underwear. I had one skirt, one jumper and one coat. At school we wore uniform. For gym we had to wear brown flannel knickers – surely the baggiest, most unfashionable undergarment ever – and these gym knickers were the only ones I possessed. I had no other underwear.

I wore those knickers every day for years. Every night I washed them in the bath, squeezed as much water out as I could and hung them to dry overnight in my room. As we had no central heating, they rarely dried much, so I went to school every day wearing damp knickers.

I did ask her for more pairs of knickers and my mother said she would buy some for me, but she never did.

However, my mother loved knitting, so she unpicked an old mohair cardigan and decided to knit me a new jumper out of the wool. Whenever she unpicked something, I had to hold my hands up so she could rewind the wool around them. The mohair made my skin prickle, and within moments my fingers reddened and started to itch. Before long my hands were on fire. Finally the day came when my mother had finished knitting this revolting dark grey prickly jumper and I had to wear it. It was purgatory having to wear it so often. I always came out in an angry rash and have been allergic to wool ever since.

The fact that I didn't possess a dress of my own made it particularly exciting when George and Joan asked me to be a bridesmaid at their wedding, alongside Joan's two sisters. They had set the date for their marriage for July 1962 – a full white wedding. We were measured up for our dresses and went to have regular fittings, which I loved. Joan also wanted us to wear white, kitten-heeled shoes, so my mother reluctantly took me to town to buy some.

'Don't tell your father, mind,' she warned. 'If he finds out, he won't let you wear them.'

He always had to approve everything I wore. He banned anything fashionable or pretty, so these shoes would be sure to enrage him.

The day approached and I couldn't wait. Joan told me to get everything I needed ready the day before to take round to her parents' house the next morning, so that we could all get dressed together. I asked my mother what I would need. 'Have a bath,' was all she said, so I did. Then I went to bed, but I hardly slept that night. It would be such a happy occasion, and very special to me to see George marry his sweetheart.

I got up and walked to my future sister-in-law's house to get ready, carrying the box with my precious kitten-heeled shoes. When I arrived, Joan's mother opened the door. She looked me up and down with a sneer. I was terrified.

She grabbed my arm. 'Come here,' she said, and dragged me upstairs to the large front bedroom where Joan and her two sisters were getting ready. 'And what am I going to do with this?' she said as she propelled me through the door.

They all stopped what they were doing and looked at me. I felt like a street urchin, small and ugly.

Joan broke the spell. 'Hello, Helen, pet. Come and join us.' She grinned, then turned to her mother. 'It's all right, Mum. We'll soon turn Helen into a princess.'

Perhaps it was going to be all right after all, though it seemed like an impossible task.

'Now, don't worry,' Joan said, smiling sympathetically at me as she dampened my hair and set it in rollers. She put my dress out for me and helped me to get ready, in between doing her own make-up. I noticed Joan's sisters had beautifully curled hair with Alice bands in place. They had had their nails manicured with delicate pink nail polish and wore pretty necklaces to go with their dresses. Joan put a necklace out for me too, and I smiled gratefully. No wonder her mother was so shocked to see my straggly, straight auburn hair, my shabby clothes and my forlorn look.

One of Joan's sisters dried my hair, took my curlers out and tucked in an Alice band to match theirs. I put on the beautiful dress and my white kitten-heeled shoes. I had never worn such a dress or such feminine shoes, and Joan was right – I felt like a princess. I tried to forget that underneath it all were the hated brown knickers. And I dreaded the moment when my dad caught sight of my shoes. I hoped he wouldn't, but I was sure he would. I knew he was capable of murder. I dared not think about it.

As we walked down the aisle in the church, everyone turned to look. Joan was radiant, beautiful, and everyone smiled at us. I enjoyed that moment. I wanted to remember this feeling for ever. Then it happened. I saw Tommy, to my right, turning his head to look at me, and his eyes went straight down to my shoes. I saw that familiar black cloud of fury cross his face. Even as we sang the first hymn, I knew I was in big trouble.

I don't remember the rest of the service, but I do remember the rest of the day. I was miserable, scared beyond belief. Years later, Joan asked me why I hadn't smiled in any of the wedding photos. I couldn't tell her.

When we got home, the row began as soon as we walked in through our front door. First, Tommy shouted at my mother. 'Why the hell did you buy those shoes for her?' He prodded her in the chest with his outstretched finger. 'You did it on purpose, didn't you?' He pushed her down into the chair. Then he turned to me and yelled a torrent of abuse.

'You look ridiculous in those common shoes. You can forget any ideas of walking around Whitley Bay trying to get the lads' attention in those. They'd probably just laugh at you anyway.' His voice was rising and his face was turning redder by the second. 'I won't have you flirting and mincing around in them.' He clenched his fists and his eyes bulged with anger. 'Take those bloody shoes off!'

I trembled as I obeyed him. He tore them from my hands, dragged me outside by the arm, and made sure I was watching as he threw my precious white kitten-heels into the bin, right into the ashes and embers from the fire. He brushed his hands against each other, to rid himself of contamination from the shameless shoes. 'That's the last time you will wear anything like that!'

Not long after their wedding, George had to go away to sea again. They had rented a flat in the next street to us, so I went to see Joan as often as I could. We were always close. She taught me how to do my hair, use make-up and do my nails, but of course I had to scrub it all off before I went home. Every week she came round for Sunday lunch, which cheered me up. It was such a relief to have a day without rows.

I'll always remember one particular Sunday with a smile. My parents were, as so often, not speaking to each other. I can't remember what it was about – I was so used to it. On this Sunday my father had been on an early shift and arrived home at two o'clock. We had already eaten, and put his meal in the oven. When he came in we were sitting in the living room, so I fetched his dinner for him. He put his plate down on a chair, in front of the television, and went to the kitchen to collect a knife and fork. When he came back through, he turned on the television and sat down on the chair . . . on his dinner.

Joan and I were wide-eyed. We didn't dare move, or speak, let alone laugh. When he realized what he had done, he stormed back into the kitchen in a rage. Our last view of him before he turned and slammed the door was the Brussels sprouts and Yorkshire pudding stuck firmly to the seat of his pants. We could hold out no longer and collapsed into fits of giggles. He charged out of the house and didn't return for the rest of the day. He didn't speak to me for another six weeks. Bliss.

Soon I had my first 'boyfriend', John. We were in the same class at school and we used to walk home every day holding hands. We went to his house and had tea with his parents. They were lovely people. I was ashamed and embarrassed that I couldn't invite John to tea at our house. I didn't dare tell my parents about him; my father would have forbidden it. In fact, at the age of thirteen, I had to be in the house by seven-thirty every evening and in bed with the lights out by nine. However, my friends and I used to spend time together down by the sea at weekends and in school holidays, swimming for hours in the natural seawater bathing pool on Table Rocks, having fun together amongst the fish and crabs.

I loved my years at the secondary school. I was selected for the school netball, gymnastics and hockey teams and travelled all over the country to sports meetings with the netball team. I was also a member of the school choir and joined in the recitals and concerts. That was very special to me as it was another way to feel part of a big group – an important part of something. Everyone else's parents came to watch these events, but mine never did.

The next boy I went out with was Terry – my first 'young love'. I met him one Sunday afternoon and he asked me to go out with him. I was almost fourteen by this time, and he was sixteen. We walked together for hours along the Whitley Bay seafront. I never had any pocket money and Terry had no money to spend either, so we just walked. A few weeks after we met, he got his first job on a trawler. He was away for days or weeks at a time, and I never knew when he was due to come home.

One day, when I got back from school, my father was waiting for me. I could see something was wrong. He held a letter in his hand, addressed to me from Terry. It was to tell me when he was due to come home. I could see the envelope had been torn open and my father had obviously read it.

'Who is this Terry?' he demanded.

I told him. It was no use trying to lie about him. It must have been obvious from the letter that he was my boyfriend.

For the next few hours I was closely interrogated. He wanted to know every detail.

'Where did you meet him? How old is he? Where does he live?'

I answered the first two questions truthfully, but I didn't tell him where Terry lived.

'You listen to me, lass,' he said, raising his voice and wagging his finger in my face. 'You've got to tell me where he lives, so I can go round there . . .'

'I don't know,' I lied, in an attempt to protect Terry and his parents from my father's wrath.

'How long have you known him? What does he do?'

And so it went on – so many questions. I answered them all as best I could, but most of my answers were monosyllabic. I knew what was coming next.

He waved my letter about. 'Any mail addressed to you,' he shouted in my face, 'belongs to me. I'm head of this house. You have no right to any private mail. Go to your room and stay there. You will not be allowed out for the next six weeks.'

I knew this would not be the end of the matter, and I was right. He rampaged downstairs like a caged gorilla, roaring and crashing things in the hall. Finally I heard him stamping up the stairs. I felt sick with fear, terrified, like a cornered animal. As soon as I saw his popping eyes I knew what would happen.

'How dare you walk down the seafront like a prostitute, wiggling your tail?' he yelled. I was so naive I didn't know what a prostitute was. He threw me onto my bed and wound his belt round his fist. This time he used the buckle end. He swung it from above his head down onto my bare legs again and again and again, with the greatest force he could muster. Then my back and my arms, each lash a searing pain. I had changed into my baby-doll pyjamas, a birthday present, so I had no protection from this onslaught. After a bit, everything went into slow motion and I stopped screaming. The pain somehow receded as I developed a kind of detachment from it in my mind. The terror overrode it. I tried to make myself as small as I could, and sobbed and whimpered as he flogged me again and again with his buckle.

As he lashed me, he bellowed, 'You will never see that bugger again. If he ever comes to this house I will kill him.' I knew he would.

The verbal abuse slowed as he became breathless from the flogging, until finally he had to stop. As he left, he slammed my bedroom door and locked it from the outside.

I don't know how long I was there, completely still, my

lacerated legs and arms oozing blood onto the bedcover. My back burned with the pain. I think I must have passed out. It was several hours before I came to, retching with nausea. More mess for me to clean up. I drifted in and out of consciousness. Then suddenly it was morning, the door opened and my mother came in with a cloth and a bowl of water.

'I had to wait till your father went out to work,' she said through tight lips. I was astonished. She had never before come to help me. She bathed my wounds, but by this time the bleeding had formed dry crusts over the lacerations and my pyjamas had stuck to them.

'You're too badly marked to go to school,' she said. She made me a cup of tea and left me to sleep.

I can still remember those baby-doll pyjamas – the palest blue with tiny cornflowers strewn across them. I loved them, but they were so badly blood-stained that my mother had to throw them away.

True to my father's word, I was not allowed to go out anywhere but to school for six weeks, and I never saw Terry again. Apart from the household chores, I was banished to my bedroom. Alone again, with no one to talk to. I did think about trying to run away, but I could not get out of my head what he had said to me that day as he interrogated me.

He had pushed his face up close to mine.

'You will never get away from me. Wherever you go, I will track you down. I will never give up until I find you. I will make you suffer for the rest of your life, you and whoever else has helped you.'

I knew he meant every word. I would never be free of his tyranny.

CHAPTER 15

Jenny
A Shock Discovery

The moment that is branded on my memory started out as a very ordinary squabble between three teenage cousins – Auntie Dorothy's daughters Marilyn, Barbara and Andrea. I was at their house for the day and the four of us were in their bedroom when a dispute broke out about a misplaced book. The argument raged about who had moved it. Finally, the other two rounded on the middle sister, Barbara. I had remained a silent onlooker till then, but I rankled at this injustice.

'It's not her fault,' I interrupted.

They all three turned round to face me.

'Well, you can just stay out of this,' Marilyn, the eldest cousin, snarled at me. 'It's got nothing to do with you. What are you interfering for?' She paused for effect, then produced her killer-blow. 'You're not even part of this family. Your mam is not your real mother.'

There was a sharp intake of breath from the other two and a long silence as they watched me with anxious faces.

I couldn't say anything. A gaping hole opened up inside

and my life imploded. I was fourteen and I'd never had any clue of this before. Obviously they all knew about it. Everyone knew about it except me.

The anger boiled inside me, but I couldn't speak. It was as if I'd turned into stone and couldn't move. There were no words, no thoughts, just an echoing howl of emptiness within.

I can't remember anything else of that day until I was in the car going home with my mother. That was when the questions started to crowd my mind. Was it true? I wanted to see her reaction, needing to gauge her response. Would she try to explain it away? Why had I not known anything about this? What actually happened and, most importantly of all, who were my parents?

I couldn't wait. As she was driving along the dark country lanes back to Embleton, I told her what my cousin had said.

Even in the darkness, I could tell her face drained of colour.

'Is it true? Am I adopted?'

'Well . . . er . . . we chose you . . .'

'Were you ever going to tell me?'

She paused and took in a gulp of air, then composed herself. 'Well, you know, I have told you. I told you the story . . .'

'What story?'

She pulled over to the side of the road by a gateway, then turned to face me. 'I told you that we chose you. Remember?'

'No.'

'We went to the town and it had a castle on the hill. We went up the hill, up a winding path. There were blue cots on the left and pink cots on the right, and we chose you and brought you home.'

What a way of telling me I was adopted! I was stunned. I did have a vague memory of this story, but I'd thought it was just that – a story. It was a kind of fairy tale, like Sleeping Beauty. A story about a young couple choosing a baby. I couldn't believe that my mother really thought she had told me I was adopted when she'd told me this.

I felt as if my whole childhood had been a lie. I had never had any thoughts about being adopted, or any idea that the people I had known as my loving parents all this time were not my parents. Who were the parents who had given birth to me? Where were they and why had they rejected me? I felt I'd been duped. By not telling me I was adopted, the very people I thought loved me best had betrayed me.

'Who were my real parents?' I asked her.

Silence. She turned her head to look down the moonlit lane into the middle distance. I couldn't tell whether she intended to answer or not.

'Who was my mother?' I persisted.

Another pause. 'I'm your mother. I'm the one who chose you, who looked after you. We brought you up, your dad and I, and we've done everything for you. We're your real parents.' She had a look of genuine anguish. 'We chose you. You must have known you were special to us.'

The rest of the journey was silent. She refused to say anything more on the subject.

From that point on, my mother stuck her head in the sand and that was that. If I ever asked her a question about it, she became agitated and upset. She gave me no answers. I knew now that she wasn't my real mother, but I did accept that she had given up so much because she loved me and wanted me to have all the opportunities she could provide.

Having no one in my family to talk to about this revelation had a profound effect on me. More than ever before, I wished I had a sister or brother to share this burden with, or at least to talk it through with. I felt very alone, having nobody to help me and no one to confide in apart from my spaniel Janie. I had so many one-sided conversations with her about it. I told her my woes, my fears and insecurities, and she tilted her head to listen, one ear cocked and her brown eyes full of sympathy, then wagged her tail to cheer me up.

I didn't feel ready, at that stage, to tell any of my friends I was adopted. Not yet. The wound was too raw and I needed to sort it out in my own mind first, to come to terms with it all somehow.

Although my father had died two years before, I missed him more than ever, now that I knew. I wanted so much to discuss it with him. There were times at night when I did talk to him. I lay in bed and whispered to him in the darkness. 'Why didn't you tell me? Why did you leave me like this?' I believe he would have answered my questions if he'd been alive; told me all I wanted to know. I'm sure he would have. But he wasn't there. He'd gone, my mother was in denial, and I had to cope with this shock on my own.

For several days I couldn't concentrate on anything. As a teenager building my own identity, it was the worst time for me to find out. Suddenly I wasn't the person I thought I was. Who was I? Who were the people who'd given birth to me? What had they passed on to me? Surely *that* was who I was, but how could I know what that was when I didn't know who they were? Everything had been taken away – my heritage, my genetic make-up, my origins – and I had nothing else to put in its place. The part of my life that was being the daughter of Mam and Dad was over, and I restarted as somebody else.

CHAPTER 16

Helen

All Work and No Play

The early sixties were a fun time to live in the north of England. The area teemed with new young pop bands, some fast becoming famous, whilst others were not so lucky. We had the best local band – the Animals. They were well-known in Whitley Bay and Tynemouth, our side of Newcastle, and my friends and I regularly saw them drive past in their battered old psychedelic Ford Transit van, driven by their road manager, Tappy Wright, who was our milkman. He used to run up our back stairs every Friday evening for the milk money and demand a cup of tea.

My mother always invited him in and put on her best act as she passed him the biscuits. 'I've opened the chocolate bourbons for you,' she would say, tilting her head and smiling.

Tappy always wore a trendy denim jacket and scruffy jeans, even under his milkman's white coat. If my father was there, he used to tell him, 'Get that hat off in my house!' This was his joke. The 'hat' was the milkman's thick, curly hair. Thick or long hair on a young man shocked many of the older generation in those days, but Tommy had taken to this maverick and enjoyed chatting with him.

Tappy used to tell me about the Animals and what gigs they were playing. Then fame took him away, but I still felt like I was part of it. Many years later I would hear about Tappy again. He worked with all the top artists, including Elvis, Barbara Streisand and Jimmy Hendrix. In fact, it was Tappy who brought Hendrix over to Britain for the first time and made him internationally famous.

My friends and I used to spend quite a bit of time at the funfair, and those of us with money to spare used to go on the rides, listening to rock music playing in the background. It was the best place to hear all the latest groups. When the Animals went to number one in the charts, it was announced over the loudspeakers and we all cheered for our local lads.

I was fortunate to have such great friends to take me out of my turbulent home life. As well as sharing the school activities, my friends and I went swimming when we could, and I got heavily involved in ice skating. Horse riding, too, though I didn't have to pay. I was the kid that hung around and helped to clean out the stables. For that privilege I would get a free ride.

Soon I found myself a part-time Saturday job as an 'assistant shop assistant' in a local fashion shop called Michelle Boutique. It was next door to Woolworths and there was a solicitor's office upstairs. The fire station was down the back lane, so fire engines often came flying past, with their big silver bells ringing when we were least expecting them.

I was the junior, responsible for cleaning the shop inside and out first thing in the morning. I had to polish the door handle and clean the windows till they sparkled. I swept the

pavement from the shop to the kerb and sluiced it down
when it was particularly bad. Next, I vacuumed the floor
throughout, removed the dust covers from the clothes rails,
dusted the surfaces and tidied the back of the shop from the
previous day. Finally I had to make sure that all the hangers
pointed in the same direction. No deviation allowed.

Once we were open, I was sent down to the local café to
collect the bacon butties for us and for the solicitors upstairs.
I still remember them – salty, succulent and dripping with
ketchup. The lean bacon we have nowadays bears little
comparison.

We were a groovy boutique, with lots of fab clothes for
teenagers aspiring to Mary Quant fashions at a fraction of
the price. As well as bell-bottoms or cigarette-line jeans, we
sold courtelle twin-sets and the popular turtleneck sweater.
We stocked a good range of multi-patterned stockings,
including some with the Beatles woven in, which Joan loved
to wear. Our 'Mod' A-line shift dresses sold well, mainly in
black-and-white block patterns. We even had the famous paper
dress and knickers, which were a big novelty that brought
people in to look, but they didn't do very well.

Our fastest selling item was a silky nylon 'non-iron and
uncreasable' mini shift dress which came in a vast range of
paisley patterns and colours, folded into a tiny plastic bag
with a drawstring. They were cheap and sold like hot cakes.
But when you think about it, they were so short they probably didn't cost much to make.

I liked the job, but it was hard work and a long day. For
this I earned seventeen shillings and sixpence (88p), which I
thought at the time was a small fortune. It was, for a girl
whose parents never gave her pocket money. There was a

building society across the road from the shop and I opened a savings account – the first one I ever had.

Once I had saved enough, I decided to treat myself. I went to Newcastle on the bus and bought a pack of seven pairs of pants, every pair a different colour, a pair for every day of the week. As I rode home on the bus again, I smiled to myself all the way. I walked into the house clutching my pack of pants, wrapped in a little bag.

'What have you got there?' challenged my mother.

'I've bought myself some knickers. Seven pairs of pants, so that I can have a clean pair every day.'

She gave me such a look. 'Oooh,' she smirked. 'Just look at you. Aren't you the fancy one, then?'

Whitley Bay was quite a vibrant seaside town, with lots of summer visitors. There was a Scots week, when traditionally all of the factories in Scotland would close down and workers migrated south for their brief holiday. The boutique was always particularly busy then and we sold a lot of bikinis – usually cotton and no stretch.

I was gradually establishing a life of my own away from the problems at home – growing up with my friends, engaged in activities and doing a part-time job I enjoyed.

At fifteen I had to leave school. All my friends would soon be going on to college to do their A levels. I wasn't even allowed to finish my O-level year.

'You will not be going to college,' my father said. 'It's time you got out and earned some money to pay your way in this house.'

'But I have to do my exams to be a nurse,' I wailed.

'A ridiculous idea!' he said. 'You'd spend all your time cleaning up old men.'

'Can't I even do my O levels before I leave?'

'No. You have to pay your keep. You can stay in your job as shop assistant and do it full-time. I've arranged it all for you.'

This was my future. All my hopes and ambitions of training to be a nurse were wiped away in that moment. I knew it was no use protesting. I felt empty and helpless – distraught. It seemed that every good thing, every opportunity I'd ever had in my life, was snatched away from me. I did well at school. I wanted to go on to college with my friends. But no. I had to give up education the moment it was legal. No choice.

Mercia and Tommy had no aspirations for me. Except as a work-horse.

So now I worked full-time at the boutique. But my pay was not my own. I didn't even know how much I earned. Every week, when I picked up my sealed wage-packet, I had to take it home unopened and hand it over to my father. He opened it and gave me just five shillings (25p) 'pocket money'.

One day, I came home from work straight into another situation.

A few years before, my parents had applied for a council house. Today a letter had arrived to say they could have one . . . back in Seghill, the mining village, home of my first memories and the extended family all around. As I took my coat off, I heard the raised voices. The argument raged for a long time, to and fro.

'I will not go back to that bloody place,' fumed my father. 'It's a backward step. My job is here, in Whitley Bay.

Why should I travel to work when it's just round the corner here?'

'You and your precious bus-driving. What about me? Don't you think I should have a say in this? After all, it's me that has to do all the skivvying at home.'

'Listen to you! You never do any housework. Helen does it all.'

'You've no idea how hard I work every day for you, and no thanks I get for it.'

'Stop playing the martyr, pit-yacker.'

'They're offering us a whole house with a proper garden, not a flat with a shared back yard. I've never had that since we got married. Only one that I had to work my fingers to the bone for. Left to you, we could never have a house with a garden again.'

'Stop your nagging, woman. We've got a perfectly good place here. I'm not moving, and that's that.'

But in the end, my mother got her way. She wheedled him round to saying yes.

That was it. We were going to move house again. I went to my room and slumped down on my bed. I did not want to move anywhere. But I knew that, once again, I had no choice. I would be moving away from my friends, my social life, my job in the boutique.

It was a 1950s council house, a two-bed semi with a large kitchen and a through-lounge the other side of the railway tracks from where we'd lived before. A lot of the aunties and uncles still lived in the village, about ten minutes walk away.

The day we moved was a nightmare. I was at work, so I didn't see much of it. My father had got hold of a van from somewhere. My mother's family turned up to help. When I arrived home, Auntie Dorrie was there with Auntie Nancy and Uncle James. Auntie Dorrie was a person who liked to take charge.

She stood with her hands on her hips, giving orders. 'Now you bring that sideboard over here, man,' she said to James, who was coming in through the front door backwards, with Tommy at the other end. 'Put it against this wall here. Left a bit. Mind the lamp-stand.'

Auntie Nancy moved the lamp.

'No, James,' said my father. 'We'll put it over here, man. By the window.'

Auntie Dorrie scowled.

'You needn't make that face,' barked Tommy.

'Less of your lip, man,' replied Auntie Dorrie, pulling the sideboard down the wall to where she wanted it.

'You leave that sideboard alone.'

'Haaway. It'll look better here.'

'This is *my* house,' he shouted in her face. 'And I will decide where it goes.' He pulled it back over to the window.

At this point, my mother walked in from the kitchen. 'Just ignore him, Dorrie. I like it where you put it.'

'You can stay out of it,' Tommy barked, prodding her and pushing her back to the doorway.

He turned to Auntie Dorrie. 'As for you,' he stormed as he walked across the room and started to push her towards the hall, 'we don't need your help – interfering, more like. You can get yourself off home.'

'After all I've done for you!'

'Much good it did,' he scoffed.

As he gave her a final shove, she stumbled and collided with a tea chest full of pots and pans. She picked up the frying pan on the top. 'How dare you treat me like that!' she yelled and hit Tommy over the head with it.

He yelped, put his hand up and steadied himself, then took hold of her arm and frog-marched her to the door.

'Let go of my arm,' she spluttered. 'You're hurting me.'

Tommy's face was set and his eyes started to bulge. He propelled her down the front path to the gate and shoved her through it so hard that she had to hold onto the post to stop herself from falling. Then he slammed the gate behind her. 'And you needn't bother coming back! I won't have any interfering in this house. You can tell them all. This is *my* house and I'll have it how I like.'

This was the start to life in our new home. From then on, the aunties and uncles kept their distance. Most of my older cousins had moved away, and the ones remaining in Seghill were a tight-knit group. They had their lives here, but all my friends and my social life were in Whitley Bay. I felt marooned. That evening my father sat me down. 'I've arranged an interview for you tomorrow. Fill in this application form tonight.'

It was for another job as a shop assistant, but this time it was in Newcastle. I filled in the application form as instructed and was asked to go for an interview. On the long bus journey I built up a sense of excitement at the idea of going to work in the 'big city'.

The interview went well and I was duly offered the job. I travelled to work every day on the bus and soon made new friends. I was in the ladies' coats department of C&A in Northumberland Street. It was a popular store in those days, with all the latest fashions at reasonable prices. I remember the huge window displays and snooty-looking mannequins positioned throughout the store. I had to wear a formal black dress or skirt and top, with black shoes and stockings. We had to look smart at all times.

My supervisor was a real-life version of Mrs Slocombe from *Are You Being Served?* She looked immaculate every day, with lots of make-up and permed hair in a bouffant style. She wore one of those gold chains on her spectacles and watched us like a hawk. If she saw any of us doing something wrong, she slowly raised the spectacles in the air and placed them on the bridge of her nose, with the expression of someone lining us up to face a firing squad. She was very strict, but not unkind, always making sure we took our breaks at the proper time, which she timed to the second. It was quite old-fashioned in some ways. We were all required to call each other 'Miss so and so' or 'Mrs so and so'. If she caught us using first names, she sent us to the stockroom to tidy and dust the shelves.

'Customer service must be second to none,' she insisted. 'If the customer requires you to stand on your head, you must do so immediately!'

We had half-hour breaks for lunch. I usually went to the staff dining room and had a cup of tea, maybe with a packet of crisps or an apple. I had to be careful because I had my bus fare home to pay and if I ate lunch I wouldn't have enough money left.

The job was tolerable, but nothing special. However, it was fun to be in Newcastle, an exhilarating place for a teenager in those days. I loved the bustling atmosphere, and there always seemed to be something going on: buskers, street people, mods and rockers, hippies. We used to go to a coffee bar called The Pit in the basement of a shop on the main street and stay for hours to watch all the Bohemian characters congregating there. They fascinated me. I don't know how that coffee bar ever made any money, as we kids only ever bought one cup of coffee and made it last for ages. The other club I loved going to when I could afford it was the Club A'Gogo on Percy Street, where the Animals had begun their career.

One morning I was on my way to work when the bus jolted over a railway crossing much faster than usual. It juddered and shook, and the next thing I remember is lying on the floor in the centre aisle. I had fainted. I levered myself up gently, sharp pains shooting down my spine. The conductor helped me off the bus at my stop and I forced my legs to walk me to work. It was clear to everyone when I arrived that I was struggling. By now my back was on fire and I could barely move. I tried to find a comfortable position to alleviate the worst of the pain, but it was no good. Suddenly I felt nauseous, and my supervisor was called.

'Fainting on the bus like that first thing in the morning,' she said. 'And feeling sick. It means you've been a bad girl, and now you're expecting.'

I was shocked; indignant that she could say that. Although stern, she was usually very fair.

'But it's not true,' I protested. 'It's not even possible.'

'Nonsense. I don't believe you. I know you girls and what you get up to. What else could it be?'

'I hurt my back . . .'

'That's enough of that,' she interrupted. 'I won't have you talking back at me. You're obviously in no fit state to work. Go off home. Now.' She pointed at the door. I could see there was nothing else I could say, so I left.

I had to get myself back to the bus stop, somehow, bent

over with pain. It was a nightmare journey home, but I was glad when I stumbled in through the front door at last.

When I told my father what this woman had said, he went to Newcastle and stormed into the store.

'I demand to see the manager,' he bellowed as all the shoppers turned to see what was up. He made a huge scene and was ordered to leave the building.

'Get out!' A security guard was called. 'And you can tell Miss Lumsden she's fired!' was the manager's parting shot.

So that was it. The next day a letter arrived to confirm my dismissal on the grounds that I had failed to attend work and therefore my services were no longer required.

'That's so unfair,' I protested.

'Forget it! That was a rubbish job anyway,' said my father. 'I'll find you a better one.'

I spent all week on painkillers, flat on my back on the floor. At the time, nobody but me seemed concerned by my back problem. Many years later, a consultant diagnosed bilateral fractures of my spine on both sides, caused by an old injury. This was presumably from the time when I was slammed against the wall at the age of about six, or maybe when I was thrown downstairs a few years later. I have since developed serious arthritis all the way down my spine.

The pain gradually abated, and I was left in no doubt that I needed to start another job to keep the money coming in.

'The amount of tax the government takes out of the working man's wage – it's outrageous,' grumbled Tommy. 'How do they expect us to make ends meet?' Then he turned to me. 'You're not helping, mind – lounging around here day after day. It's time you got back to work and earned your keep again.'

My father was now a fitter at MacGregor's, an engineering company in Whitley Bay. Next door was the Shirt Factory. The following day was a Friday and, without a word to me, Tommy spoke to the manager and came home to make his announcement.

'I've got you a new job as a machinist, making shirts. It's piecework, so you can make a lot more money than that bloody shop. You'll start work on Monday.'

For a girl who loved to be active, help people and use my brain, this was a calamity. To sit still all day, conversation impossible against the noise of the machines, no contact with customers, doing this repetitive job sounded like the worst sort of work for me. But I had no choice.

For the first week they trained me to use the industrial sewing machines. After that I worked on the production line, making shirt collars. This was a miserable occupation – mindless and unfulfilling piecework. I was paid according to the number of collars I produced. I tried hard to be positive, to think of the good points of the job, but nothing came to mind. It wouldn't have been so bad if I could have made whole shirts, but just doing collars all day was stultifying; teenage drudgery. I hated it to such an extent that I stopped eating and lost a lot of weight. Nobody noticed.

I was very unhappy at the time, of course. My spirit and my hopes for the future had all been completely trampled on. My work was so boring and the constant noise ground me down. I couldn't even go to the toilet without asking permission and being timed. I just didn't feel like eating all the time I worked there. I didn't think of it as any kind of protest, though maybe it could have been, subconsciously. I don't know how much weight I lost as we didn't have any scales at home, but my clothes were hanging off me.

As my father worked next door, he insisted I meet him every Friday lunchtime to hand over my pay packet. As in my previous jobs, I was not allowed to open it, so I had no idea what I earned. But the Shirt Factory must have paid more than C&A because he raised my 'pocket money' to ten shillings (50p). I worked very hard for this meagre 'privilege'.

The high points in my week were the evenings when I was allowed to go out. I took the bus back to Whitley Bay and met up with my old friends, and for a few short hours could be a normal teenager again. We met at the fairground in winter, or on the beach in summer. Sometimes we went to one of the three teenage clubs in town, where we danced to live music on Saturday and Sunday nights. Our favourite was The 45 Club. It was non-alcoholic, just for teenagers. There was a soft-drinks bar and the whole place was run like a battleship by a middle-aged matron called Betty. There was never any trouble when Betty was there – we were all terrified of her!

The 45 Club had a dance floor and a stage at the front. The lower half of the walls was painted black and the top part was like a sheet of music, with notes on all the lines. During the week it was a disco, with the DJ and his record decks up on the stage. The regular DJ was a boy called Simon. He was older than me; good-looking, with dark hair, a Manfred Mann beard and a warm smile, always smartly dressed in a sharp suit with a shirt and tie. Simon played all the groovy pop music of the sixties, such as the Rolling Stones, the Kinks, the Small Faces, Long John Baldry and the Who.

At the weekends we danced to some fab live groups, including the Junco Partners (still performing today), the Brethren, who later changed their name to Lindisfarne, the Silver Dollars, and many other great groups. Sometimes, if he wasn't DJ-ing somewhere else, Simon came to join us too. We were all local kids and we all knew each other. It was a unique atmosphere, and so packed that it was sometimes impossible to find a space on the dance floor, even to stand still. On those evenings, people just stood outside on the street and listened to the music, dancing the Shake or the Locomotive on the pavement.

I knew all the boys in the bands in those innocent, crazy days before fame came calling. They were great times and it was always good to catch up with my old school friends. But I was in a dead-end factory job that I hated. They went to college, studied new subjects, went out on field-trips, lived the student life and planned their future careers. We lived in different worlds.

The highlight in my life at this time was my growing friendship with Simon. Soon we were going out together and we really clicked. As well as The 45 Club, he was heavily involved in the hospital radio service and had his own programme. He took me several times, to his studio in the basement of the hospital, which was always dark and spooky, but he dispelled the gloom with his hugs. Once inside the studio it was fine. He had stuck a variety of old egg boxes all over the studio walls to insulate the sound.

'I know it looks wacky,' said Simon. 'But it really works.'

He was dedicated to his work for the hospital service. Once or twice I sat with him as he broadcast his programme, full of pride at how good he was. The patients loved him.

As an apprentice motor mechanic, Simon was very keen on cars. He had a tiny maroon Ford Popular van of a certain vintage. Of course it didn't have a built-in radio, so he decided to mount a full-size transistor radio inside the roof, between the driver and passenger seats. This was hilarious. As we drove along, Radio Caroline faded in and out so much that we could only catch short clips of each song!

At weekends, to boost the household finances, my father was a part-time bus-driver. He drove the ten o'clock bus back from Whitley Bay to Seghill in the evening, which gave him yet more control over me. I had to be on that bus. On the rare occasion that I lost track of time and failed to be at the bus stop in time, he would park the bus outside and storm into The 45 Club, where he would humiliate me in front of my friends. I would be sitting at a table or dancing to the music when he charged through the door in his bus-driver's uniform and came straight for me.

'C'mon home *now*.' He would grab me roughly by the arm and drag me through the club as my friends, their faces aghast, parted to let us through. When he first did it, everyone was shocked, their mouths hanging open and their eyes wide. I had the feeling they had never seen anything like this happening before. But they never said anything, never tried to stop him. They were probably as frightened as I was.

Once we were outside he didn't say a word. In a way this was more alarming than if he'd berated me. He kept his vice-like grip on my upper arm all the way to the bus, pushing me along in front of him, thumping me in the middle of my back as we went. I was pushed up the steps of the bus and had to sit in silence all the way home, re-enacting in my mind the humiliating scene and trying to quell the embarrassment and indignation that welled up inside me.

He withheld my pocket money that week, so I couldn't go out at all the following weekend.

My mother, at this stage, had a job in a cardboard box factory, so both my parents worked full-time now. Their earnings plus Dad's overtime and my wages on top meant there was a lot of money coming into the household, but where it went I have no idea. I never saw any of it and there were no luxuries. It was a mystery to me. Were they saving it up? Was there something I didn't know about?

CHAPTER 17

Jenny

Home on the Range

At fifteen I was selected to swim freestyle for the county. I felt both surprised and honoured. My mother wasn't surprised at all, but she beamed with pride when I told her. She had spent a fortune, as well as so much of her own time, taking me everywhere in all weathers, often late at night or before anyone else was up in the morning. She felt we'd both earned this accolade.

But once the county coach had picked the final team of swimmers, he realized we had a problem. Five swimmers with the same name – Smith!

'Four of you will have to change your names, mind.'

'What can we change them to?' asked one girl.

'Have you got any other names? A nickname, maybe, or another family name?'

We all tried to think of alternatives.

'What about you, Jenny?' He looked at me. 'What's your middle name?'

'I'm Jennifer Constance Lee Smith.'

'Ee, that's easy. You can be Jenny Lee Smith. How's that?'

'Fine.' I nodded. And that was how I came to be known

throughout my competitive career. Even now, after all these years with my married surname, Jenny Lee Smith is what I'm still known as in the sports world.

By now I was training in the mornings before school, at lunchtimes and in the evenings after school. Swimming was my life and there wasn't much room for anything else.

But we continued to go to Embleton for weekends whenever there was a gap in the schedules. In fact, it was about the time I was selected to swim for the county, aged fifteen, that I won my first golf competition. Once again it was at my home golf course, Dunstanburgh Golf Club, and as before it was against people much older than me. My mother had beaten me the previous year, but now it was my turn – my first golfing victory. My mother didn't mind that I had beaten her, and I felt elated. I think it's brilliant when you win an adult competition that young. It's such an incentive. I told myself, 'If you can win this, you can win other things.' It opened the door for me.

There was a big dinner-dance that evening – all adults except for me. I had to go up on stage, where they presented the women's trophy to me. Here was I, a teenager, winning the annual prize. Mind you, I could only keep the trophy for a year, but my name is on it and I believe it's still being awarded now.

Whilst it felt great to do so well at golf, I didn't see it as anything special, as the swimming continued to be my priority for another year or so, but once you get to around sixteen, you're often finished as a swimmer, and I gradually turned back to the golf over that year, though I didn't see it as any kind of a career opportunity until quite a bit later. It was just a pleasure to go around the course and talk to people as I went from one hole to the next. It was a sociable activity, outdoors in the freshest air I knew, by the sea at Embleton, which I loved.

Without noticing any great difference myself, others began to see an improvement in my game. The more I enjoyed it, the more I played, and the more I played, the more skilful a golfer I became, so the quality of my game increased without any great effort on my part, just lots of carefree practice. I smiled to myself when I thought about what Dad would say if he knew what those little cut-down clubs he'd made for me when I was three had started. It seemed I was getting better and better.

When I was selected to represent Northumberland in their junior golf team, it was a great surprise to me, but of course I was very pleased.

One day my mother looked up from reading the local newspaper and said, 'Haaway pet, listen to this: "The famous golfer, John Jacobs, has opened a golf centre at Gosforth",' she read out to me. 'He's going to give lessons – they say he's the best teacher. They call him Dr Golf. Would you like to go and have a lesson?'

Well, of course I said, 'Yes, please.' I'd heard of John Jacobs. Everyone who played the game had heard of Dr Golf. 'But won't it be very expensive?'

'Let's go. You can have one lesson and we'll see how you get on.' Mam smiled. 'You know, it's important that you take your opportunities when they come, so don't worry about the cost, mind. I'll open the salon for longer hours, now that you're not swimming any more. That will help.'

I knew how lucky I was to have my mother's support.

'Pass the paper, Mam,' I said. 'I want to go through the job vacancies.'

I had left school after O levels. I was never very academic, and anyway I wanted to help my mother support us both. Turning to the jobs page, I saw the perfect opportunity for me.

'I don't believe it. John Jacobs wants a receptionist at his new golf centre!' I exclaimed.

'That's just the job for you, pet,' she laughed.

I rang up straightaway and got an interview.

So it was that I never had to pay for a lesson from Dr Golf. I got the job. It was wonderful to work on a golf-range and have a free practice whenever I liked – I would often go out at lunchtime or after work in the summer.

I had a twenty-eight handicap then, aged sixteen. When John came out on the range and saw me hitting balls for the first time, he stopped to watch. I was quite a powerful girl and I could hit the ball very hard. Golf builds up muscles, and I'd been hitting golf balls all my life.

John used to call me Shorty. 'Come on, Shorty. Let's see you hit this.' He coached me and advised me on different ways to improve my swing. In the first five minutes he got me hitting the ball even harder than I had before! He was a brilliant teacher.

'Do you know what I think?' he said to me at the end of my first free lesson.

'No.'

'One day, young lady, you'll play for England.'

I laughed out loud and said to myself, 'This guy's crazy!

He doesn't know what he's on about.' How could he make such a ridiculous prophecy when he hardly knew me?

When I told my mother what he'd said that night, she laughed and laughed, and I joined in. It seemed so absurd.

John often came out to give me tips and a bit of free coaching when I was out practising on the range. I hit thousands of balls under his watchful eye. He didn't so much look at my swing as the flight of the ball, which told him what I needed to do to improve. He was a lovely man, and very compassionate. He became quite fatherly towards me, which I really appreciated. I'm sure his kindness helped me personally as much as his coaching helped my golf.

During the two years I worked at John's golf range, I became quite friendly with a lot of the regular golfers who came to practise there. We often met up as a group in the restaurant at the range, or at the busy bar, which was quite a social hub, hosting quizzes, dances and film evenings. Nearly all the members who regularly attended these events were lovely people and we always enjoyed ourselves there.

One of these regulars was Richard, an attractive man and a keen golfer, a few years older than me, as most of them were. He was great fun and we played a lot of golf together, both at the range and with other friends at various golf clubs in the area. Playing so much with him really helped strengthen my game. In between we often spent evenings together amongst our golfing friends, so we all got to know each other very well. I knew Richard for a long time before he asked me out, by which time we were already firm friends, so it just seemed a natural next step.

Meanwhile, my golf continued to improve so much that,

by the end of the two years I worked there, my handicap was down to four. I was winning tournaments and was well on my way to bigger things.

In between tournaments, I attended the local college and trained to be a hairdresser so that I could be more useful to my mother and take on some of her work whenever I could, which was a great comfort to her now that she was getting older and suffering from arthritis. What with college, work in my mother's salon and golf, I didn't have much time for joining in with the 'swinging Sixties' and I wasn't much into music, but I did once go with some friends to see the Rolling Stones at the Newcastle City Hall. They had amazing energy as they blasted out their songs, filling the whole hall with a storm of sound. I can still hear them now!

Throughout these mid-to-late teenage years, the fact that I was adopted was always in my mind, subdued for my mother Connie's sake. It felt like a continuous dull ache in the background, and at times turned into a shard of glass that pierced my consciousness and overshadowed everything I achieved.

I didn't tell anyone I was adopted for another three or four years. I couldn't say it. I hardly understood it myself.

I think the sports training I was involved in, the competitions and the way I had to learn to really focus when I was playing golf enabled me to move on, gradually. My determination helped too. Despite everything, I seemed to have an inner strength that carried me through and helped me slowly come to terms with what had happened. It also helped that through my growing successes in golf I was developing a greater sense of my own identity. Indeed, the whole situation might have played a part in strengthening my resolve to be my own person when I was competing – to do well, to show the world.

When I spoke to another cousin about my adoption years later, she admitted that everyone in the family had known from the beginning, but they'd all been sworn to silence. She told me that apparently it was the rule at the time of my birth in 1948 that my real mother had to keep me and feed me till I was six weeks old, and only then could I be given for adoption, which solved the mystery of my first six weeks. The health visitor who brought me to my adoptive parents when my real mother was finally allowed to relinquish me had managed to arrange it all because she was also the health visitor to my birth mother. How strange is that? The health visitor became my godmother.

'You know,' said my cousin, 'I remember that whenever your mam was at our house when you were little and we were playing with you, my mother was persistently trying to persuade Connie to tell you. "When are you going to tell Jennifer about her adoption? You must tell her about it. She needs to know." But Connie always refused. "I can't talk about it," she'd answer with her lips pursed. "And nor must you. I'm her mother. She doesn't need anyone else."'

Eventually, by the time I was a young adult, I had come to terms with my situation enough to tell new friends that I was adopted. I felt quite brave about it outwardly, but for many years could not shake off the feeling of being bereft, detached, a lost soul. And I still retained some of my original anger and resentment against my adoptive mother. It was something that never really left me, but I didn't tell her how I felt. My father's death when I was twelve had been a devastating loss, but to find out in that cruel way that I was adopted and wasn't who I thought I was turned out to be the more acute and enduring bereavement.

I determined to find out one day who I really was. Maybe not while Connie was alive, but one day.

CHAPTER 18

Helen

Life on the Balcony

The talk in our house was suddenly all about emigration. The talk between my parents, that is. I wasn't consulted, of course. They looked at various brochures and showed them to me. I didn't know what to think, but I wasn't too alarmed as I didn't think it would really happen.

Their preference was for South Africa. I have no idea why, but as this came to seem like a serious possibility, the whole thing horrified me. It was the last place I wanted to go just then.

When you have a difficult home life, friendships are all the more important. My friends were more of a family to me than my parents. But that was the problem. My parents didn't want me to have a life of my own, or have fun with my friends. It seemed that whenever I made a life for myself outside work and things were going well, they chose to remove me from it and exert their control over me.

They insisted I go on the bus with them to Newcastle to have an interview at the South African Immigration Department. I remember feeling both resentful and nervous that day. I was fuming inside – I didn't want to be there; I didn't want to go – but I was only sixteen and that meant I probably wouldn't have much choice, unless I could persuade them somehow to leave me behind.

Partway through our family interview, I was just thinking about how I could achieve that when I heard my name. The immigration officer had turned to face me. They all looked expectant.

'I'm sorry,' I mumbled, red-faced. 'Did you ask me a question? Could you repeat it, please?'

'Yes, of course.' There was kindness in his smile. 'And what do you think about going to South Africa, Miss Lumsden. Are you excited about going?'

My father tightened his lips and clenched his fists as he stared at me, oozing menace should I dare to let him down. I knew that look and hesitated, trying desperately to think of something honest to say without angering him any more than necessary.

'I'm . . .' I paused, plucking up courage. 'I don't really want to go.'

In my peripheral vision, my father's face reddened.

'Why is that?' asked the officer in surprise.

'Because . . . I'm frightened of insects,' I blurted out.

Immediately everyone relaxed and laughed together at my childish answer. I managed a weak smile, but inside I felt desperate.

Suddenly it was a reality. The application to emigrate to South Africa had been approved. All my hopes deserted me at that moment. My parents were now free to take me, against my will, to a foreign country where I knew no one.

By this stage, my boyfriend Simon and I were going steady.

We'd been going out for six months now. We spent a lot of our time together and I couldn't bear the thought of being parted from him. We loved each other and had plans for our future. How could I leave him to go so far away? What would happen to us? Would I ever see him again?

'I don't want to go to South Africa,' I told my father one day when I thought he was in a good mood. 'Can't I stay behind? I could go and live with George and Joan, or maybe Uncle James and Auntie Gladys.'

'No. You are coming with us. There's nothing to stop you.'

'Yes there is,' I dared. 'I don't want to leave Simon.'

My father was dismissive. 'Get rid of him!' That's what he said. That's how little he cared about me.

I railed inwardly against this for several days and sleepless nights. I didn't know what to do. I couldn't cry or beg, because it would probably provoke a backlash. I considered running away, but I knew how risky that would be. I was sure I couldn't finish with Simon. We were a couple. Nor could I tell him I had to leave him to go with my parents to live on another continent.

I finally mustered the courage to confront my parents. 'I will not leave Simon behind,' I began. 'I will stay in England on my own if I have to. You can go to South Africa without me!'

This was the first time in my life that I had faced up to them. I stood firm and tried not to flinch, waiting for the explosion. I might be sixteen, but that wouldn't stop my father's wrath. He could be as violent now as he'd always been.

'You can't stay behind,' my father said in a reasonable voice, a tone I was not used to hearing. 'But I tell you what

– invite this Simon round for tea so that we can meet him.'

I couldn't believe it. My first feeling was of relief, but that was short-lived as things reordered themselves in my mind. Suspicion besieged me – I didn't trust my father's motives. I couldn't. I had seen only bad things come out of this sort of situation in the past. I didn't want Simon to see what my parents were like, but I had little choice, so I did as my father asked. This bizarre meeting was sure to be uncomfortable. Or worse.

The day came. Simon arrived and my father was charming. I believe I sat with my mouth wide open in amazement. Surely there would be a killer blow at the end of this tea party? But that didn't happen. The whole thing was a happy occasion, carried along by my father's bonhomie. I couldn't understand it.

A day or two later, Dad announced his idea: 'Your boyfriend will finish his mechanic's apprenticeship next year. Then he can come out and join us in South Africa.'

It seemed such a simple plan. Not an easy one, I know, with a year's separation in between, but it did seem to resolve the impasse between us. Simon and I discussed it later and realized it was probably the best solution I could have hoped for. My father agreed that Simon should come and live with us in South Africa and he would even find him a job for when he arrived.

Everyone was content with this proposal . . . apart from me. If only I was legally old enough to stay behind. My protests had gone unheeded and there was nothing I could do now but go along with it, for the sake of peace, though I continued to have nagging doubts.

The build-up to our departure depressed me more than I can say. Everything had to be sold or disposed of and I was allowed to take only one suitcase with me. I squeezed in as much as I could during the last few days. While I was out, my mother threw away all of my remaining possessions, including my one-eared teddy, which I had kept all these years – a cherished friend, now gone.

'What about your savings account?' asked my dad.

I had kept this account since I'd left school. There was £6 in it, which was a lot of money to me. It meant nothing to my father, who marched me off to the bank and stood over me while I withdrew my hard-earned savings.

'Right, give it to me,' he ordered. He took *my* money and I never saw a penny of it again.

Finally the day came. The day I would leave behind everything and everyone I knew. My brother George drove us to London, to Heathrow airport. It was a miserable journey for me and I didn't speak the whole way there.

We said our goodbyes to George at the departures gate and were soon on board the twelve-hour flight to South Africa.

As we walked down the steps of the plane and across the tarmac, the dry summer heat smothered us in its rasping grip and the brilliance of the sunshine blinded us. It was a huge contrast to the cold, dark winter we'd left behind a few hours before.

My father had a job arranged as transport manager of a removals company in Pretoria, so the boss's wife, Mrs Ashman, met us at Johannesburg's Jan Smuts Airport and led us to her car. I couldn't believe my eyes when I saw it – a huge, metallic blue Chevrolet station-wagon. It burbled like a monster as she drove us onto the main road. We had all the car windows open and the rich mix of scents, sounds and colours overwhelmed all my senses.

Mrs Ashman drove us the thirty miles to Pretoria, chatting away and pointing out some of the sights as we drove through the tree-lined streets, the trees dusted with lilac jacaranda blossom. Everything seemed particularly foreign to me, as I'd never left the north-east of England till now. There was one thing that surprised me more than anything else – I had never seen so many black people before, and they all seemed to be doing menial jobs. I didn't understand why. I'd not yet heard of apartheid.

Finally, Mrs Ashman dropped us off at the Jacaranda Hotel, our temporary home until our permanent accommodation was ready for us.

The hotel itself seemed fine, but I was dismayed when I saw our bedroom – a double room with a double bed for my parents and a small single put-you-up shoved into the corner for me. I was sixteen years old and I had to share with my parents, just like I had done as a small child. Was this what it would be like everywhere we went?

The answer soon materialized when, a few days later, we were supplied with a one-bedroomed furnished apartment.

'You can sleep on the balcony,' said my father.

It was a small second-floor balcony with no furniture except a 'shake-down' bed which doubled as a sofa during the day. The concrete floor of the balcony was painted glossy red, and on the outer side there was a waist-high, rough brick wall. The only privacy was afforded by a canvas roller-blind which pulled down at night.

This set-up was surreal I was like Rapunzel in her tower, except that it was no fairy-tale – I was trapped with no hope of escape. I'd been transported to a strange land, and my bed was outside in the open air in all weathers, with hardly any privacy, even less security, and an insect problem. My parents closed the doors from the inside at night, so I was out there on my own. That balcony was a metaphor for my life – looking out at the world, but not part of it, excluded by my family. A reject. Mere property, to be stored out of the way.

The air on my balcony was hot and still, the fragrance of semi-tropical flowers a consolation for the constant clicking sound of the cicadas in the undergrowth beneath. Lizards and chameleons made their homes on my balcony, where they basked in the sun during the day. Being a fair-skinned English girl, the insects zeroed in on me like torpedoes at night. There were cockroaches and a whole variety of Africa's larger creepy-crawlies. I became used to them all in time. But worst of all were the mosquitoes. They'd won the lottery; they attacked me every night, so I was plagued with mosquito bites for weeks.

Tommy's new boss invited us to the RAF club, where all the company's employees met on Saturday nights. On that first evening I found myself stuck with a group of unknown adults swapping stories about their time in the war. I concentrated on trying not to yawn.

Soon I became aware of a 'what shall we do about her?' situation. I was being talked about, within earshot, and it wasn't complimentary.

'Helen's sitting around at home, being lazy and useless,' moaned my father. 'She needs to get a job – something easy that even she can do.'

My father asked around to see if there were any shirt factories for me to work at. Everyone looked shocked. In the sixties, under apartheid, only 'blacks' were allowed to do that kind of job.

On one of these Saturday evenings, I met a student called Mike.

'Hi. You must be Helen? I'm the boss's son,' he said with a rueful smile. 'Just home from uni for the long vacation.'

'I'd love to do a degree, but I'm not allowed to study.'

'No, I gathered that.' He tilted his head in sympathy. 'Why don't you come and meet some of my friends tomorrow?'

'That would be great.'

We talked and talked. He listened to my troubles and seemed to understand those problems I chose to share with him. But of course I kept a lot back.

Mike came and called for me the following day. He had the sweetest car – a vintage Austin 7 that he had restored himself.

'Would you like me to take you on a drive around Pretoria?'

I didn't hesitate. 'Yes please.'

He showed me the sights of the city and then took me to meet up with some of his friends. I was so relieved to come across people nearer my age and began to feel more at home.

I started to hang out with Mike. Sometimes he borrowed his dad's Chevrolet truck and we took his two younger brothers to the drive-in. We sat in the back of the truck on those hot African nights watching movies and eating snacks. I didn't have a job yet, so Mike and I were free to spend every day together. His dad had the removals contract for the embassies, and he let us have the keys and free access to some of the grandest buildings in Pretoria with their luxury swimming pools. I had an idyllic summer swimming and sunbathing with Mike and his friends in those plush surroundings. In between, he taught me to drive the Morris Minor he had restored. My life was definitely improving.

But despite South Africa's blue skies, dark clouds never stayed away long in my family. My father didn't like his job and his resentment exacerbated his instability. The long-distance driving that kept him away for days at a time didn't help. I'd never really thought about the implications. I took things at face value most of the time – the easiest way to stay out of trouble.

One Saturday, when Tommy was away on one of his long trips, Mike and I were stopped by another company driver.

'Go and buy two cinema tickets for me, will you?' he said to Mike. Then he turned to me. 'I'm going to take your mother to a movie.' He paused and put his finger to his nose. 'Keep this to yourself. No questions asked. Right?'

He could have been straight out of a rubbish gangster film. I would have laughed about it if it hadn't been such a serious situation.

Mike had to do as he was asked, so my mother went to the cinema with this man. We went to a different cinema that evening and I didn't get home till quite late, so I tiptoed onto my balcony and shut the door.

I don't know when my mother got home.

All she said the next morning was, 'Don't you dare tell your dad.'

I was alarmed that she was dating while my father was away. I knew what it would lead to if my father found out.

*

My first New Year's Eve in South Africa started full of promise. It was a beautiful summer's evening. Mike took me out for a meal. After dinner we drove into the centre of Pretoria, the traditional focus of celebrations, and arrived to a carnival atmosphere with everyone laughing as they sang and danced to live music. Some of the revellers rocked our car and shouted 'Happy New Year' greetings to us as we inched our way around Church Square. We laughed with them, carefree and full of hope. At midnight we drove to the Union Buildings, high above the city, and watched the fireworks dance in the velvet sky.

On the way home we chatted and laughed in the car until we turned the corner into the street where I lived. The road was empty apart from a lone man standing in the middle of the street. As he saw us, he jumped up and down and waved his arms wildly.

'Look at that guy,' said Mike. 'He's a lunatic, isn't he?' We laughed.

Then our headlights lit up the grimace on the man's face. His shouts were soundless above the noise of our engine.

In an instant, my laughter turned to dread. 'It's my father, Mike,' I whispered, and, more urgently, 'Don't stop the car!' A cold fear crushed my heart in a vice and acid rose into my mouth. I knew my father. I knew what he was like, what he could do. Seeing him now, like this, I knew it was imperative that we drive away. If we stopped I felt sure he would kill me . . . and Mike too. 'Please, Mike,' I pleaded. 'Don't stop!'

I suppose Mike was concerned about my father – he did stop the car. As he pulled up, the lunatic rushed over to us. I shrank back into my seat and he flung open the passenger door. In one movement, he grabbed me by my arm, pulled me out of the car and threw me to the ground.

'Get into the house, *now*!' he screamed.

I ran for my life. I could barely make it up the stairs – my legs gave away beneath me with every step. I focused on our front door. I had to get there, fast.

The last time I saw Mike, he was sitting in the car, stunned by the shock of what he saw unfolding.

When I reached our apartment, I found my mother sitting up in bed, her bedroom door open wide. She watched me, wordless, the hint of a smile playing on her lips as I staggered out to the balcony. I knew what that meant. She had wound my father up again, as she always did. She couldn't resist it.

I went to bed, but couldn't sleep for ages. Mike's car had gone from the road and I hadn't heard whether my father had come in or not. I couldn't get his maniacal expression out of my mind. Finally I must have drifted off, but not for long.

As dawn broke I lay sleepless, in fear of what had happened to Mike.

CHAPTER 19

Helen

An Education

A few days after New Year, my dad erupted again with grave consequences. When he was told to take another long trip away from home, he refused to go, but he didn't refuse quietly. Oh no. He made a big scene, accusing his boss, Mike's dad, of employing him under false pretences. Mike's dad, shocked, responded with an ultimatum: either my father did this trip, or he would not get paid what he was owed. It was a stalemate, and neither of them would give in. Tommy refused to go, and his boss refused to pay his wages.

We had no money, not even for food, and there was almost nothing left to eat in the apartment.

Mike had called me to tell me he was OK, my father hadn't hurt him. 'His anger just seemed to drain away after you had left,' said Mike. 'It was uncanny, as if he had lost his purpose.'

I was so relieved to know he was safe. We went out together again on the night of Tommy's row at work – it was Mike who told me about it. I think his father was fond of me, and he invited me to come round to their house to join them for dinner in the evenings. He said nothing about the argument with my father, but I knew that was why. I was pleased to accept, and grateful for their kindness.

So Mike picked me up each evening and I had dinner with his family. One day, while we were sitting at table, Mike's father turned to me. 'Why don't you come and stay with us? You spend enough time here already!'

I smiled.

'I mean it,' he continued. 'You'd be very welcome to come and stay with us full-time. We would love to take care of you.'

I couldn't believe it. I looked at his wife, who beamed and nodded in agreement.

I was flustered, torn between what I wanted to do and what I knew I would have to do.

'That's very kind. Thank you so much. I'd love to accept . . . but I'm afraid I can't.' I dared not agree to this tempting arrangement, as I knew how my father would react if I did, and I wouldn't be the only one to suffer.

The conflict at Tommy's work deteriorated further. Out of funds, he stormed round to Mike's dad's office and demanded to be paid what he was owed. Mike told me that his dad refused again. Tommy erupted into a violent rage and threatened Mike's father with such menace that Mike's father drew his gun.

'I'll shoot you if you don't leave the premises,' he said, his finger on the trigger. 'Right now! And don't ever come back here again.'

Tommy stormed home and turned on me. 'I forbid you to see that bastard's son ever again.'

I was in a difficult position. Mike and his family were my dear friends, yet his father was at loggerheads with mine.

'No, Dad. I can't do that,' I said. For only the second time in my life I stood up to him. I stayed as calm as I could, though I felt far from calm inside. 'Mike is my friend. You don't have any argument with him, or with me.'

'We'll see about that!'

When I told Mike, he came round to our apartment to talk to my father. With grave misgivings, I let him in.

He faced up to Tommy. 'I've no wish to be involved in this matter,' Mike began. 'It's between you and my father. It's nothing to do with Helen and me. It's a private matter and I don't wish to take sides. I'm sure Helen doesn't either.'

'No, I don't,' I shook my head.

'So I would like you to agree that I continue to go out with Helen and our friends as usual. I think that's reasonable. I hope you know that I would do nothing to upset you or Helen, so I would like your agreement on this.'

There was an ominous silence. I tried not to show my fear as I watched the cogs turn in my father's brain. Finally he seemed to make up his mind.

'Thank you for coming round to talk this through,' he began. 'You're right. It has nothing to do with you, and I agree to what you ask. But I would prefer you not to come here again.'

Another silence while I took that in. Mike thanked my father and we went off to meet some friends. So nothing had changed, but Mike never entered my home again.

I was still out of work at this time. All the menial jobs were apparently the province of black Africans, so there was nothing I was qualified to do. My father, always so forceful about my working for my keep, seemed to be stumped. What I was desperate to do, of course, was to further my education, which had stopped as soon as I had turned fifteen. I wrote letters to various colleges and was finally accepted to do a two-year commercial subjects course in Pretoria. This was a great boost to my confidence. I wouldn't have chosen secretarial work, but I did want an education, and a qualification. I was elated to be offered this opportunity and couldn't wait to start.

There was one obstacle. I kept putting it off, but the evening before I was due to start the course I had to tell my father about it. The conversation did not go well.

'How long is this course for?' he asked, his face dark as thunder.

'Two years.'

'*Two years?*' he shrieked. 'And who is going to pay for this? Who is going to pay for your keep?'

I said nothing.

'You should be out working,' he ranted. 'I will not allow this. I forbid it.'

His one-sided outburst continued for most of the evening.

'You have no right to any more education. You've had all you need; all you're fit for. It would be a waste of time. How dare you think you can just be allowed to waste your time on such nonsense for two years while I slave away?'

I didn't dare mention that he didn't have a job.

The row escalated. He yelled, screamed, stomped around and slammed doors far into the night. My mother went to bed, and I crept off too as soon as I dared. I lay awake nearly all that night, tears streaming down my face, my hopes dashed. I was desperate to do this course. What could I do?

The following morning I was resolute. I went to the bus

stop early, and when I arrived at the college, I asked to see the Principal.

He had a kindly manner. He must have noticed my red eyes and sensed some anxiety. 'Come and sit down,' he said. 'What can I do for you?'

I explained the problem about my father's anger when I told him about doing this course.

'He really needs me to get a job and bring some money into the house,' I said. 'He refuses to let me study for two years. But I really do want to do this course.'

He sat in thought for a few seconds, twitched his nose and considered what I'd said. Finally he leaned forward and smiled. 'Don't worry, my dear. Let's talk this through and see if there is some way you can do the course – perhaps an arrangement that your father will agree to?'

I nodded, grateful that he seemed so sympathetic to my situation. We discussed the course itself and different options there might be that would be more likely to satisfy my father. Finally he proposed a solution.

'It will be a big pressure for you – a lot of intensive work – but I think we could arrange for you to do the whole course compressed into just one year, if you are willing to do all the extra studying in that time. You'll have to work twice as hard. Do you think you could manage that?'

I didn't hesitate. 'Yes, I don't mind working hard. I really want to do it – this is my big chance. Thank you.'

'And you'll talk about it with your father?'

'Yes, I'll tell him when I get home,' I agreed. 'Thank you so much.'

I didn't say that I was still afraid of what his answer might be. I'd have to deal with that on my own.

That evening, quaking, I approached my father when he was relaxing in the lounge.

'I went to see the Principal at the college today,' I began in trepidation. 'I told him you don't want me to do the course in two years, and he said I could do the whole thing in one year, if you agree. This is the one thing I really want to do, more than anything, and I'm prepared to work twice as hard to achieve it in one year, if you'll let me.'

My father's reply was adamant. 'No. I cannot allow it. There is no way you can do this course. I forbid you to go to that college again. You have to get a job and earn some money. The sooner the better.'

I used all of my teenage negotiating skills to try and bring my father round to at least consider my point of view. I explained the potential benefits to the household if I gained a qualification that would enable me to earn more. Gradually he calmed down a little.

Finally I consolidated my plea. 'I promise that, if you will allow me to do this course, I will get a part-time job somewhere in the evenings or at the weekends.' I realized this was an impossible ask. I could never successfully complete an intensive course, with so much extra study, while at the same time doing a part-time job. But it was my only chance. To my great relief, this was the decider.

'All right. As long as you pay towards your board and keep. You'll have to pay for all your own books and study materials too, mind.'

I had no other option but to agree. 'Yes, I will. Thank you, Dad.'

That year remains a blur to me. All I can remember is the extreme fatigue and stress, the intensity of balancing my coursework with my part-time job in a supermarket, not to mention my dysfunctional family. I had no time for a social life, although Mike remained a good friend in the background, nothing more. My health suffered. Always tired, I caught one thing after another: throat infections, stomach upsets and colds. To make it worse, there were many nights when insomnia set in and I couldn't sleep. But somehow I kept on going. I lurched from one day to the next, utterly determined to achieve my goal. How I managed to get through it all I don't know, but I did. At last I had earned a qualification.

I was elated, and now the bright light on my horizon, the thing I most looked forward to, was my boyfriend Simon's arrival from England. We had continued writing to each other throughout my time in South Africa, and now he was ready to come and join me. My parents agreed that he should move in with us and get a mechanic's job in Pretoria, as planned. How we were going to manage on my balcony, I couldn't imagine.

CHAPTER 20

Helen

Tales of the Unexpected

My father's new job, working as a fitter for the South African Iron and Steel company, came with a three-bedroom house in Pretoria West. Thank goodness! I had a proper bedroom at last, and, with my newly acquired qualification, I had found myself a good job as secretary to the manager of a major car dealership in the west of the city. My newfound confidence gave me great hope for the future.

I was impatient to see Simon again after all this time. I had qualms, of course, following such a long absence – would we still feel the same about each other when we met? Or had we grown apart? Could our relationship survive, living in the 'madhouse' of my family life?

I needn't have worried as we immediately re-established our former closeness. He was excited about his future – his new job and our life together in South Africa. We both were. We paid board and lodging to my father every week, a separate bedroom for each of us. After all, we weren't married and this was my parents' home.

My father's behaviour, always unpredictable, now became

increasingly bizarre. His practical jokes in particular took on a macabre quality.

I came out of the bathroom one morning and walked straight into a scene from a horror movie. Tommy was hanging from the door frame. He had a noose around his neck and hung with his head to one side, his face contorted into a fixed grimace and his tongue lolling out. A wave of nausea hit me. My hands became clammy, my legs weakened, and I fainted to the floor. What I failed to notice was that my father was holding onto the door frame as he hung. I came to as he let himself down and burst into laughter.

'No sense of humour – that's your trouble!' he berated me. 'Can't you take a joke?'

On another occasion, one hot African night, a bat flew into our house. Dad picked up the fly-swatter and chased the bat from room to room. It might have been funny to some people watching this grotesque pantomime, but when he cornered the bat he laughed in a manic frenzy as he beat it to death.

'Stop it!' I pleaded repeatedly, in vain.

Tommy pounded the creature to pulp. The memory of his demented laughter as he finally stopped still has the power to send shivers through me.

After work one evening a neighbour stopped at our gate for a chat with him. It seemed an unlikely coincidence, but apparently this man was the hangman for Pretoria, and he told my dad that he was due to hang someone the following day. My father was fascinated, but the hangman expressed some emotional difficulty with the nature of his job, which surprised my father. I rather suspect he would have relished the hangman's work.

The following day the hangman performed the execution as required. 'It was a good job I talked him round,' said Tommy that evening. 'I knew it would help.'

His smug expression left me cold. Simon, who was getting to know my father better, shuddered with distaste.

It wasn't easy living with my parents – and their demands. 'Cook the dinner, do the washing up, iron my shirts . . .' My father always had to give the orders in our house. He had to be the boss and exert his authority on Simon as well: 'You will not smoke in this house without my permission.' Even though he smoked himself. We couldn't even play the radio quietly without him shouting at us to 'turn that rubbish off'.

Simon and I talked of our dream – to set up a home of our own one day. This spurred us on as we worked hard and planned our future together. We went out as much as we could, to get away from my parents.

Out of nowhere, our plans were jolted once again.

'I've got a new job in Johannesburg,' announced my father when he got home one evening. 'We're all going to move there next week.'

Simon looked the way I felt – shocked and devastated.

'We don't want to go to Johannesburg,' I began. 'We've both got good jobs and friends here. We could get our own apartment and stay here.'

'No you bloody won't.' He slammed his fist down on the arm of his chair. 'You're only eighteen. Much too young. There's no way you're going to leave home yet. Not till you're at least twenty-one.' He gave a cruel laugh. 'I will not allow it.'

'But . . .'

'I will not allow it,' he repeated. 'You will both get new

jobs in Johannesburg, and that's all I'm going to bloody well say on the matter!'

Simon and I talked about this over the next two or three days. Although he was twenty-one, I was still considered to be a minor. Lots of people were allowed to leave home at eighteen, especially if they could earn their own living, but my father wanted to continue his ownership and control of me. There had to be a way.

I phoned the British Embassy and talked it through with someone there.

'The trouble is,' said the kindly voice, 'that if you were in England, you could legally leave home. But here in South Africa, you are not considered an adult until you reach the age of twenty-one.'

'But I'm a British citizen.'

'Yes, but I'm afraid that makes no difference here. You live here, so you have to abide by South African law. I'm really sorry that I cannot help you further.'

We should have left there and then to go back to England. We nearly did, but my mother heard us talking.

'How could you possibly think of leaving me?' she wailed. That made me feel really guilty, as I knew my living with them made things easier for her. I was torn. Simon voiced what I had already acknowledged to myself: we'd have to go to Johannesburg.

Luckily, we all found good jobs when we arrived, which helped us settle in. Simon and my dad worked together at British Leyland as final vehicle assembly inspectors. I cannot imagine how difficult that was for Simon. By now he had recognized what my father was and disliked him intensely.

The only way we could find some privacy for talking in

Mercia aged about twenty-one.
She was a beautiful young woman.

Baby Helen chuckling
in her grandma's arms.

Helen, aged about three,
with Tommy.

And Mercia posing with Helen on her
knee – note the restraining hand.

Above left Baby Jenny, about eighteen months' old, with adoptive parents Connie and Sid at Embleton.

Above centre Jenny goes bumpy down the steps at Embleton.

Above right Jenny's grandpa wearing his favourite beret.

Left School photo of Jenny aged six.

Right School photo of Helen aged six.

Below left Helen on the beach at Embleton, with a reluctant Mercia coerced into the picture.

Below centre Mercia in a silky black georgette dress, posing by the front gate at Murton, ready to go out for a Sunday drive and picnic.

Below right George aged about eighteen.

JENNY LEAVES HER RIVALS TRAILING

THREE victories, four runner-up spots and, for good measure, two third-place cheques enabled Jenny Lee Smith to dominate the Women's Professional Golf Association tour in 1981.

Only twice in the 11 tournaments she played did the 33-year old Newcastle girl finish outside the top ten. A remarkably consistent record that earned Jenny record prize money of nearly £13,519 and made her runaway winner of the Hambro Life Order of Merit.

Jenny won the Sports Space tournament at Dyrham Park and the McEwan's Lager Welsh Classic at Whitchurch, but saved her best for last.

That came at the end of the season at Moor Park, where she claimed the Lambert and Butler match-play championship crown — and £3,000 - by beating Beverly Lewis in the final.

On two occasions Jenny finished just one stroke off the top. Her biggest disappointment, however, was on home ground in the British Women's Open Championship.

Bidding to win the title, she captured in 1976 and playing over the Northumberland Golf Club course just five minutes drive from her birthplace, she went into the fourth and final round holding a two-shot lead.

Even the backing of local supporters failed to lift her. A shattering return of 79 forced Jenny back into third place as American Debbie Massey retained the trophy, four strokes clear of Belle Robertson.

For the second year in succession Jenny was leading British professional in the Championship.

Above left Jenny, with her spaniel Janie, practising golf on the grass outside her bungalow at Embleton. The third hole of the golf course is nearby.

Above Jenny being awarded the silver candlesticks and tray as the winner of the inaugural Women's British Open in 1976.

Left Jenny dominates the Women's Professional Golf Association tour in 1981.

Helen standing on her balcony and Mercia sitting in
the living room of their first flat in South Africa.

Helen and Simon's wedding in South Africa, with
Tommy and Mercia – note her fixed expression.

Above top Jenny and her children – Katie, Ben and Josh in the foreground – with Mercia in her flat.

Above Jenny with Mercia outside her flat – their first and only meeting.

Left Jenny (*right*) with her cousin Wendy who helped her search for her birth family.

Jenny and Sam.

Helen and Dennis.

Left Wilfred Harrison,
Helen and Jenny's biological father.

Above Jenny and Helen in 2012 – twins
who are happy to be together at last.

the evenings was to go and sit in the car. Simon was exasperated living with my parents, particularly my father, but he found my mother difficult too. She demanded that he call her Mam. Well, she wasn't his Mam, but she demanded it, so he always had to call her that. To his credit, he put up with an awful lot. Life with my parents was a roller coaster that we couldn't get off.

At this stage, my mother, not having a job, became increasingly possessive of me. Perhaps she feared that the day was approaching when I would leave home and abandon her. Though she had never shown me any love, I recognized that she was needy and tried to pacify her, mostly to give us an easier life. Every lunchtime Mercia expected me to call her from work and spend my whole lunch-break talking to her while the other girls went out or did some shopping, as girls do. It was quite ridiculous, really. I had only seen her that morning, so we rarely had anything new to talk about.

One particularly busy day, we all had to work through lunchtime with only coffee to keep us going, so I didn't have a chance to call her. When I got home that evening, she refused to speak to me. During dinner, she turned to Dad.

'Do you know? Helen couldn't even be bothered to call me at lunchtime today and I was alone all day. I didn't have a soul to speak to.'

'Really?' sympathized my father

'I waited all afternoon for her to call. But she didn't give me a thought; neglected her own mother.' She paused and gave me her 'martyr' look.

'I couldn't get to the phone,' I explained. 'We had to work all through lunch today so I couldn't call you.'

'She didn't even apologize properly when she got home.' She puckered her brow and drew her lips together.

My father slammed his knife down on the table and turned to me. 'It's your duty to think of your mother. You must call her every day, no matter what, to make sure she's all right here, on her own.'

My mother continued her sullen silence with me, so I stopped making lunchtime calls. One less apron string.

Some weeks later, we had just finished dinner when Dad turned to Simon and me. 'So when are you two going to get married?'

We were stunned! We had talked about it from time to time, of course, but we always came to the conclusion that he would never agree to our marriage, not until after I was twenty-one. We were so surprised by this unexpected question that we didn't answer. Just looked at each other.

'It's about time you got married. Of course, you would have to stay living here, and you're both earning good money, so when you get married you can pay half the rent and all the bills.'

We should have seen the signs, but we were too excited to notice. We weren't going to miss this opportunity.

The date was set for five months away, when I would be nineteen. We had lots of things to think about and began to get organized. We planned a full church wedding, followed by a reception at home. I tried to involve my mother, but she showed no interest at all. Indeed, she wouldn't even talk about it. I got the feeling she was resentful about our getting married. Even when I went to have a fitting for my wedding dress, she refused to come with me, so I asked a friend from

work to come instead. We had to pay for everything, Simon
and I. My parents contributed nothing, though my father did
begrudgingly agree to pay for the simple reception buffet
which we ordered from the caterers.

'What are you going to wear?' I asked my mother as the
day approached.

'I don't know, and I don't care,' was her reply.

I persuaded her to come into town with me and try on
some clothes, thinking this might make her feel more positive. But no, it was an awful day. She didn't like any of the
outfits she tried on. I don't think she wanted to like them.
Finally, we found a silver-grey dress and matching jacket. She
didn't actively dislike it, so I bought it for her with my own
money, and the hat, gloves and shoes to go with it. She didn't
thank me.

When everyone had left for the church, it was just me and
my father in the house. Finally I was ready. I was both excited
and nervous, and I hoped I looked my best. My father would
surely be proud of me as the radiant bride today.

I went into the living room wearing my wedding dress
with the veil down and holding my bouquet.

Tommy looked at me, his face expressionless. 'You look
very nice,' he muttered and turned his back on me. He seemed
almost embarrassed at seeing me and couldn't wait to get
out of the house. 'Come on, then.'

As we went out to the car, I was struck by a terrible empty
feeling of disappointment, as if he'd let me down again. He
could have tried to show some pride in me, even if he didn't
feel it.

On the way to the church, we sat side by side with a silent
chasm separating us. Finally, without turning his head, he

muttered in a sullen voice, 'You can change your mind, you know. If you want to change your mind, I'll back you all the way.'

I was speechless with shock. It was as if he was pouring icy water on the happiest day I'd ever had. I couldn't think why he'd said it, but I was sure I didn't want to change my mind, so I said nothing and tried to put it out of my thoughts, determined to enjoy my special day.

The church wedding was a lovely ceremony and everything went well. Sadly, none of Simon's family nor George and Joan could afford the fares to come and help us celebrate, but they sent telegrams, and we had some good friends there to share our joy, as well as my parents.

All our guests seemed happy, apart from my mother. She just stood around when we went outside for photographs. She talked to no one and stayed on the edge, passive, ignoring everything. Even when cajoled kindly by the photographer, she barely managed a straight-mouthed smile. She kept her lips firmly clamped together and her eyes on the middle distance, beyond the churchyard.

We had a wonderful afternoon at the reception until the catering lady approached me. Loud enough to be overheard, she told me my father had refused to pay her. There I was on my special day, in my beautiful dress, surrounded by all our friends . . . humiliated. Naturally I didn't have any money on me, so I had to ask Simon to take care of it. We could not believe that Tommy would do this to us on our wedding day.

The great news that came a few days later made up for it. My father told us he had found himself another job working for a company that was building a landing strip at Windhoek airport. My heart sank at first on hearing this: not another battle. But I was amazed to find that neither of my parents seemed to expect us to go. Apparently, now that we were married, my father could no longer exert any control over me by law. He must have known this, because he didn't even try. It was such a relief when we waved them off to Windhoek. Now Simon and I would be left to our own devices.

At last we moved into a brand new apartment of our own at Germiston, near Johannesburg. This was the first time in my life that I'd been allowed to live outside my parental home, and the sense of freedom was intoxicating. We were thrilled to have this beautiful flat to ourselves, to be able to do what we liked, when we liked. We planned with great excitement how we would have it, ordered furniture and arranged our lives to suit ourselves. One of our greatest treats was inviting friends to visit our home. I had never been able to do this before, so now we enjoyed relaxing evenings, eating with friends and chatting as late as we wished.

We lived on the fourth floor, with a balcony overlooking the bustling main street below. Shortly after we moved there I found out that all the flats were 'serviced', which meant that someone would come and clean our apartment every day. It was included in the rent, so it wouldn't cost us anything extra, but I felt deeply uncomfortable with this. It was our home, and it didn't feel right for a stranger to be there when we were out. I suppose I was a little naive, because I decided to tell the African man who was our cleaner that I didn't need a cleaner and would therefore not require his services. It didn't occur to me this might have an effect on him, but of course this was South Africa, the apartheid regime.

The man began to cry, great tears running down his cheeks.

I didn't know why, so I asked him, 'What's the matter?'

'If I do not clean the flat, madam, I will lose my job.'

I could have kicked myself for being so insensitive to this gentle man. I realized I must change my mind straightaway. 'I'm sorry. I didn't know. Please ignore what I said. You are welcome to come and clean our flat every day.'

'Thank you, madam,' he said, smiling through his tears. I thought for a moment he was going to shake my hand or give me a hug, but then I realized this would be forbidden.

Of course, it still felt wrong and I didn't really want him to do our cleaning, but I couldn't see him out of a job, just because of me.

Shortly after we moved into our apartment, it was Simon's birthday. I remember it so clearly – 20 July 1969, a momentous day, celebrated across the world as the day of the first moon landing. Sadly, South Africa did not permit televisions as they were meant to be a corrupting influence. I recall the frustration of knowing that back home in Northumberland we would have been able to watch Neil Armstrong taking that first step, that 'giant leap', as it happened, whereas here we could only hear about it on the radio. Strangely, though, we found it almost more riveting because we couldn't see it and had to imagine the scenes as they happened.

That night, as the silver light shone through our bedroom window, I was so excited to think that men were actually walking on the moon that I got up at 3 a.m. and slipped out onto the balcony. I was amazed to see the revelry in the street below. It was like a carnival atmosphere, with people dancing and bands playing music. I woke Simon and we ran out of the flat and down in the lift to join in. We all bought the newspapers next morning to see the pictures of men on the moon and read all about it.

As well as spending evenings with friends, we sometimes drove thirty miles through the scented evening air to the nearest drive-in cinema so that we could see the latest movies. These were such carefree days for us.

One morning, there was a white envelope amongst the bills As soon as I recognized the writing, I knew something was wrong. The blood drained from my face and my skin turned cold. Once a week my parents wrote us a letter and my father always addressed it. This letter was out of turn, and the writing on the envelope was my mother's.

I held it and stared at it for a few seconds, not wanting to open it, but eventually I reached for a knife and carefully made a slit along the top. In trepidation, I pulled out the single, thin sheet of paper. There were only a few lines to read, but they were enough to threaten our newfound happiness. I had known it would be something bad, but it was worse than I could have expected. My father, aged only fifty-one, had suffered a heart attack and was dangerously ill in hospital.

'You have to come and see him,' my mother wrote. 'I don't know what to do.' Then, plaintively, 'He asked for you.'

I gulped. My father had never asked for me in his life. Now he wanted me to come to him, and my mother was almost begging me to go at once. A flood of confused emotions hit me. My dad was seriously ill in a strange town hundreds of miles away. I began to tremble from the shock of this news. Of course I must go.

I wanted to go anyway, beset by fear for him and for us all. What would happen if . . .? No, I couldn't think about that now. I was surprised to feel love for this man who had been the monster of my childhood years. At this moment he was my dad in a foreign land and he needed my help.

The company I worked for were fantastic when I told them and immediately arranged a flight on their own private plane to get me to Windhoek. I gazed out in wonder at the stunning African panorama below, the 'Big Hole' in Kimberley caused by diamond mining, the Kalahari desert and the wildlife scattered across the plain.

When I arrived, I got a taxi straight to the hospital. Dad was gravely ill, in coronary care, wearing an oxygen mask and attached to a heart monitor. He was in a private room with a crucifix above his bed. Mum and I stayed with him for a long time and he seemed to improve slightly. Finally, exhausted, we went back to their house for a change of clothes and something to eat. As we sat down, my mother told me what had happened.

'When he came home from work, he was in terrible pain. I think that's when he was having a heart attack.'

'What did you do?'

'I called an ambulance and they rushed him to the hospital.'

'It's quite a small hospital. Do you think they're treating him properly?'

'Well, I know it looks basic, but everything is very clean and the nuns care for the patients well. They seem to have all the equipment they need to help Dad.'

'Why are there nuns?'

'It's a Catholic hospital,' she said. 'When we got there, even through his pain, Dad saw the cross and demanded it be taken down. He told them he's an atheist, but they said they couldn't take it down. He was angry about that, which didn't help.'

'Have you spoken to a heart consultant?' I asked.

'Aye. He said Dad's in a bad way, but he's holding his own.'

Just then, the phone rang. Mum went to answer it.

'Quick. We have to go back. He's very poorly.'

We rushed back to the hospital and found him alone in his room. Suddenly, right there in front of us, my father arrested – he turned blue and stopped breathing. We called for the nurse, but no one came, and I realized I had to do something fast. I was nineteen years old and had no training at all, but instinct kicked in.

I thumped his chest with my fist. Then I applied regular pressure and tried to encourage his breathing. 'Come on, Dad,' I said. 'Breathe. Breathe for me. You have to breathe. You can't leave now. You're my dad.'

I worked and worked on him. I didn't know whether I was doing the right thing, but I kept on with it anyway. Then the miracle happened. Well, that's how it seemed to me. He started to breathe again. I could feel his chest moving and his heart started beating steadily once more.

He opened his eyes. 'I've been watching you,' he said. 'From up there.' He looked up at the ceiling. 'I saw you pounding my chest. I saw it all.' Then he looked at the crucifix. 'And there was someone else there.'

His eyes watered and tears ran down his cheeks as he turned to me. 'You saved my life.' He held my hand and wept openly.

All of those years of violence and neglect faded away in

that moment. I looked down at him and felt nothing but compassion for him.

The nuns eventually came in and took over his care, as I sat down, shaking and weak. One of them brought me a cup of sweet tea.

'She saved his life,' said my mother. It was the first time I had ever heard pride in her voice when talking about me.

The nun who had brought me the tea placed her hand on my head. 'Bless you, my child.' Then she was gone.

For my whole life, from the time when I was a small child, I had always believed, hoped, that if I could be 'good', the best I could possibly be, it might change things. That by being a good daughter, I could make my mother love me and my father change for the better. I just wanted to be special to them. Sitting there, holding my father's hand, I supposed this powerful experience we had shared was for a reason. Perhaps now things would change between us all.

In those days, in South Africa, if someone had a long-term health problem, there was no extended 'sick leave' or care provided. Since my father was considered too unwell to do his job, when he was discharged from hospital, his employer fired him. With a sense of dread, I realized that the only solution was for my parents to come to Johannesburg and live with us. We would look after them until my father recovered. My mother was not working and had no qualifications to obtain any work, so we would have to pay for everything, as usual.

We found a three-bedroomed house in Benoni and arranged to move in the day they arrived in Johannesburg. Dad was still very weak, and when we opened the front door of our new house, the house for which Simon and I were going to pay the rent, my parents walked into the master bedroom.

'We'll have this room,' said my father. 'You two can choose one of the other rooms.'

I was about to say something, but I bit my lip. He was a sick man who needed some comfort to help him get better. I couldn't deny him that. We'd be fine in the small spare room.

As we unpacked our things, my parents took over the lounge and kitchen. A great sadness engulfed me. Simon and I had only been allowed to revel in our freedom for such a short time.

CHAPTER 21

Helen

The Gun Chase

'I'm pregnant,' I grinned. I was bubbling over with excitement.

'That's wonderful.' Simon gave me a huge hug.

'Hey, not so tight,' I teased him, then held his hand to my tummy.

He looked almost reverent as he exclaimed, 'I'm going to be a dad!'

We were both absolutely thrilled with our news, and realized that sharing the house with my parents would make it difficult to keep a secret. So we decided to tell them after dinner. 'We're going to have a baby,' I announced.

After a flicker of surprise, my father grunted and went straight back to reading his newspaper. You'd think I had told him a fly had died.

Simon took my hand in his and turned to my mother. 'We thought you'd be pleased.'

She looked from one to the other of us. 'Well, one thing about being pregnant,' she smirked. 'Everyone knows what you've been doing, don't they?'

Our happiness turned to shock. How could she say such

a terrible thing, especially in front of my husband? I squirmed. It was naive, I suppose, but we both thought they would be happy. Not at all – I was stunned at their indifference, their lack of support.

At fifty-two, Tommy's chronic health problems made him subdued, even withdrawn some days. Conversely, my mother brightened. She had reprised her role as mistress of the house. Of course, it was our house and we paid for everything. But my mother took over.

This situation could never have worked out for long, but we felt we had no other option. Why did I continue to do as they commanded, without question? Simon was the same. Anything to keep the fragile peace, I suppose.

I hoped things would improve, but I was wrong. The only positive was that my father recuperated enough to work again and he found another job in Johannesburg. This boosted our finances, and Tommy's mood. He regained some of his old strength . . . and all of his dominance. That was the challenge. Out in the car one evening, Simon and I discussed our future. We'd talked about it often, and now we decided. We would return to England as soon as we could. To be fair, this was not only because of my parents. We did not want our child to be brought up under the apartheid regime.

Our beautiful baby was born in August 1970 – a boy we called Scott, with the finest blond hair. As the midwife handed him to me I burst into tears, completely overwhelmed with joy. I had never understood how fierce maternal love would be, but the urge to protect him was overpowering. It was our moment – my son and me. I looked with adoration into his deep blue eyes and he looked back at me in puzzlement.

Simon, beside me, was now in floods of grinning tears, desperate to have his turn. I handed the baby to him, the most beautiful baby in the world. He was now the number-one priority in our lives.

Simon and I talked almost every day of our plans to return to England. We would have to save up to pay for our tickets. We worked out that if we saved a little every week, we could be free by the time Scott was a year old. That was our goal. It was what kept us going through all the tensions of life with my parents, now that they'd taken root in our house, and regained control of our lives.

I expected that my mother would take an interest in her new grandchild and was happy for her to dote on him, as grandmothers do. We wanted her to be involved, but from the beginning, my mother overstepped her role and interfered between me and my baby. She became fiercely possessive of him, disregarding our feelings and wishes completely. This situation was overbearing, but we could see no way to end it without causing a huge row, and maybe worse. We wanted a calm and peaceful home to bring our family up in, and we dared not do anything that would threaten that.

Every time Scott cried, she rushed and picked him up before I got there. She took him over – he was her baby now. I was both devastated and bewildered. I fumed inwardly with indignation and fear. How could this happen? How could we stop her?

If we three could have left then, we would have done. But we had only one salary between us, and still paid most of the household bills for five people. It became a struggle to save, so we would just have to be patient. We had no choice.

One Sunday, I wanted to make a cake. It was so hot and

airless in the kitchen that I took the mixing bowl into the dining room and sat down. I beat the mixture vigorously with a wooden spoon.

Tommy stormed in. 'Stop making that bloody noise!'

'I'm just making a cake.'

He glared at me, grabbed the glass bowl, complete with mixture and spoon, and threw it out of the window. It landed upside down in the garden, unbroken. I could see it on the lawn. If the atmosphere hadn't been so tense, I would have laughed to see blobs of the thick mixture slowly fall onto the grass.

Stunned and fearful, I said nothing. He was back to his old self, as if possessed, raging and stamping around the house.

'I am master of this house and you *will* do as you are told.'

'But I was only making a cake.'

He poked me hard in the chest with every syllable as he said, 'I am sick of the sight of you!'

A torrent of verbal abuse rained down on me. His face went red, then purple, and his eyes stood out like organ stops. I sat still, transfixed.

'You've always been a bloody slut. A slut and a leech. A pit-yacker, just like your mother. That's all you'll ever be. All this is your fault. You made all that bloody noise on purpose, to annoy me. You can't do anything right. You will regret it – I'll make sure of that. I'll make your life a misery.'

I stood up to get away from his anger.

He waved his arms wildly as he shrieked. He poked and prodded me in the chest again and again, pushing me across the room.

'I'm sick of the sight of you!' he carried on goading. 'Get out of my house. Get out and don't come back.'

I had remained quiet and that hadn't worked, so I calmly replied, 'If that is what you want, then we'll move out until we return to England.'

'Just get out of this house. *Now*.'

Simon had heard all this. He called a good friend and arranged for us to go and stay with them for a while. We packed our things and piled them into the car. He left with the first load. 'I'll be straight back for you and the baby,' he promised as he pulled away. 'As quick as I can.'

Tommy screamed, 'I'm going to end all of this.' He ran into the bedroom and rushed back with a gun in his hand.

I was in the living room when he ran past the door towards the kitchen, where he thought I had gone. This gave me just enough time to pick up the baby and run, barefoot, out of the house. Petrified, I ran as fast as I could down the road, my breath rasping. Panic gripped me. My heart thumped so hard it hurt. I had to get Scott away from that madman. Simon would be back in a minute and he would save us. I stared into the distance, but the road was empty. I continued to run, stumbling, my breath halting, the baby crying.

I heard sounds behind and glanced over my shoulder to see my father reversing his car out of the driveway. Panic. I tried to speed up, sobbing in terror. The gleam of that gun was all I could see now. I knew my father would catch us and shoot me – maybe kill me, and the baby too.

It was no use. He came up alongside me and slowed to my pace.

'Get in the car!'

'No.' I kept running.

The car came up parallel again and I took a sideways look. The gun was lying in his lap, ready for use.

'Get in the bloody car!' His voice more urgent now.

'No. Go away. Leave us alone.' I was sure he was ready to shoot me. Why didn't he do it? I was close enough. I looked for an alleyway, some way of escape, but there was none. I ran on again. He cruised by and slowed once more.

This time he leaned out of the car. 'I'm not going to shoot you. Look.'

I saw him put the gun in the glove box. I lurched with relief.

'I beg you, Helen. Get in the car. I am not going to hurt you.'

I couldn't escape, so I slowed down and stopped. He opened the car door for me. Defeated, I climbed in, desperate to catch my breath, Scott still whimpering in my arms.

'I'm sorry,' he said. 'I just can't help it. When I get like this, I just can't control myself.' He put his head in his hands. 'My head is hot. It feels like my brain is on fire.'

I said nothing. It was the first time he had ever spoken to me like this; the first time he had acknowledged his own weakness.

After a few moments, he looked up at me. 'Please don't move out,' he pleaded. 'You know your mother will never let me hear the end of it if you move out.'

I thought about this, confused by the sudden change in him. I was still hardly able to breathe normally, let alone speak. He waited like a schoolboy needing reassurance after some misdemeanour.

Finally I found my voice. 'I'll have to speak to Simon.'

We went back to the house just as Simon returned. We were all met at the door by my mother.

She stood directly in front of me. 'How can you move out and leave *me*?' she screamed. 'I will not let you take my bairn away from me.'

Simon stepped forward. 'He's *our* baby, not yours.'

I walked into the bedroom with Simon and explained very briefly what had happened.

'We can't stay here. It isn't safe,' he said, gathering some more things up. 'I can't trust him.'

'Nor can I.'

'We're moving out – now!' He picked up a case. 'This is dangerous. We have to move out.'

"He'll come after us wherever we are. We might as well stay here until we can go back to England.'

'Let's at least stay away for a few days.'

'I don't know.' I wavered, the memory of my father's plea fresh in my mind. 'If we leave, my mother will make Tommy's life hell and he'll never be allowed to forget it.'

Simon was crestfallen. He just stood there. His instinct to take us away and keep us safe warred with his desire to support me in what I felt was right that day.

'We must go to England as soon as we can,' I said.

'Yes.' He put the case down, 'If you really think we have to stay, I'll support you, but I'm not happy about it. He's an evil man. Your mother's not much better.'

'I know.' I nodded. 'It's a no-win situation. But it won't be for a day longer than necessary.'

So we agreed to stay on. As so often in the past, my parents settled into a cold silence and neither of them spoke to me for weeks. It was quiet, but that suited us fine. We had our baby to protect. Scott was my focus and I didn't care if they never spoke to me again.

We usually ate our main meal at about five o'clock. One day, while Simon was still at work, my father made an announcement.

'You must wash the dishes at six o'clock every evening. That's your job.'

'I can't do it then.'

'You will do it then. You'll do as I say. If you want to continue living in my house.'

So it was his house now, was it? The rent book was in our name.

'But six o'clock is when I feed Scott. I'll do it after I've finished feeding him.'

'I want the dishes washed at six o'clock. Not a moment later. Your mother will take over the feeding.'

So that was the reason. My mother sat there triumphant.

From that day on, I stood in the kitchen at six o'clock washing the dishes. Simon helped me to make it quicker, but we were never finished soon enough. Meanwhile, my mother sat in the living room, smiling like the Cheshire cat. She fed my baby and put him to bed for the night before I could finish. When I did go up to say goodnight, it was always too late. He was asleep. Too late for him to know my lingering kiss.

My mother became his mother more and more each day. She was determined to push me out, and I could do nothing to stop her without rocking the dynamics of our household. Tommy still had that gun. The consequences would be unthink-able.

I can't understand now why I was so passive. I just coped

one day at a time, as I always had, to keep a tenuous peace. It must have been a nightmare for Simon. He was wonderful. He supported me through each day, staying against all his instincts.

Fearful for Scott's welfare, for our bond with him and our sanity, we got through it together, determined to leave at the earliest opportunity we could find.

CHAPTER 22

Jenny

The Eighteenth Hole

I finally got used to wearing shoes whenever I played golf. At nineteen, I partnered Neil Moir to win the Hoylake Open Scratch Mixed Foursomes. I joined the Ponteland Golf Club the same year. At this stage I still had only four golf clubs, and one of those was a conversion job.

One day, when I was playing in the Ponteland championship, a lady member turned to me.

'My dear. Don't you think you ought to get yourself a decent set of clubs?'

I ended up playing her in the final . . . and I beat her! That felt good. Then of course I did buy myself a set of clubs.

After that, I joined Gosforth Golf Club. It was nearer home, and everybody there was so friendly and encouraging. They all came to watch me when I won the Northumberland Championship. That was fantastic. There was a big celebration for me in the Gosforth Clubhouse that night!

My game just kept getting better. Of course I practised a lot, whenever I could, and worked hard – but I loved it. I loved the challenge. I think that was down to the utter determination I learned from my mother and the enthusiasm I caught from my father. When I was young, I had always thought I had inherited these qualities from them. I now knew that wasn't true. Nonetheless, I recognized that Mam and Dad had both been instrumental in my growing success, and I was grateful for that.

Mam and I settled into a happy, companionable phase. I didn't mention the adoption, and she remained in denial. I had to accept that I would never coax any answers out of her, though the questions were all still there jostling for attention at the back of my mind. I couldn't ignore them, but they had to wait their turn, when the time was right.

Richard and I had now been going out for quite a while and spent time together whenever we could. This became increasingly difficult in between my golf commitments and his job, which took him travelling all over the north-east of England so, although we were definitely a couple, it was rather an on–off relationship, with one of us often away when the other was home and vice versa. I suppose we each thought we were in love, though we didn't really talk about it, or about our future together. It was a convenient relationship for us both. We enjoyed each other's company all the more whenever we could, and I think we just assumed it would continue that way.

For the next few years, golf was my life. In 1973 I was selected to play for England in Home Internationals, so I played a lot of big tournaments. Then I was asked to join the main team practices over the winter period. The first tournament the following year was the British Championship. I knew that the Curtis Cup selectors were watching me and expecting me to do well, so I was keen to do my best.

I was knocked out in the second round. I assumed that was it.

As I drove home, I thought, 'What an idiot – the last tournament before the selection. I could kick myself.' In bed that night, I relived all the holes. In the early hours I woke up with a start, annoyed with myself. 'How did I miss that shot?'

A couple of days later, a friend rang me. 'I see you've been selected to play for Great Britain and Northern Ireland in the Curtis Cup team . . .'

'You're joking!' I said. I thought he was playing a trick on me.

'No. It says so in the Football Pink.'

I went straight out and bought a copy of the newspaper, and there it was, right on the front page! This was either a scoop, or a sham, and I didn't know which as nobody had contacted me about it. I had to wait till the next day before one of the selectors called to notify me officially that I had been selected. I didn't think it was very well managed, but it was fantastic to know I had a place in the team, especially as the tournament was to be in San Francisco. For a girl who had never been further than Edinburgh Zoo till a few months before, this was a dream.

In the following months, I played in the England team at the European Championships and in the winning British team at the Commonwealth Championships, won the Wills Match Play tournament and played for Great Britain in California and Columbia, as well as in the Home Internationals.

1976 saw the peak of my amateur career – I won the first ever Women's British Open at Fulford. Only a few days before, in bed with a rasping chest infection, I thought I wouldn't be able to play. The antibiotics helped me on the way to recovery, but I was still quite congested and muggy right up to the day, and I dithered about whether to withdraw. In the end, I thought, 'Oh, what the heck. I'll go.' I'm glad I did!

It seems strange to say it now, but I started out that first day of the tournament knowing I could win. I believed in myself and thought anything was possible. I've always just played my own game, unconcerned about what others are doing around me or how the crowds are responding. The only time I was conscious of feeling nerves was on the first tee, with the crowds all around me – that's when the butter-flies fluttered. But once I got under way, I was always fully intent on what I was doing there – I just played the game, shot by shot. I kept a complete focus on making a par at every hole. If I managed a birdie, fine. I never considered dropping any shots. Even if I did, I knew I could always make it up on the next hole. I was always very positive, like my Dad, and I maintained that strong attitude at every point of the match.

I was two shots behind the leader at the start of the final round, but I was so concentrated on my own game that I didn't notice how the other players were doing. I was blink-ered, always focusing on the next shot throughout the final day.

Fulford is a great golf course. I've played there many times since and I always love it, but because it was the first Women's British Open, there were not enough leader boards around the course, so we often couldn't see who was up or down the board, or what the scores were. That's why I arrived at the last tee thinking I had to make a four.

It was a par five hole, which meant, or so I thought, that I had to make a birdie to win. I was positive that I could do this hole in four because that's what I'd done the day before, so it would simply be a repeat. I focused on my game as usual and reached quite close to the green in two. Then I chipped onto the green and holed a five-footer to win. Of course I thought I had only just made it, but in fact I'd won by two strokes.

The crowd roared and applauded enthusiastically. It was only then that I noticed them and started to feel elated. The golfing press hadn't forecast me to win. Although I'd beaten many of the other players in the past, they had been seeded higher than me, so it was a surprise to many of the experts when I won over the half a dozen people who were thought to have more chance to win than I did, and who were probably a bit miffed, but they were all very gracious about my stealing it away from them.

Everybody came up to shake my hand, and the officials around the green were all clapping and cheering. Friends ran onto the green to congratulate me and it would have been easy to get carried away with it all, but I knew I had to go and sign my card and hand it in or I would forfeit the title, so that kept me grounded. At the award ceremony which followed, in front of all the crowds, I wasn't able to accept the money, being an amateur, so I was just presented with the trophy – a plinth holding two Edwardian candlesticks. I could only keep this for a year, till the next British Open. The only thing I was allowed to keep for ever was a gold pin that says 'British Open Winner'. I still have that.

There was one sad thing about winning the British Open, and that was that Mam, who had worked so hard and for so long to make this possible for me, wasn't there to see it. She would have been so proud to be part of the crowd that day, but she had to work to earn our keep, so I phoned her straightaway from the clubhouse. She was thrilled and I think the bush telegraph went into overdrive after that!

The day after my British Open win, I received a surprise telegram from my former coach, mentor and friend, Dr Golf himself, John Jacobs. It said:

> I told you you'd play for England one day. You've done far better than that, haven't you? Congratulations. Well done. John.

I was moved to tears and treasured this special message throughout my career.

After my Open win and some Curtis Cup matches as the British Champion, I was amazed to receive an invitation to go to Buckingham Palace with other members of the British and USA teams.

The day for the visit came and I was strangely nervous, much more than I ever felt playing golf! It was a weekend, the day of the Trooping of the Colour, and we were meant to meet the Queen at half past ten. We were taken into an ante-room and, moments later, the Master of the Queen's Household walked in. He explained to us what to do, how to curtsey and that we shouldn't speak unless spoken to. We were told to say only 'Good morning, Your Majesty' when she came to us. After that it had to be 'Yes, ma'am' or 'No, ma'am.'

The Queen had been out to practise riding side-saddle earlier that morning, and as she dismounted her horse had given her a kick, so the royal doctor had been called to check her over and make sure she was all right. Fortunately she was fine.

After some delay, we were taken into the richly decorated room to have our audience. It was fantastic – a wonderful experience. We all had these tiny coffee cups and silver spoons engraved with ER. One of my team colleagues whispered to me: 'Do you think they'd miss this if . . .?' She paused, then added, 'Better not, or they'll put me in the Tower!'

The Queen was a lot smaller than I had imagined, and was carrying the eternal handbag. She knew all our names and what we had won. She asked how we were and made some general conversation. At that point no one in the Royal Family was really into golf. However, I do remember that she said, 'I think golf should be in the Olympics again. It used to be in the early years, but it hasn't been since, has it? It's much more important than cycling. I can't understand why cycling is now an Olympic sport but golf isn't.'

Of course, that was before cycling really took off.

She spoke to us all for quite a long time, asking a lot of questions, especially to the American team, headed by Nancy Lopez. It was a very positive meeting and she was charming, lovely – and well genned up on our careers. I remember it as a really happy morning.

Later that year I was voted joint Daks Woman Golfer of the Year by the golf journalists. I was quite surprised to be chosen for this award, but at the same time I just took everything in my stride. There was a lot of positive press reaction towards me, and that was helpful in preparation for the next exciting stage in my career.

Meanwhile, my relationship with Richard was closer than ever. Connie got on well with him and they were both avid Newcastle supporters, so that helped. We spent happy weekends at Embleton together whenever we could, mainly on the golf course, followed by an early evening drink in the village pub about a mile inland.

My life was too busy with golf commitments to have a normal social life, but Richard never complained about all the times I was travelling away to tournaments – he was always very supportive of everything I did. I felt very lucky to have such a strong relationship. Perhaps I should have read something into the fact that we didn't mind being apart.

CHAPTER 23

Jenny

A Professional Career

The following year, in 1977, just as I was approaching thirty, I was offered sponsorship to go to the Ladies Professional Golf Association, or LPGA, in the USA and attend their qualifying school. This was a great opportunity and I discussed it with Mam. If I accepted the sponsorship offer, I couldn't continue to work for her, to help her out and to earn us some extra income between amateur golf tours. This would mean there would be less money coming in to begin with, though the sponsorship money would support me through qualifying school. Of course, there was a small chance I could make the grade to become a professional, which should lead to higher earning opportunities. It was a risk for us financially.

'I don't want to leave you in the lurch, Mam,' I said.

'Don't worry about that, pet. Of course you must do this. It's a wonderful opportunity. We'll manage.' She smiled. 'We always have up to now, Jen, and it's time for you to step out and take the chance.'

'Are you sure?'

'Of course I'm sure. If you don't give it a go, you'll always regret it.'

I was glad of her encouragement and support, and Richard's too, but I still wasn't sure. As I learned more about what would be involved, I mulled it over. There was in those days a chasm between amateur players in Britain and professional players in America, which was where my sponsorship would take me. It was a daunting prospect, going from being the top golfer in the UK to one of the crowd in the USA. I'd had a taste of it before, when I'd played in a Curtis Cup tournament in San Francisco, but as a professional it would be very different.

I still hadn't made up my mind when one of the British amateur selectors called me a few days later and launched straight in: 'We think you might be turning pro,' he said, as if it might be a crime.

'Well, where did you hear that?' I was shocked that he was so confrontational about it. But then I realized that of course this situation would mean I could no longer be available for selection for any of their amateur teams. However, this decision had to be about my own future.

Do you know what? I must have been a bit blasé about the whole thing, because I really didn't know how many top players would be competing for a small number of places when I decided to go for it. It turned out there were about 120 girls playing for very few places. Just those few would get a player's card to turn professional. It was a bigger risk, and a greater challenge, than I'd realized.

It was a four-round tournament, with a cut after the first two rounds. The officials said they'd accept any player who played four rounds of 75 or better. I got through the first two days, one round a day, and made it into the last seventy-five. That was when they changed their minds and said that only twelve of us would be awarded professional players' cards. The top twelve scorers at the end of the fourth round.

My English playing partner, Christine Langford, and I went out for a fish supper the night before the final round. That was a mistake. She chose the crab and was sick all night, poor kid. Really, really sick. The other English girl still in with a chance did her best, but it didn't work out for her.

I was lucky enough to sail through the early holes. I'd never hit the ball as well in my life as I did that week. I was feeling very competitive and stayed positive, as usual.

My playing partner that last day was an American girl called Sylvia Ferdon. We got on really well, but by the eighteenth hole we were both feeling the tension of needing to make par or only one over to make the grade. That was a lot of pressure.

The last hole was a par five. There was water on the right, trees on the left, and more water just in front of the green. We'd have to hit near enough to the water on the right-hand side to make it an easier right-angled shot onto the green. We both hit our shots way left. Fortunately, we each found ourselves with reasonable lies – a golfing term for the way the ball sits on the grass. I looked at Sylvia and she looked at me, and that was it! We both burst into hysterics, which eased the tension. We calmed ourselves down and both made our pars on the hole, so we waltzed through and have been great friends every since.

When reporters questioned me during the interviews that followed throughout my career and asked what characteristics I relied on to help me win, I always thought back to that fit of hysteria with Sylvia when we were approaching the final hole, and I always gave the same answer.

'Humour – that's the best thing. You know, whether you've hit a bad shot or a good shot, being able to laugh at yourself, to laugh at your awful score and not to let it get you down, that's the important part of it. I always managed to laugh at myself, not to take myself too seriously. It's good to be able to talk to people on the way round; another way to break the tension – switch off for a few moments, then switch on again. You've got to be very determined, of course, and get back into that cocoon again.'

So I was now a professional golfer, the only English girl to get in that year, but still as naive as ever. I really didn't know what I was letting myself in for. Fortunately, the fact that I was playing probably the best golf I'd ever played was a strong buffer for the gruelling tournaments to come, as I flew back and forth to the States on my own. It was a lot to take on, but I got used to it. I paid my way and got on well.

But I missed the calm normality of home times with Richard or with my Mam. Richard came out to join me on his holidays and I introduced him to some of my new golfing friends. We had some good breaks being holiday tourists in some of my favourite places. I treasured those brief interludes with Richard, but most of the time it was a long-distance relationship. The strange thing was, he didn't seem to mind. I don't think I questioned this at first. We'd never actually lived together, so these separations didn't perhaps seem as hard as they might have done. Many of my golfing friends, like me, had dedicated their lives so much to their sport that we all shared that disconnect from everyday life, popular culture and close relationships. Few of us thought ahead any wider than our golf careers. I think this must have been why I was unaware of the years passing by.

I was lucky enough to be the highest earning woman golfer in Europe for two years running, winning the Order of Merit each time. I played as a professional for several years, during which time I did well in most of my matches and won twelve tournaments on the European tour. Fortunately, Richard was able to join me for some of these events.

In one European tournament I mistook my tee-time following a rain delay. Everything was confused with the interruption in play, and the officials had said we would continue at ten o'clock the following morning. What I didn't know was that they later decided to split the players into two groups, one to start earlier on the first tee, and the other to start on the ninth. My group were now due to start at nine-fifteen. I arrived at the course with what I thought was plenty of time to spare to do some practice shots.

I had a great American caddy at that time, nicknamed 'Neat Pete'. As I was walking across from my car to the practice area, I spotted Pete beckoning me.

'Come on,' he yelled. 'You've got to go straight on the tee.'

So off we went and, with no practice at all, I hit a cracking shot from the tee, straight down the middle of the fairway.

'Well,' said Pete. 'You certainly don't have to warm up a Royce Rolls!'

I made a great many friends on the tour, including some of the regular spectators. There was one American couple, Pat and Mike Eckstein, who were like a mam and dad to me and came to watch me play whenever they could. On the day of the last round of the World Championship, I knew they planned to be there. For some reason, I hit the most horrific shot from the tee – it went shooting off to the right, going straight for where the crowds of spectators were walking.

'Fore on the right,' yelled a marshal. Everyone ducked or dived out of the way. It was quite a melee. Despite the warning, my ball did hit one of the onlookers, and I was really concerned about it, but by the time I had walked over there, everyone had been moved away. I hit a good shot onto the front edge of the green and carried on with the match. Every now and then, while waiting to take my shots, I looked around for Pat and Mike, but I couldn't spot them in the crowds until we got to the fifth hole. I was partnering Nancy Lopez that day and we finished our round together and signed our cards.

Then Pat and Mike came over. 'We're here. We're fine!'

It was the first chance I'd had to talk to them. As Pat approached, I couldn't help but notice her arm, swollen black and blue.

'My God, Pat! What's happened to your arm?'

'You happened to it,' she laughed. 'You hit me on the first hole!'

Somehow, out of the many thousands of people watching us tee off on that first hole, I'd managed to find and hit the one person who was a good friend.

'I didn't want them to let you know,' she explained. 'They wanted to take me away to the hospital to have my arm checked, but I refused because I knew it would upset you if you found out. And anyway, I wanted to stay and watch you, and I knew you'd be looking out for us.'

Fortunately, there was no serious damage, though I think the bruising took weeks to disappear completely.

At home, life was happy, I thought, whenever I managed to spend time there. My mother had by now retired and seemed to be coping well, surrounded by her sister and brothers and their families, and after all those years when she'd worked so hard to support my swimming and golf coaching, it was my turn to help her financially, which was a great relief and pleasure for me when I was often so far from home. Richard continued to be very supportive of my career and never complained at my long absences. When I was back with him, our relationship always seemed happy and comfortable, focused on everyday things. But we never looked ahead much, and something was beginning to niggle me.

CHAPTER 24

Helen

The World's Not Wide Enough

As we flew back to England with our baby to ourselves at last, the sense of relief transformed us into giddy teenagers. Our spirits lightened with every passing mile as we travelled further and further away from my parents. I was twenty-one, I was married with a baby, and I was free.

Back in Northumberland, we moved straight into the house that used to belong to Simon's grandfather, who had recently died. It was a traditional two up, two down semi in North Shields, full of old-fashioned furniture, but we were grateful for a home of our own. That first night back in Northumberland was the first time that Scott had ever slept through the night. It seemed like such a good omen. Simon's parents lived close by, as did some of his other relations, and I enjoyed getting to know them all.

George and Joan regularly came to visit and we spent a lot of time with them and their children. We renewed old friendships and enjoyed the life of a young married couple again. It was such a relief. I was happy, for two months . . . until we received a letter from South Africa.

'Your mother is pining away,' Tommy wrote. 'She's missing the bairn. So we're coming back to live with you.'

My body tightened up. Just when we had rebuilt our lives as a small family unit, with our own plans and aspirations, our own future to relish, the hammer had fallen on us. Would I never be free of them?

I put down the letter and gave Scott a cuddle. He wanted to get down again, of course, to be free to continue his crawling exploration of the uncharted corners of our living room, but I needed his warmth, his zest for life to lighten my mood. The one and only good thing about this letter was that my parents couldn't afford to come till the following year. We had some time, at least, to cement our own relationships with each other, the three of us, and to enjoy our remaining freedom.

Over the next few days, Simon and I discussed this situation and agreed that we really had no choice but to accept the inevitable. We wanted to refuse to have them to live with us, but my father had by now had three heart attacks and would never get a mortgage or be able to afford the rent on a place on their own. They wouldn't even qualify for a council house, no longer being resident in the area.

I did write back and tell them we only had a two-bedroomed house, but they made no response to that.

One evening, as we walked back from Simon's parents' house, a familiar car passed us in a hurry.

'That's odd,' said Simon. 'Isn't that George's car?'

We quickened our stride and turned the corner into our road. There he was, parked outside our house. We rushed towards him as he got out of his car. The grim look on his face was an omen, and I knew it wasn't a good one.

We went in together.

'Sit down,' he told me in a gentle voice betrayed by the anxiety behind his eyes. 'I had a phone call from Mam.'

My heart jolted. I didn't want to hear this.

'There's no easy way to say it.' He paused. 'Dad died a few hours ago.'

I sat there, stunned. My father was only fifty-three, the same age as my mother. I think I went into shock. He was too young to die. Of course I knew he had nearly died that time when I had resuscitated him, but now it had happened when I was far away and he really was dead. I should have been there. Perhaps I could have saved him again. Yes, he was a tyrant, but he was my dad. My eyes welled up with tears, thinking about him and about the rare good times we had enjoyed together – those trips in his brick lorry when I was a small child in Seghill. Sorrow and guilt battled against my relief that I would never again suffer his bullying control, but most of all, I felt I had lost someone important in my life and my first tears were for him.

Inevitably, as it all sank in, my thoughts turned to my mother. I felt for her, as I realized she would be devastated. What would she do? I knew the answer to that question, of course. Our lives and all our hopes were about to be changed again.

The rest of that day was a blur.

Mercia was staying with friends in Johannesburg when she phoned me.

'He had a massive heart attack at home,' she said. 'And by the time they got him to the hospital, it was too late. He was dead.'

I could hear the tears. I knew they were tears for herself as much as for him.

'I asked your dad only a few days ago what I should do if anything happened to him.'

'What did he say?' I didn't need to ask, but I wanted to make it easier for her.

'He said, "Make your way to Helen. She will look after you."'

'So are you going to come back to England?' I asked, groaning inside.

'Yes. The people I'm staying with will arrange it all for me. I'll let you know the details and you can meet me at the airport.'

That's it, I thought. I'm twenty-one years old. We've just set up our own home and our own lives with our first baby, and my mother is going to move back in with us, ready to take over when we've hardly begun.

I wept most of the evening, and no matter how hard I tried, I could not get to sleep that night. In the early hours, and most of the following nights, I suffered a recurrence of the old panic attacks I'd had at the age of ten when we lived at Whitley Bay. Simon was so worried about me that he called the doctor, who said I was in shock.

My mother left South Africa a few days later, in January 1972. She left all their furniture, all her personal possessions and our family photographs behind, to be disposed of by strangers. She arrived back in England with one suitcase and no money.

'I'm going to devote the rest of my life to this family,' she vowed.

I tried to smile, but every cell groaned, 'Oh no! Do I really need this?'

In May 1973, three weeks late, Simon took me to the maternity unit of the hospital to be induced.

'Would you like to stay with your wife for the birth?' the midwife asked Simon.

'I don't think so,' he grinned. 'I would pass out.'

The nurse laughed. 'That's OK. We'd just leave you on the floor till you woke up!'

Our daughter Donna was born the double of Scott, except for the blackest of black hair – a beautiful baby. When she was handed to me I was overwhelmed with so many feelings. This precious, beautiful little girl was ours. She was gorgeous and I immediately loved her to bits.

A few days later the nursery nurse whispered to me, 'Your Donna is the most beautiful of all my babies. But don't tell any of the other mothers I said so, or I shall be in trouble.'

In the months and years that followed, I finally had the chance to go for a job I wanted to do. I did my nurse's training and built up a good career for myself. We had my mother as well as the two children to keep now, so I worked long hours at the Nuffield Hospital in Newcastle – many twelve- to sixteen-hour days. But work was no problem compared with trying to do the right thing in my mother's eyes. I had long been accustomed to not being good enough.

My mother once said to me, 'It's your duty to take care of me, because I don't have another life. You're my only daughter, so it's your job to look after me.'

George worked for a company called Schat Davit, who wanted to open up a new base in the USA. They appointed

George the taskmaster for this move, which was the opportunity he needed, and he took his family away to a new life in Florida. Of course, the job was only part of the reason for the move. I think he felt for me, because I was the one who was left with the burden of Mercia. I appreciated that he had his life and he had to make choices for his family. My time would come one day, but it didn't come for many years. Simon joined the police force and we both worked shifts, but we tried hard to have one of us there when the children came home from school. We didn't want my mother always to have them to herself. Nor did we want to lose the new closeness we had begun to achieve with them. This meant that one of us arrived home just as the other was going out, and we hardly had any time together. The only opportunities for all four of us to be a family together were on holidays away with the children – but my mother came too.

She took over the running of our home and looked after our children. We didn't get much of a look in. The miracle was that she became the mother figure to them that she had never been to me. I remember one occasion, not long after she came back to England, when Scott was a toddler and he wasn't well. He woke up during the evening and I heard him crying, so I stood up to go up and see him. My mother leapt forward, pushed me out of the way, rushed up the stairs and got to Scott first.

'Oh, sweetheart!' I heard her say as she picked him up and cuddled him. There were many occasions like that.

Simon had a chat with her. 'I don't think it's right that you push Helen aside when the children are crying.'

'Why?' she huffed. 'Have I done something wrong? I didn't think I was doing anything wrong.'

'Well, no. You're not doing anything wrong, but Helen is their mother. She wants to see to them and have that time with them.'

'Oh,' she sulked. Mercia didn't speak to me for a long time after that.

It made no difference. My mother continued to push me out at every opportunity, and sadly I allowed her to do this. I don't know why – perhaps I felt sorry for her. It sapped my morale to the point where I was distraught at times. She made me feel I owed her something, and that I should be grateful to her for being my mother.

One Mother's Day, I was up first, before anybody else. When Scott and Donna came down I gave them their breakfast, then my mother started down the stairs. The children both ran to the hall.

'Happy Mother's Day, Grandma,' they chimed in unison. They ran up a few steps to meet her and gave her cards and presents.

I thought, this is not right! It wasn't jealousy. I just thought, these are my children and I am their mother.

I think she did have the grace to say, 'Your mother's downstairs as well.' They realized it was my day too after that.

On these special occasions, she always claimed the children for herself. And I worked such long hours that, to my shame, I let it happen. Sometimes it was the only way to cope. But I wouldn't have had to work so hard if we didn't have that extra mouth to feed. She had a gravy train at our house for many years. We bought her everything she needed.

Of course, with us both working so hard, it was good to

know that the children had someone always there for them. Simon was often there when they got home from school, before he went off to work. He sat and watched TV with them and knew all the children's programmes.

I'd say, 'Who's Bagpuss?' They'd all look at me as if I was a dunce.

As they grew older, they were able to stay up later, so when I arrived home they were keen to tell me things. I used to sit and do their homework with them and I went to all their parents' evenings at school. It wasn't easy to fit everything in, but they were good times, especially with the children.

I liked to do the things that my parents never did. I wanted the children to have experiences and opportunities I'd never had – birthday parties, Christmas presents under the tree, outings, activities of all kinds. Most of all, I gave them lots of cuddles. When I was that child alone in my bedroom, unloved, I used to think to myself, when I have my babies, it's going to be different for them. I learned from my parents' mistakes. I knew, even then, what a child needs – all the things I hadn't known. I knew I wanted to be hugged, so I hugged my children a lot and told them 'I love you' all the time.

They hated it. They'd say, 'Get off, Mummy!'

There were occasions when my mother would do the old thing of saying, 'I'm going to tell your mother when she comes in and you're going to get a hiding for that.'

Of course, when I came in through the door, I'd get, 'Scott has done this and Donna has done that.'

'You have to deal with that at the time,' I said. 'Don't

expect me to do it when I come in from work, because I want to have a happy time with them. Don't hand it all over to me.' She took no notice of course.

In 1980, when the children were ten and eight, Simon and I decided to move our family to Australia as '£10 poms'. Our main reason was to provide the best future for Scott and Donna, but it was also to have a life of our own, far away from my mother. We were optimistic about this new start. 'But what about me?' wailed Mercia when we told her.

'We've made our decision,' I explained calmly. 'It's up to you to decide what you are going to do.'

Her response was immediate. 'I'll come with you, of course.'

The tide was pulling me down, like a drowning man. 'You could have a good home here, with kind people living around you,' I struggled. 'There is no need for you to come halfway round the world just because we're going there.'

'I have to come. You can't leave me behind. The bairns need me.'

At this time, Mercia was more or less estranged from all her siblings. She had wrapped herself entirely in the lives of my children, to the extent that she was no longer close to any of her own sisters and brothers. I had tried to encourage her to get on the bus to Seghill and visit them, but she always refused. We had even offered to drive her over, but she was always totally against the idea. As a result, she had deliberately put herself in the position of having no one but us.

Simon and I tried to think of a way out of this, but we

couldn't be that cruel to her, so, once again, we made it easy for her to make our lives difficult.

We spent two good years in Melbourne, despite Mercia's manipulative endeavours and the extra shifts we both had to do to support her, but Donna's asthma gradually worsened. Doctors told us she was allergic to something in the air, and it devastated us to see her struggle so hard to breathe. We had to return to England and, of course, mother came too.

CHAPTER 25

Jenny
The Knife

At the age of thirty-three, I had now earned enough in prize money to buy myself a house, and that's when things went unexpectedly out of balance. My mother had an absolute fit. She went berserk.

'How could you do this to me?'

'What do you mean?'

'It's a disgrace to the family, a single woman moving into a house on your own . . . to live with him.'

She obviously meant my partner, Richard, the man I'd been with for many years and whom she had always liked. I couldn't believe how extreme her reaction was to my buying my own house. Especially since my relationship with Richard had very little to do with buying the house at all. My accountant had advised investing my money in a property and it seemed the sensible thing. That was the main reason.

'I'm not going to live with him, Mam. He has his own house, so we're not moving in together.'

She didn't seem to have heard what I said. She certainly didn't take it in. 'I'll never speak to you again!' She was livid, her face almost as red as her hair.

While the house purchase was going through and I was still living at home with Mam, it was increasingly difficult. I couldn't have a normal conversation with her any more, and our warm relationship shattered, for the time being at least.

She constantly jibed at me. 'Of course, you know I'll never come to this house you've bought. It's a disgrace, bringing shame on me . . .'

It was as if she wanted to hurt me. In fact, she hit well below the belt when she said, 'My cousin and his wife adopted a child. He warned me, you know. I should have listened to him, mind. He said, "You should never adopt a child. They always do you wrong." I never thought that would come true with you. But now it has.'

This was not only the most hurtful thing she could say to me, but it was the only time she had ever made direct reference to the fact that she had adopted me. What a time to do it!

The day for me to move was approaching. One night, around two in the morning, something woke me. I realized it was the front door opening, so I went down and looked out through the open doorway to see her walking down the street, with nothing on but a skimpy shift. I went after her, struggled to turn her round and guided her back into the house, with great difficulty. I didn't know what to think – it was very alarming.

A couple of nights later, as I was lying awake worrying about whether I should go and tell her doctor about this, I heard some movement outside my bedroom. We had glazed doors, so I turned to look across my bedroom to my dressing table, where I saw reflections in the mirrors of a person's shape walking around on the landing. My mouth went dry and I kept very still for a few moments, wondering what was happening. Then I realized it must be my mother. I got out of bed and opened my door to find her wandering about with a glazed look in her eyes and a vacant expression on her face, holding a carving knife.

'What are you doing?' I asked. But she made no response. At first I thought she might be sleepwalking, but she was obviously awake because she paused when she heard my voice the second time. 'What's the matter?' She was clearly distressed and made no attempt to answer me. She just stood still with the knife held firmly in her hand. I was struck with fear and started to edge backwards, a step at a time, into my bedroom. I quickly closed the door and wedged a chair under the handle.

I listened in silence as she moved again, this time going back into her bedroom. I was wide awake now and couldn't sleep. I dared not sleep, worrying about her and what she might do, but I didn't dare move the chair and go to see if she was all right either. I lay in the dark and turned it all over in my mind, distraught to see my mother in such a state and with that frightening vacant stare. I couldn't get it out of my mind.

I was still awake when, an hour or two later, in the early hours of the morning before dawn, I heard her get up again and walk along the landing and down the stairs, and then the sound of the front door opening. I jumped out of bed and rushed down to see what she was doing, though I kept my distance, just in case. As I looked out of our front window, I could see her outside, walking down the road again, moving along in the moonlight like a ghost. Then she turned round, walked back into the house, up the stairs and into her bedroom.

I barricaded myself back into my own bedroom, but now I was shaking with shock as well as the cold. I feared for myself, but I feared even more for her. I lay awake worrying about what I should do, and it was a long time before I heard her snores and could begin to relax. I eventually fell into a fitful sleep of nightmares no more frightening than what I'd just witnessed.

In the morning, I tried to think it all through. What was wrong with her? Was she ill, or was it all, as she tried to make me believe, her extreme anguish at my decision to 'disgrace' her by moving into a house of my own. I reflected ruefully on the irony of this situation, since she had herself bought a house before she was married, though she had rented hers out for financial reasons. What really upset her was that I would be living in my house as a single woman, or worse, as a single woman with a partner to whom I wasn't married, even though he wouldn't be living there.

I rang my closest cousin, Wendy, and told her about the walkabouts and last night's incident with the knife.

'I don't know what's wrong with her. It's all come on very suddenly. When she went out walking down the street the first time, I thought perhaps she was putting it on, to show me how hurt she felt, but last night was different. She looked so detached, as if she was in a trance. She almost seemed not to know who I was.'

'Oh dear, it doesn't sound like Auntie Connie at all,' agreed Wendy.

'I don't know what to do. What should I do?'

'You've got to do something, Jen. You can't go through

another night like that. For your own sake, your safety, you've got to call the doctor. It sounds like some sort of nervous breakdown to me, mind, but whatever the reason, she's a danger to you and to herself. She needs specialist help.'

Wendy was a tower of strength, the closest thing I had to a sister. Though of course we didn't share the same domestic problems, we were always there for each other. On that occasion, I don't know what I would have done if I hadn't been able to talk it through with her. She held me together.

The doctor straightaway decided to section my mother and admitted her to the psychiatric unit at St Nicholas's Hospital in Gosforth. 'I believe she is having a nervous breakdown,' he said. 'Although it can be frightening for the relatives, it is usually a short-lived situation and they will help her to get better at the unit.'

I felt awful, almost guilty, though I knew it was the only option. At first, when I visited her, she seemed unaware of what had happened to her. She was heavily medicated, in a zombie state. I visited her in a room where all the people were sitting in a circle, most of them in a daze. One man stood up every now and then to drop his trousers. It was both shocking and depressing. Gradually, as they reduced the dosage, she became more aware, and more resentful. She didn't remember how she came to be there, but blamed me anyway. I blamed myself too.

As the weeks went by, she became more herself, and every time I went in to see her, she would plead, 'Get me out of here!' It was heartbreaking to have to turn my back on her and walk out of the door.

*

Finally the day came when I collected the keys to my first house, a three-bedroomed brick-built townhouse in a row of eight in Cramlington, a new town built round an old mining village about a twenty-minute drive from our family home at West Jesmond and just a couple of miles away from the pit villages of Seghill and Seaton Delaval.

I still felt slightly uncomfortable and perhaps even a little guilty that I was going against my mother's wishes in moving into this house – 'betraying' her, as she called it – but I was determined to make it my home and hoped to persuade her to get over the 'disgrace' and accept my living there. To be honest, what seemed to be her main concern, the fact that Richard and I weren't married, was something that didn't look likely to be resolved, but it had never worried us. In fact, we hadn't at any point discussed or planned our future, let along the idea of marriage or having children. We just drifted along as we were, content in our relationship. I suppose all our friends and relatives thought we would get married when the time was right, as people did in those days, but I think I probably felt it wouldn't be fair while I was away so much. In the back of my mind, however, I was becoming more and more aware of time going by.

Putting such thoughts out of my head, I was buzzing with excitement when I first opened the front door to my new house and started to plan how I would have it all. Over the next few days I took my cousin Wendy with me to choose furnishings and colour schemes, and we had a lot of laughs trying out chairs and beds in the showrooms. It was such a joy buying things for my own home. I spent several more days painting and decorating the rooms, with great help from Wendy and my friend Val.

In between these home-making sessions and golfing trips abroad, I made frequent visits to my mother in the psychiatric unit, where she seemed to be making good progress. She lived for my visits, so I always tried to be light-hearted and think of silly things to talk about – maybe something one of my aunties had done, or a funny incident on the golf course. It was very difficult to keep off the subject, but somehow I managed not to mention my house at all. I wanted to wait till she was well enough to be discharged before we could talk about that.

When the decor was finished and all the furniture had finally arrived and was arranged how I wanted it, I walked round and round the house on my own, just looking at everything with amazement. It was a fantastic feeling, like walking on air. I had earned this house by my own hard work . . . and had a lot of enjoyment in doing it. My over-riding feeling as I drove back to Jesmond that night was of a special sort of freedom that I would soon be living there.

After seven weeks my mother was nearly ready to be discharged, and in preparation she came home to our Jesmond house for the weekend. I had everything ready for her and she seemed pleased. I stayed awake for a long time the first night, but Mam never moved, and finally I drifted off. The next day she was bright and breezy, as if she hadn't been away. But that evening she became subdued. I wanted to cheer her up.

'I think you'll be home for good soon.'

'Ee, I would have been here all the time if you hadn't upset me so much. It was the shock.'

'Let's not worry about that now.'

'I suppose you've gone ahead and bought the house?' she blurted.

'Yes,' I nodded. 'Shall I take you over to see it tomorrow?'

Her quiet mood melted away as her whole body suddenly shook with sharp anger. 'I said I wouldn't ever come to your house, and I won't.' She looked away. 'You bring shame on me, and on yourself, moving in before you're even married.'

'But it's my own home I'm moving into.'

'Well, don't expect me to come round, because I never will.'

That week my mother reluctantly spent her last few days in the unit while I was away playing a tournament in the States, and then I helped her settle in back home, which was difficult because she would barely talk to me by now.

Finally I took the last of my stuff over to Cramlington and spent my first night there. It was an exciting new start, but it was marred by my mother's attitude. As I lay in bed that night, I felt sad about her apparent inability to accept the situation and I worried about her. I still couldn't shake off the feeling of guilt, but it was clear I could do nothing to change her. Maybe she never would come round to see me, but this was my life now and it was a wonderful feeling to sleep in my own home at last.

The day after I moved in, there she was knocking brightly at the front door! I could hardly believe it. I let her in with a huge grin.

'Hello, Mam.' I gave her a hug. 'I'm so glad you came. You're my first visitor!'

'Ee, that's good. Do you need any help?'

The next few weeks were up and down. She had her resentful moments still, and had to continue taking medication for a long time, but she was regaining her emotional strength now and I was glad that at the age of seventy-eight she could finally relax and enjoy her retirement, spending time with friends and relations and watching golf on the TV whenever it was on. Our relationship got back to normal and we put that disturbed period behind us.

I loved living at Cramlington. Richard came over quite a lot and we both continued with our independent lives in between. My neighbours were all very friendly and we often socialized together when I was at home. Some of them took care of the house for me while I was away, so I never needed to worry.

In my friendly new community, I suddenly felt I wanted to go back to church. I started to believe again, for the first time since that terrible day my father died. We had a lovely old church at Cramlington, with a fantastic vicar who was very welcoming, and the first time I attended a service there, the church was absolutely packed with friendly families, full of smiles and singing brightly. I felt like I was coming home. A tremendous warmth radiated through the church, an atmosphere of complete acceptance of one another regardless of background or circumstances. I felt so enriched by the whole experience that I went regularly when I could after that and have been a firm believer in God ever since.

Most of the families in the houses around me had children and I used to watch them play outside just as we had done when I was young. Sometimes they would wave at me as I went out in the car, or when I was doing some gardening. I loved hearing their laughter and I couldn't help thinking: what would it be like to have children of my own? Richard and I had never really talked about it, so maybe it was time

I broached the subject with him. I didn't even know if he wanted children. But I didn't feel the time was right while I was still away on tour so much, so I put it off for a while.

The following year, 1982, I was voted North-East Sports Personality of the Year. This was one of my highlights, as it was voted for by the sports journalists across our region, who apparently wanted to show their support for a local woman achieving across the world in her sport and raising the profile of the north-east region. That was the important factor. It was a big thing, so it was all televised and I was to be presented with a big trophy, but sadly, wasn't able to be there because of a tournament, so my mother was thrilled to bits to receive it on my behalf. I couldn't believe all this fuss was for me, just for doing something I loved – playing golf with my friends on tour on the best courses in the world.

The following year was even better, when I attended the ceremony myself to pass on my trophy. I was delighted to present it to a certain young footballer then making a name for himself playing for Newcastle United – Kevin Keegan. I have to confess I was rather star-struck, though I tried not to show it. The press carried photos of us together and I still have one of them in a frame on my sideboard, Not because it's of me, but because it's with Kevin and my mother. As a lifetime Newcastle supporter, Connie was even more excited to meet him than I was.

The risk of aiming for a professional career had certainly paid dividends. I could now support my mother and provide extra comforts for her. Despite her arthritis, she was quite fit and active for her age. I occasionally took her with me on tours, and we'd hire a car and have a holiday in California or wherever was reachable between tournaments. She loved it, and I know my dad would have been very proud of his 'little girl' doing so well at the game he had taught me.

But of course, in one important way, I wasn't his little girl. Whatever I did and wherever I went, there was still that ache that never left me, always gnawing away in the back of my mind, impatient to get out. One of these days I'd pay more attention to it and start on the journey to seek answers about my adoption, my real origins, maybe even find my own blood family. Would I feel I belonged? Could I have been any happier there? Might I have become a different person?

CHAPTER 26

Jenny
A Visit to Seghill

A few years earlier, in 1975, a change in the law had made it possible for adopted children to gain access to their original birth certificates and adoption records. All I had possessed up to then was a shortened form of birth certificate, issued after my adoption, and with only my adoptive parents' names on it. At last there was a way to access my true birth certificate.

When this law was passed, I was heavily involved in professional golf tours and tournaments, so I filed it away in my brain for a time when I could start on that journey. Finally, one day in 1980 after a day's matchplay, I spoke to my friend Jane about it.

'I really want to find out where I came from; who my real mother was.'

'I don't know why you want to do that!' she said, sharp as a knife. 'Why can't you just be happy with the parent you've got? Your mother has given you a good life, hasn't she?'

'Yes, she has. Both of my parents were great. But that's not the point.'

'Well, I was adopted too, and there's no way I'm going to look for my birth parents.'

Jane was a great friend, but she had her own view and that was fine. We agreed to differ. Hers was a common response in those days, when everyone brushed such situations away, and her matter-of-fact perspective had some sense to it – I had to acknowledge that. I changed the subject, but I couldn't forget it. Out of sight it might be, but it certainly wasn't out of mind. There was always this void. I felt there was something vital that I was missing. I suppose it came down to one thing: Who was I? Every time this question surfaced in my mind, it became more and more insistent.

Finally, I could ignore it no longer. I didn't want to upset my mother, but she was alive and well and it seemed as if she was going to live for ever. At this rate, I might go before her. I had to do something about it, so finally I applied to see my records. I could do this without telling Mam. I felt sure I could keep it quiet. She need never know.

I applied for the records and they were sent, not directly to me, but to the adoption counsellor. This was the standard process, because anyone in my situation had to have counselling to prepare them to receive the information.

I remember so clearly the day I went to see the counsellor. The street was wet with rain outside the tall brick building, but the sun's rays bled out from behind the clouds.

I strode into the room, heart pounding, and the counsellor sat me down at a table.

'Right,' she began, straight to the point, rather like me, I suppose. 'It's my role to make you aware that there is a possibility of a double rejection.'

'What do you mean?'

'Well, you could find out who your mother is, and, as she's already given you away once, you might find she doesn't want to talk to you, or have anything to do with you.'

'Oh.' I tried to take this in. I had thought about this possibility, but had chosen to blank it out.

'You might have other siblings who don't know you exist.'

She continued along this line, and my head reeled at the thought that I might have brothers and sisters – something I'd always wanted, always missed. Maybe I hadn't been an only child after all. But then the double deprivation of that hit me – not knowing they existed, if they did, and at the same time being deprived of their company and support throughout my childhood.

She paused to let me consider all this and how I felt about it.

I didn't wait for her to speak again. 'Yes, I do want to do it. I definitely want to know. Even if they don't want me, I need to know.'

She nodded. 'Are you sure?'

'Definitely. Absolutely sure.'

'You could always wait a while if you like, to prepare yourself emotionally for what might happen. Nobody knows how your parents will take it when they find out.'

'No, there's no need to wait. I've had a long time to think about this and have made up my mind, so I'm sure I'll be fine.'

'OK. Now, before we go any further, I must tell you that I'm here to help you. If you're certain you want to go ahead and find your family, I'm here to support you and I will help as best I can.'

'Thank you.'

'I must start by saying that here, in the north-east of England, we normally find it's easy to trace families, because when girls get married, they move one door along the same street.'

'That's true.' I smiled, relieved that this would be a straight-forward task.

She took from her lap a document of some kind and passed it across the table to me. I unfolded it and held it up to read. There it was – my birth certificate, printed out – a simple document, but the most important of my life so far. The date in 1948 was certainly my birthday. Jennifer was my given name, the name I had now. Obviously my adoptive parents must have decided to keep it. Perhaps they liked it themselves, as it was a popular name at the time. They had added two middle names, but my first name, Jennifer, was the only thing my real mother had ever given me. I wish I'd known that when I was younger. All those years of thinking I had nothing of hers, and now I discovered that she gave me my name.

I looked at the dash surrounded by empty space in the next column with a hollow feeling – utter dismay. The column was headed 'Name and surname of father'. It was blank. I had no father, according to my original birth certificate – a terrible disappointment. This could mean only one thing, something I had always wondered about, and presumably the reason why I was adopted. Perhaps my birth mother had had no choice. She might have been forced to give me away, which would mean she hadn't rejected me after all. Maybe she really loved me . . . I stopped myself. I was getting carried away with fanciful thoughts.

I moved on to the next and most important column. 'Name, surname and maiden name of mother', and underneath was written: 'Mercia Dick, formerly Bradshaw.' Mercia – what an unusual name. Distinctive.

'Mercia,' I heard my voice saying. The counsellor sitting opposite me nodded and gave a half smile of encouragement, as if she understood my reactions. I suppose she had seen it before in others. She must have gone through a lot of these sessions.

There was more below the name: '. . . a shop assistant of 6 Northcott Gardens, Seghill.' I knew Seghill very well – it was just two miles down the road from my house in Cramlington. How amazing. I'm sure Mam used to go there with her corsets – she probably had clients there. She'd have visited them, gone into their houses to fit their corsets and chatted with them. Connie was always very good at talking with strangers and putting them at their ease, which of course helped her to sell a lot of corsets. Perhaps she had even been inside Mercia's house, or her mother's? This thought warmed me in an odd way. A coincidence maybe?

I moved on across the columns. The 'father's occupation' was of course blank. Next was the person who registered the birth. 'M. Dick. Mother.' Finally the date of registration, just eight days after I was born. Was this because she was keen to register me, or because she had to? Was I still with her then? Perhaps she was feeding me and making a bond between us that made it more difficult for her to give me away?

My mind turned everything over and examined every possible clue.

I had been born as Jennifer Dick, with no named father and a mother called Mercia. At first it seemed odd that she'd had a former surname, but then I realized that maybe she'd been married, possibly widowed or divorced. I was born after the war, so her husband couldn't have been killed in the war . . . or could he? Yes, of course he could, since he clearly wasn't my father . . . I was going off at tangents into the realms of fancy again, so I deliberately brought my mind back to focus on the present, on the woman sitting opposite me and the piece of paper in my hands. There would be plenty of time to think around it all when I got home and over the days to come. The main thing was that this woman on the certificate, my birth mother, Mercia, presumably wasn't a teenager when she had me, unless she'd been born with a different name herself, and . . . No, I'd think about all of that later.

'So there's no father's name registered,' I said.

'No.' Her face was expressionless. 'That suggests to me that maybe your mother had an affair . . .'

'Yes, I suppose so.'

I looked at the certificate one more time, then carefully folded it and tucked it into my bag.

'One last thing,' I said. 'Do you have any record of where she lives now?'

'No.' The counsellor shook her head. 'But I have some contacts who can look into that sort of thing. If you like, I'll try to find out for you?'

'Yes, please!' I was new to all this and had no idea where to start, so her offer of help was a great boon.

'I'll get back to you within a fortnight.'

It was a long fortnight. Every day it felt like I was at the mercy of the lead weight under an old grandfather clock that was swinging very slowly. And at the end of each day there was still no news. Nothing. I moaned about the delay to Richard.

'Well, if you're too impatient to wait,' he said, 'give her a call.'

'She's obviously having difficulty finding this Mercia. Maybe she died young. Or maybe she emigrated or something,' I wondered aloud.

'Well, you won't know if you don't call her.'

'But I don't want to be too pushy – it might put her off helping me.'

It was another two weeks, a month after our initial meeting, before I finally gave the counsellor a ring.

'Yes, I'm sorry I haven't got back to you yet. I've been trying to find some news for you, but I'm not getting anywhere.' She paused. 'Do you want me to carry on?'

I'd had a lot of time to think about this, so I said, 'Not really.' It seemed to me that this woman probably hadn't done much.

Right, I thought, I'll just to have to get on with trying to locate Mercia myself.

I went back to my original birth certificate and started from there, at the address in Seghill, so amazingly close to my own home. I looked on a Seghill street-map and marked the address.

I'll go and find the house,' I said to Richard.

'You must be mad. You're going to go looking for a stranger, a woman you've never met, with your name emblazoned all over your car.'

I smiled – it did sound preposterous. I had forgotten that I was currently driving a sponsored car.

'She won't live there any more,' he continued. 'She could have moved lots of times. You won't find her and you'll only be more upset.'

This fired me up. 'Well, I'm definitely going anyway. I have to start somewhere.'

'And what if you do find her . . . and she denies it all, or doesn't want to have anything to do with you?'

'I guess I'll just have to deal with that if it happens.' Ever the optimist, I couldn't see the heartache I was letting myself in for.

The following day, I drove to the street on the birth certificate, 6 Northcott Gardens, not far from the old pit-head, and parked outside the small, neat-looking semi. I sat there for a moment, trying to imagine this place in 1948, the year of my birth. I walked up the short path in a daze, wondering what to say. For some reason, I hadn't thought about that before and I wished now that I'd planned my visit better. I had been assuming it would all go well, but what if it didn't?

I knocked on the glazed wooden front door, tentatively at first, then again with more determination, though I wasn't feeling that inside. As I waited I began to shake with anticipation, or perhaps fear, at what I would find out. My heart beat wildly as I stood on the front doorstep and leaned in to hear the slightest noise. But there was none. I knocked once more, even louder this time. Finally, as I turned, an elderly chap doing his garden next door stood up. I froze.

'There's nobody in,' he said. He put his head to one side. 'Can I help you?'

'Well, I'm not sure. I'm looking for the family of Mercia Dick.'

'Ee, she's long gone.'

I went cold. 'You mean she has died?'

'Haaway, no. She doesn't live here any more.'

A wave of relief flooded through me.

'But her sister Dorrie lives in the next road.' He told me the number and pointed in the general direction.

I trembled as I walked round the corner to a very similar house with a painted wooden door. I rang the bell and stood there for what seemed an eternity, watching for any movement in the net curtains at the window. I rang again. But once again it was a disappointing result – there was no one at home.

The next day, first thing in the morning, I went back to Seghill, parked my car down the road and approached Dorrie's front door. I rang the bell and rapped the knocker too, just in case. Immediately I heard a bustle inside as someone's fast footsteps approached, almost as if the resident had been expecting me.

The large figure of a woman opened the door and loomed over me. She looked about sixtyish. She had a determined expression, and was wearing a pretty dress with a working pinny over the top, as older Northumberland housewives still did in those days.

'Are you the lady who came here asking questions yesterday?' she asked, unable to hide her blunt curiosity.

Word had obviously got round. I smiled because I knew that in these narrow village streets, everyone knew everybody else's business. It was the same in Jesmond, though they didn't make it as obvious there.

'Yes, I am,' I said, almost gasping for breath in nervous anticipation. 'I knocked on your door, but there was no answer.'

She said nothing; just stood there, waiting for me to speak.

Embarrassed, I blurted out, 'My name is Jennifer . . .'

There was a loud intake of breath as she gazed intently at my face. What I didn't know at that moment was how greatly I resembled my birth mother.

She breathed out. 'Hhhh. We knew you'd come back. We knew you'd find us one day.'

She almost jumped forward and wrapped her arms round me. 'I'm so glad you came back.'

It was as if all my worries just dropped away at that moment. This was immediately followed by a strange inner confusion that I was glad of such a warm welcome from someone I didn't know.

She must have sensed this as she stood back. 'I'm your mother's sister, Dorrie.' Then she took my arm. 'Come on in, hinny. Step inside and have a cup of tea.'

She ushered me into her small front room, dark and old-fashioned, but tidy, with everything in its place, lots of photos on display, pictures on the walls and glass vases on the mantelpiece. Although it was warm outside, it felt cold in the room, but I expect that was just me and my apprehension.

The kindly woman gave me a cup of tea and showed me some of the photos. I was overwhelmed as she pointed out various relations whose names, of course, I'd never heard of. They went in one ear and immediately flowed out of the other, missing out my brain completely. The more photos she showed me, the more confused I became. It seemed to be a very large family.

Dorrie showed me a photo of Mercia, taken when she was about my age. I missed a breath. It was the first time I'd ever seen my birth mother. It was an amazing feeling to have a face to go with the name. And even I could see a resemblance between us, though another photo of her as a young woman showed that she had once been a real beauty, with a look of knowing it.

It suddenly struck me how bizarre this situation was. Here I was sitting in my birth mother's sister's front room, with this woman who was my aunt, and who knew so much about my mother whilst I knew nothing but her name. Dorrie was very relaxed and genuinely welcoming, but I couldn't quite adjust to this new concept.

And now that I'd seen Mercia's photos, I wanted to know more.

'What about my father?' I asked tentatively.

Immediately her expression hardened. 'Oh, he's long gone. He was a bad bugger. He's six foot under. You don't want to bother about him. You're better off not knowing him.'

She seemed so definite that I didn't doubt her. In my usual trusting way, I took this information at face value and changed tack.

'Where does Mercia live?'

'In Tynemouth,' she said.

That was about ten miles away. I must have looked a little disappointed.

'It isn't far, pet.' She stood up. 'Let me call Mercia now and tell her about you.'

My hopes soared. After more than half a lifetime, I was now only a phone call away.

She obviously got through as there was quite a conversation going on, but of course I could only hear one side of it, and that was indistinct because the phone was out in the hall.

'Jennifer came this morning. She came back, looking for you.'

'Aye, Jennifer is here. You see, I told you she'd come back.'

'Aye, she's in ma front room now.'

'She wants to see you.'

'Oh, don't you think . . .?'

'I could bring her to the phone to speak to you . . .'

'Are you sure?'

'All right, pet. I'll tell her.'

It didn't take me long to work out what was happening. Dorrie came back into the room, wringing her hands.

I couldn't wait. 'What did she say? Can I go and see her?' My heart was pounding with hope, despite what I'd heard.

'No, I'm afraid not. I'm sorry,' she shrugged. 'She doesn't want to see you. She says too much water has gone under the bridge and it's best left alone.'

'Ohhhh.' My hopes deflated and my whole body turned suddenly cold and clammy, shocked by the mixture of emotions that flooded through me – disappointment, anger, defeat, betrayal . . . and yes, the terrible pain of rejection.

'Please forgive her.' Dorrie looked anguished. 'It was the end of the war and times were hard . . .'

I said nothing at first, only nodded in a non-committal way. I was born well after the war. But then I felt sorry for this woman who had given me such a warm welcome. She seemed to have done her best.

'It's OK. I had a happy childhood with great parents. I don't feel bitter.'

She appeared relieved, but I was suffering. I felt dazed and numb, in a sort of bubble, rather like swimming under water – I could hear a muffled voice from outside, but not what it was saying. I felt sick and faint. I tried to take deep breaths to calm myself down.

For the second time in my life, my birth mother had rejected me with barely a moment's hesitation. That hurt desperately. Yet, in a strange way, I also felt a sense of relief, that I could walk away from this overpowering stranger who was related to me. It was uncomfortable to think she had seen me as a baby, knew all about me, was part of the secret and yet was the barrier between me and my birth mother. Could I really be sure that was what my mother had said? Maybe this aunt had made it all up? For a moment I saw a chink of light, but then it disappeared. No, the conversation had sounded genuine. It must be so.

As I was leaving, Dorrie gave me a photo of Mercia to keep, the pretty young Mercia's photo. So at least I would have that. But I knew I had to accept that my birth mother didn't want to know, and there was nothing I could do about it.

As I turned on the doorstep to thank her for the tea, she seemed to make a sudden decision. 'Wait.' She turned back to fetch something and handed it to me. 'You have a brother and a sister,' she announced, pointing at a second photo she had just slipped into my hand. It was like a sudden electric shock. Transfixed by this news, I could not move for a minute, or perhaps it was only a moment. Then I gave in to the overwhelming urge to run up the road to my car. I did not look back, knowing this person was still at the open door, staring at me.

Only when I was in the car did I look at the small photo of Mercia, middle-aged, looking rather dour, with two young adults, one either side. So these were my brother and my sister, he good-looking with a broad grin and she pretty with a half smile. So now not only did I know I had siblings – a huge shock in itself, but I could also see what they looked like. However, I didn't know when the photo was taken, how old they were or whether they were born before or after me. I didn't even know their names.

I wondered if they knew about me; if they'd seen me as a baby. Dorrie had simply said they were my sister and brother, but I presumed she probably meant half-sister and half-brother. Perhaps they had been born of Mercia's marriage, unlike me. Perhaps she had kept them.

As I drove away, my head pounded as I repeated to myself, 'I have a brother and a sister, a brother and a sister.' I should have been jubilant, but all I felt was a great sense of loss that I hadn't known about them for all those years, that I hadn't shared those usual sibling things with them. Where were they now? Could I ever find them? The tears flowed down my face and I drove the last mile home in a blur.

Thinking back now, I don't know why I didn't turn back to ask the important questions, or at least why I didn't go back later. But for some reason I didn't. Perhaps it was the finality of Dorrie's swift gesture with the photo, or the fact that I could feel her stare boring through my back as I left. It felt to me that she was banishing me from her life after Mercia's refusal to see or even speak to me.

As soon as I got back home, with a splitting headache, I made myself a strong cup of tea, took some paracetamol, half closed the curtains to darken the room and sat down. My birth father had died and my birth mother didn't want to meet me. Who was I? It was all too much. My surface composure collapsed and I started sobbing uncontrollably. Hours passed before the torrent ceased. I was completely drained.

When Richard came round that evening, I related it all to him. He was always supportive and listened patiently, but I knew he didn't really understand how I felt.

'I knew it wouldn't end happily,' he said. 'I told you.'

Of course it was true. I hadn't heeded his warning. But I felt resentful that he seemed to be scoring points out of my distress.

Over the following days, I kept picking up the photos and putting them down, over and over again. Every time I looked, I was overcome with indignation and frustration. It sharpened my sense of loss. This was all I had been left with, the dregs, when all the good wine had been drunk. I looked and looked at these people. It brought into focus the feeling of not belonging, being detached, cast aside. It troubled me every time I held that photo that there they were, together, and here was I, apart, discarded, searching for scraps of information about the one person who should have loved me, but clearly didn't want to have anything to do with me. Equally hurtful, I had siblings I'd never seen or known about. I thought back to all those years of longing for a sister or brother to share my childhood.

I showed the photo to my cousin Wendy when she came round. 'I've found the family,' I said. 'But my mother won't talk to me.'

She gave me a hug. There was nothing she could say, but the warmth of her support helped me more than any words.

After that I just set it all aside. My mam would be very troubled if she ever found out, so she didn't need to know. My busy tournament schedule continued. But wherever I was and whatever I was doing, a phrase kept resurfacing: 'Mercia Dick is a real person, living in Tyneside.'

I kept the photo of the three of them, my mother, sister and brother, for a long time until one day, in sheer frustration, I tore it up, along with my original birth certificate. In my mind, that was that. If they didn't want to know me, I would forget about them too. But of course I could not forget. The revelation of my nameless siblings stayed lodged in the back of my mind for years.

CHAPTER 27

Helen

Three People in This Marriage

When we arrived back in England from Melbourne, we bought a house and settled into life more or less as it was before. We caught up with friends and occasionally went over to George and Joan's house in Cramlington for a meal and the chance to get away from Mercia, but there wasn't time for much socializing.

Every day when I came home from my shifts at the hospital I had to continue with the almost unbearable situation at home: the fact that there were three people in my marriage. My mother lived in our house, ruled our roost, sat on her throne in our living room. It was difficult, at best. We were not able to have a private conversation in our own home because she was always there, always listening, hoping for some drama. She loved being the centre of a good drama. If we wanted to have an argument, or discuss something serious, we had go outside and stand in the garden shed, or sit in the car as we had done for years.

Whenever she could, she would listen to our private conversations. Occasionally she couldn't resist butting in. For example, if I was complaining about some slight from Simon she would interrupt and take his side against me. 'He didn't say that. I was there. You are completely wrong, Helen, and very unfair to poor Simon.'

Or she would bide her time until a chance arose for her to pour salt on existing niggles or instigate new ones. 'Simon, I thought Helen was very rude to you this morning,' or, 'Helen, did you notice Simon was late home tonight? What do you think he's up to?' The glint in her eye when she was stirring up such mischief reminded me of the many times she had goaded my father into his rages. Mostly, she couldn't endure her curiosity and would came straight out with direct questions we couldn't answer. 'You were talking about me in the shed this morning, weren't you?' She must have crept up outside the door to know that.

That's no way to carry on a marriage, is it? We hardly spent much time with each other as it was; we didn't really have a proper husband-wife relationship – and it took a terrible toll on us both. I was sad and angry about all these things. It didn't seem fair. But I suppose we both reached the point when you think: this is the way it is; just get on with it. We had to. That's how we thought at the time, anyway, oppressed by all those years of servitude and forbearance.

I was working at the Newcastle Nuffield Hospital as a theatre nurse at this time, mostly supporting surgeons oper-ating on orthopaedic or gastro-intestinal patients. David Stainsby, the Consultant Orthopaedic Surgeon there who specialized in sports injuries, especially spinal injuries, always used to request me as his theatre nurse and I enjoyed working with him. We did many operations together. But the long hours and my own worsening back problems ground me down.

As our children approached their teenage years, we realized we needed more space – physical space so that the children could have separate rooms. We had a three-bedroom house, but, because of my mother, they had to share, which we thought wasn't right at their ages – Scott was thirteen and Donna was ten or eleven. You know what it's like when teenagers get to be teenagers. They needed their privacy.

One day, I mentioned it to my mother.

For her the solution was simple: 'If that's the case, you'll have to buy a bigger house, won't you?'

'Well, no. We can't really afford to do that.'

'It's the only answer. You'll just have to buy a four-bedroomed house.'

When I told Simon later, he said, 'We can't continue like this. It's terrible.'

We made a decision. It had taken us long enough, I know. Simon was right. It could not go on any longer.

I chose my moment with care and broached the subject.

'It would be nice for you to have your own home, wouldn't it?' I suggested. A pause. I could see I'd caught her by surprise. 'We could find you a comfortable flat, a place of your own, with your own front door.'

She looked at me as if she'd swallowed a lemon, several lemons. 'You're pushing me out. Is that all I'm worth to you, after all these years of mothering the bairns?'

I thought: here we go again.

She pushed on: 'You want to take me away from ma bairns? To throw me out?'

'It's not like that,' I soothed.

'That's what it looks like to me.'

'I think it would be nice for you to develop your own

independence, now that the children are older.' I smiled. 'To have your own place and your own friends. You've been widowed so long. Don't you think it would be good, to have your own life again?'

'I have my own life here,' she scowled. 'You just want to take me away from *my* bairns. How ungrateful can you be?'

'No. You've got it completely wrong.'

She sulked and said nothing.

'Well, just have a think about it,' I suggested.

'I will not!' She fixed the sharpened steel of her eyes on me. 'I will not think about it at all.'

Several weeks and many conversations later, to our immense relief, she came round to the idea of having a place of her own. I put her name down with several housing associations, and one of them came up with something.

The lady from Social Services explained. 'You're actually overcrowded. We have allocated a flat for your mother.'

She had nothing to take to her new home, so we bought all her furniture, appliances, carpets, pots and pans, cutlery, crockery, bedding and everything down to a soap dish. All of it brand new. It cost us what her generation used to call a tidy sum, leaving us nearly penniless, but we rejoiced the day we moved her in. We did it all – carried the furniture and boxes up to her flat on the third floor. I vividly remember Simon struggling up the three flights of stairs with her carpet as if he was wrestling a monster. We settled her in, then went home exhausted but elated. Finally, we had made the break!

When we got back, Scott and Donna had already rearranged their furniture how they wanted it, each in their own rooms. We ordered a pizza and ate it, just the four of us, watching TV together. Simon and I couldn't stop smiling. We were a normal family at last. I did give my mother a fleeting thought at one point, wondering how she was. I didn't want her to be unhappy, but it was wonderful to have our home to ourselves at last, to relax however we wanted and not have to worry about pleasing anyone else.

Waking up the next morning was bliss, knowing we didn't have to rush to get up. It seemed almost wicked to stay in bed as long as we liked and there wasn't a sound from the children's rooms. Eventually I got up and went downstairs to make Simon and me a cup of tea to have in bed. As the kettle came to the boil, I heard the key turn in the lock. I felt that familiar, heavy feeling of dread in the pit of my stomach.

'Hello, Mam,' I sighed, trying to hide my consternation.

'I caught the bus to get here,' she said triumphantly. 'I thought you might need me.'

I got another cup out for her. 'Did you enjoy your first night in your new home?' I asked.

'It was all right, I suppose,' she grunted and hung up her coat.

From then on, this was her routine. She caught the bus every morning and spent the whole day in our house in her customary role, until either Simon or I drove her home late afternoon. She'd have stayed longer if we hadn't taken her back.

After several weeks of this, I raised it with her.

'It's very kind of you to come so early and stay all day to help us out. But really, it's not necessary now that the children are older and more independent.'

'You're trying to take my bairns away from me!' she wailed.

So we felt we had no alternative if we wanted to keep the

peace, and life continued in this vein for a few more years, with my mother in our house every day. During our annual holidays and on bank holidays when we just wanted to lie in, she would arrive early in the morning and wake us up.

We felt defeated. She was still sucking the life out of us.

CHAPTER 28

$\mathcal{J}$enny

All Change

My long golfing career and the international travelling that went with it meant I was rarely home in Northumberland for more than a few days. My focus was always on the next tournament. For some time now, these challenges had successfully hidden a fundamental hole in my life. Richard and I had enjoyed a strong relationship for about fifteen years. We had developed a lifestyle that suited us both – together yet independent. He still came to join me on US or European tours in his holidays. We went out and spent time together whenever we could, sometimes with friends when I was home. It was all working fine and it felt very easy and comfortable.

But that was the problem.

It was an easygoing, contented partnership. We talked a lot whenever we spent time together. We laughed and we chatted. But I had begun to realize that we always spoke about superficial things. Somehow we never resolved the more important issue of joint aspirations, family, children. I suppose I assumed we would get married one day, and I had intended for a while to raise my concerns about marriage and children, but somehow the time had never been right, or Richard had perhaps seen it coming and the subject had been sidestepped. I'm not sure now that I ever really believed we would marry. I was aware that some relationships can meander calmly along for ever. But it had only occurred to me recently that maybe we had fallen into that rut.

I was in my mid-thirties and becoming more and more aware of the years passing and the need for something more. I had learned to be adept at hiding things away, not just from others but from myself. I suppose I continued to do that, and the more the months slipped by, the deeper the longing became inside, eating away at me. I saw friends with their children, families in shops, on the beaches, everywhere; wherever I went I saw parents with their children. I wanted to be like them. To be a mother. My adoptive family, though wonderful, were borrowed, not really mine, and I'd been rejected by my birth family. Now I wanted a family of my own. But I began to fear I'd missed out, that maybe I'd left it too late.

My mother, Connie, made things worse.

'When are you and Richard going to get married? When are you going to have children? I want to be a grandmother. Isn't it time you gave me a grandchild? You're not young any more.'

'Thanks, Mother!'

'You mustn't leave it too late.'

I didn't know what to say.

Finally I talked about it with Richard, but nothing was resolved and we continued to drift along, but rather half-heartedly now, as my golf commitments took me away from home more frequently and we began to see each other less.

*

The years 1981 to 1982 were the most successful of my career, but by this time my body had taken years of stress. A series of surgical operations followed over the next couple of years to remedy serious back problems and foot injuries. I had the best orthopaedic surgeon, David Stainsby, renowned across the north-east, and he operated on me in the Newcastle Nuffield Hospital, with a wonderful operating team. Of course I didn't see much of them as, after an initial smile and some brief conversation, they knocked me out pretty quickly. But I always felt safe in their hands.

Eventually I had to give in to the inevitable. I couldn't continue with my professional career, so I played my last tournament in 1984. I found it enormously sad, as I'd derived such enjoyment out of the game and would miss the camaraderie of all my friends. Nearly everyone I knew was part of my golfing life. I thought that was all over now.

However, a new door opened with the offer of a job as teaching professional at the very golf centre where I began my playing career. They knew me and my reputation, and I brought in a lot of new business for them – clients came from far away for lessons. It suited me well for a while – I didn't have to travel, nor did I have to give up golf completely. I had more time to spend with my mother – and of course with Richard, but our relationship didn't alter now that I was at home all the time, and despite a few attempts by me to talk things through, we still evaded the silent questions, the unspoken truths.

One harsh Northumberland winter's day, I saw an ad in the paper. It was about a new golf development just about to start up in Tenerife, and it was advertising properties for sale. It looked quite exciting, and the thought of some all-year-round sunshine gave me a bright idea. I called the number in the advert and asked to speak to the manager.

One week later, I flew out to Tenerife to join the team at Golf del Sur. The idea was that I'd welcome potential clients, talk to them about golf and maybe play a trial round with them to give them some hints and tips. In return I'd have my own apartment and use of the course whenever I wanted.

On my first morning I got to the car park at 9 o'clock, as agreed, to meet Maurice, the manager of the complex, but he wasn't there. I waited and strolled about, but still nobody came. I was wondering what to do when a tall, good-looking man walked over to me.

'Are you Jenny?' He didn't wait for a reply. 'My name is Sam Lucas.' He smiled.

I thought he was rather brash. 'What about Maurice?' I asked.

'Oh, Maurice can't come. He asked me to look after you for the weekend. I'm playing golf today. Would you like to come and play?'

'Well actually I've just made plans to go and take some pictures.' His confidence that I would join him slightly irritated me, and anyway it was true – I had become an avid photographer and had my camera with me.

'What are you doing tonight?' he persisted. 'I've got some friends here. Would you like to join us for a drink?'

'Yes, that will be fine.'

So that was it. We met that evening and quickly got chatting, only to find we had both lived in the north-east. He told me about his background and about being a Sunderland supporter. I think he was quite interested when he learned a bit about my golf career, but he was far more impressed that I was a Newcastle United supporter. We talked and talked, and when we started to compare notes about our childhoods, there were an amazing number of similarities. We couldn't believe it when we found we had both been at the same Saturday afternoon cinema on the same day. That was spooky.

Sam and I arranged to play golf the next morning, and in the evening went out for a meal with some more of his friends. We played golf again on the Sunday, enjoying each other's company and talking endlessly. We had a good game of golf and were just walking down the eighteenth fairway when the green-keeper hurried over with an agitated expression.

'Sam. Robert . . . Robert is *morto* . . . '

The owner of the complex had apparently been driving his great Mercedes like a lunatic, as usual, and had lost control and driven over the edge of the road and down a steep bank. This was on Friday. They didn't find his body until Sunday lunchtime.

On Monday morning, Sam and I went to his funeral together. We were both shell-shocked.

It was Robert who had brought us together, asking Sam to look after me for the weekend while he was away, and we had spent most of our time in those four days in each other's company. Now that Robert had died, I didn't know where I stood jobwise, so I flew back to England.

Sam drove me to the airport and saw me off. 'I'll see you next week,' he said.

Would he? I was amazed at his impulsiveness. Wow!

Back home in Northumberland, I met up with Richard and broke off our relationship. He didn't seem too surprised as we both knew we had been drifting apart for a while – we just hadn't got round to making a decision. We were both quite sad about it all because we had shared so much over the years and were still fond of each other, but the break was inevitable.

The following weekend, true to his word, Sam flew over and drove up to Northumberland to see me, and we started going out together properly. It was instantaneous. I was hooked.

We drove up to Embleton, my favourite place, because I wanted to show Sam where I'd spent so many happy times throughout my childhood. I took him to see the clubhouse and the bungalow, and we strolled across the links and along the top of the bank above the beach, chatting non-stop. Then we walked down the steps and along the sands. We had so much to talk about.

Suddenly he stopped and turned to face me. 'What you need is babies!'

After three months, I moved south to live with Sam in Kent. It sounds so simple, and in a way it was, but of course it was a huge decision to make. I had my own house and was teaching golf at the Gosforth Park Golf Centre. My mother was getting older and I helped her with some of her errands, and most of my friends lived in Northumberland. My whole life was in the north-east. Even though I'd spent so many years travelling the world, I always came back home, so it was an enormous step to move to the other end of the country. But I was so sure about our relationship that I knew I had to make the break.

I talked to my mother about it.

'You must be mad, Jen!' she exclaimed.

'But I love him, Mam. I know this is right for me.'

'Ee, I like Sam well enough.'

'And he thinks you're great . . . apart from supporting Newcastle!'

She laughed at that, but she wasn't happy about my plans, though she had become more tolerant in her old age. Inwardly I think she knew I was determined to go and that she couldn't stop me. I knew that what she was really worried about was my reputation, and what the neighbours would think, but of course I wouldn't be around any more, so I suppose she realized they wouldn't have anything to gossip about.

Sam and I went to see her before I moved.

'I'll take very good care of your Jen,' he assured her. 'And you'll always be welcome to come down and stay with us.'

'That would be nice.'

'And we'll come and see you whenever Sunderland are playing at home!'

'Well, I'll be watching Newcastle,' she retorted with a smile. There was a twinkle in her eyes whenever Sam was around. I was so relieved that they got on well, and that she had accepted our situation so quickly.

Sam and I couldn't get married as he was going through a divorce, but we didn't want to wait. I was elated when I found out I was pregnant at the age of thirty-eight. After all those barren years, I really would be a mother at last. But life can be cruel, and I lost the baby at seven weeks. I was distraught.

A few months later I became pregnant again, but I dared not be too excited, and sure enough I miscarried this one at eleven weeks. I swung from one extreme of emotion to the other. It was a very stressful time for us both.

Just as I was doubting, at forty, that I would ever have a full-term pregnancy, I came across an article in a magazine I idly picked up in my dentist's waiting room. As I leafed through it and came to this page, I felt a sharp jolt. I suppose you could call it fate. The article described new investigations under way at St Mary's Hospital in London, involving women who had suffered numerous miscarriages. They had found that in some partnerships, the male's antibodies worked against the foetus and made the woman abort.

As soon as I got home I called the hospital and asked if we could be included in their experimental treatment. They said it was normally only for women who'd had at least five miscarriages, but in view of my age, they agreed to include us.

I became pregnant again, and with the treatment at St Mary's I went the full nine months. Katie was born in December 1989, when I was forty-one. I was ecstatic. It was Christmas Eve, and she was the best Christmas present in the world. As I held this little bundle in my arms, her eyes gazing up at mine, it hit me like a bus that this was the first time since I was born that I'd ever touched or held someone who was my own flesh and blood. She was part of me – a family of my own. I wept buckets of happiness that day, and didn't stop crying for three months.

When Katie was just one month old we took her over to Tenerife. Sam had a house out there, as he was in charge of selling properties as an agent for Golf del Sur. He went over there quite a lot and I used to go with him to help him by playing golf with prospective clients. The idea was to have a holiday in the sun for a few weeks, and for me to have a good rest after the emergency Caesarean. Sam took over from his salesman for a while and carried on with selling the houses, and we both played some golf.

I couldn't believe it when we met John Jacobs, my old mentor and coach, 'Dr Golf', out on the course one day – one of my favourite people and someone I owed a lot of my golfing success to. He had recently bought one of Sam's properties from his salesman.

Sam saw me talking to him and came over to join us. He gave John a quizzical look. 'Don't I know you?'

'No, I don't think we've met.'

'Don't you play piano in a pub somewhere?' asked Sam.

John laughed and laughed about that. We all got on well together and met up with his wife Rita for lunch. I have a photo of her holding Katie. We bumped into a friend of Rita's who told me they had adopted their two children. That got us talking, but it was nothing like my story. They had told their children right from the start that they were adopted. She was shocked to hear of my experience, and sympathetic when I explained about tracing Mercia, only to be rejected for a second time without meeting her.

We stayed a couple of months in Tenerife then returned to England, and continued to go back and forth for a while. Two years after Katie, when I was forty-three, we had Ben. That meant Katie didn't have to be an only child, like me. At last I had the family I never believed I could have. I felt I was the luckiest woman in the world.

One afternoon, Sam called me from his car. 'I'm on my way back home. Can you book a babysitter for the evening and come and meet me at the Leather Bottle at seven o'clock?'

'Why?'

'I can't talk now. I'll tell you later.' Sam is a man who often does things on impulse, so I didn't think it strange. I just assumed he'd arranged for us to meet up with some friends at our favourite pub.

When I arrived at seven, he was already there on his own with a drink waiting for me. We sat together for a while, chatting about our day. Suddenly, he produced a ring-box from his pocket and opened it. 'I think we should get married.'

We'd already lived very happily together for seven years and had two beautiful children. I'd almost forgotten we weren't married!

I was so elated that I can't remember what I said. Probably just, 'Why not?'

It all sounds quite matter-of-fact, and that's the way we are, but we were both as excited about getting married as two twenty-somethings starting out.

We wanted to keep our wedding low-key, so we decided not to tell anybody about it because we didn't want to wait or have the complications of getting all our friends and relations down to Kent from all over the country. Sam arranged a registry office ceremony more than a hundred miles away in Bournemouth – a place he knew quite well. I arranged for our babysitter to move in for a day and a night while we were gone. We needed at least two witnesses at our wedding, so we asked Danny, Sam's son from his first marriage, and his girlfriend. Sam's mate Malcolm, who was the salesman at a Mercedes garage nearby, kindly allowed us to use his address, so we invited him to come along as another witness. They were all three sworn to secrecy. The only other person I told was my cousin Wendy. We have always been close and I couldn't bear to keep it from her, but I knew she would tell no one. She was thrilled for us and sent me a lucky silver horseshoe.

The wedding was a light-hearted affair on a beautiful sunny morning in April 1992. We both enjoyed the ceremony itself, though it seemed to go very quickly. However, I do remember how nervous I felt when I was signing the register – quite out of character for me.

'This is worse than teeing up on the last hole of the British Open!' I sighed. Everybody laughed and my tension vanished.

Malcolm had brought with him the tiny round paper clippings from his office hole-puncher to use as confetti, and it fell like new snow down the registry office steps.

Sam had organized a splendid feast and champagne for the five of us in a suite of rooms at the Carlton, a posh sea-front hotel. We had a great lunch and too much champagne. I must have fallen asleep as the next thing I knew it was six o'clock in the evening. I immediately phoned Connie.

'Hello, Mam. How are you?'

'Oh, I'm fine, pet. How are the bairns?'

'They're both full of fun, as usual.' I paused momentarily, then took a breath, ready to launch into my announcement. I knew it would be a shock for her, but I needed to make sure she found out straightaway from me. 'Mam, are you sitting down?'

'Yes.' She sounded perplexed. 'Why? What's happened? Nothing bad I hope?'

'Sam and I have just got married today.' I heard her gasp, but carried on. 'It was a secret wedding and we've had a lovely day.'

'Well it's about time, mind! But why didn't you tell me, Jen?' I could hear she was hurt not to have known. 'Don't you think you should have told me and let me in on the secret? I wouldn't have told anybody.'

'I know, Mam. But we just wanted to keep it quiet and tell everyone afterwards. You're the first person I've called.'

'Ee well, that's something, I suppose.'

I wanted to cheer her up and lighten the conversation, so I changed tack. 'You're a mother-in-law now!'

'Well, I knew it would happen one day, but I always hoped it would be a lot sooner than this. You've done it all the wrong way round.'

'Yes, I know, but at least I've got married at last.'

'Thank goodness. But why did you keep me waiting till you were forty-four years old, and not even invite me to your wedding?'

'You know why. And we didn't invite anybody.' That wasn't quite true, I know, but I had to reassure her. She said nothing, so I changed direction again. 'What's it like to have a son-in-law who's a Sunderland supporter?'

That made her laugh. 'I'll convert him yet, mind,' she said. 'You'll see.'

Married at last, we stayed overnight in our beautiful hotel suite and drove home to Katie and Ben the next morning. I couldn't stop smiling all the way home. We were legally a family now – husband, wife and two wonderful children. We were overjoyed that things had gone so well and our family was complete. But of course we had no idea what the coming year would bring.

CHAPTER 29

Helen

Holding On

We used to love our holiday visits to Florida as a family to visit George and Joan – the only time we could escape from my mother. Whatever the reason, Mercia didn't ever want to come, which was a great relief. We would relax happily in George and Joan's company and enjoy meeting their friends. Their two children had grown up and gone their own ways, with good careers and happy relationships, and George and Joan were enjoying their life of retirement in the 'Sunshine State', and the warmth and comforts they had earned through many hardships. Whenever I was there, the years fell away and it was as if I was back in those fields amongst the animals with George, or giggling with Joan as she taught me to put on make-up for the first time.

In 1995, Simon and I went for a visit on our own, as our kids were now grown up too. As soon as we got there my instincts kicked in – I knew there was a problem. We had dinner together that evening, but George didn't eat much. When he went to have a lie down between courses, I realized there was something seriously wrong. After the meal, when he went to lie down again, I made him a cup of tea and took it to him. He was sleeping lightly. When he saw it was me on my own, he sat up in bed to sip his tea.

'There's something wrong, isn't there?' I asked.

'Oh, it's nothing to worry about, just a little touch of cancer.'

'OK, George.' I tried not to show my dismay. 'I'm a nurse. Tell me about it.'

We talked for a long time as he explained some of what the doctors had said and what treatment he was having. He somehow managed to tell me all this without emotion. 'It's just a little touch of cancer,' he said again. But I could see how much weight he'd lost, his fatigue showed and there was a grey tinge to his complexion. I had a huge lump in my chest which felt as if it would burst.

'It's no big deal, pet,' he continued. 'I'm going to fight it.'

'Good for you, George. You can do it.'

I know he didn't want to upset or alarm me, but of course he did both. I was sick to my stomach with fear for him, though I tried not to show it.

Joan and Simon left us together. We talked, we reminisced and we hugged. I sat with him and held his hand until he fell asleep.

Later, I talked to Joan. She told me about his diagnosis, all the details. She hid nothing, and I was grateful for that. But, as I feared, it was the worst news. My half-brother, whom I'd always adored, the one person who had stood up for me as a child, was terminally ill. He had only weeks to live.

All the time we were on holiday, every day was a worry as George insisted on going everywhere with us, even on a long day's trip to Sea World. He couldn't disguise his fatigue and, barely able to walk, soon exhausted himself with the effort.

That night my brave brother said to me, 'I can't believe this kiddo. I thought I was invincible.'

The day we left Florida, I had a last chat with Joan. 'If you need anything, Joan, if you want to talk, or think I should come, I'll be on the next plane.'

She nodded as she choked back her tears, unable to speak as we hugged goodbye.

It was only a few short weeks later when the call came. 'George is very ill. Can you come?'

I was on the next flight.

From the moment I arrived, Joan and I between us spent every minute of the day and night with my beloved brother. He was desperately ill, on maximum medication for his pain, and suffering badly. We took turns to have short naps, but he always had one of us awake with him, ready to soothe and care for him.

One morning, after I'd had a bit of sleep, I walked into his bedroom to see his face contorted with pain. He was semi-delirious.

'Get out of here!' he screamed. 'Get out. I don't want you here. I don't want to see your face. It brings all the bad memories back.'

I ran from the room in tears. I knew it was not really him talking – it was the medication – but I was distraught.

Joan soothed him and stroked him, at the same time telling him off. 'You shouldn't speak to Helen like that. She has flown a long way to be here for you. She loves you dearly.'

I composed myself as well as I could, went back into the bedroom and walked over to George's side.

He looked up at me with tears in his eyes. 'I'm sorry, sweetheart.'

In spite of having the best care we could give him, George's condition deteriorated daily. At this point we arranged for some hospice nurses to come in to take on the bulk of his nursing care and give us a break. Overwrought with emotion, we needed to have some rest so that we could be there for him whenever he was awake. One afternoon, in between nurses, I sat with him, holding him while he cried with the pain.

I stroked his forehead with the slightest touch. 'George, if I could take your pain for just one day, I would.'

'I know.' His expression took on an eerie determination. 'Go and get my gun.'

'No, George. I can't do that.'

Defeated by everything, he slumped back and began to give up.

For his fifty-fifth birthday, three days before he died, his children, Barry and Ross, brought him a huge bunch of balloons. He loved them. We tied the whole bunch to the end of his bed so he could see them.

Over the next two days, Joan and I held vigil with him in the final stages of his illness. One of the nurses beckoned me out of the room at one point. I motioned to Joan to come and join us.

'The doctors are arranging to take him into hospital,' said the nurse. 'They want to put him on a ventilator to make his breathing easier, and they will put in an intravenous line to feed him.'

'Oh no,' gasped Joan. 'Can't he stay here? Let him die here.'

'Surely it will not prolong his life more than a few days, at most?' I added. 'He wants to die in his own home, to die with dignity.'

'I'll tell them when I go back. I'm not sure what they'll say.'

When the nurse had gone, we agreed to put this new threat out of our thoughts and focus our attention on George. Thankfully, we didn't need to worry about fighting with the medics. George died peacefully in his own bed that night, at midnight, just as a Florida storm swept in.

After a few minutes of weeping together, comforting each other, Joan and I took his balloons out onto the windswept verandah. We loosened the ribbon and released them. 'We're letting him go,' Joan shouted, against the noise of the storm.

Whipped away by the gale, we watched them as they rose, buffeted by the squalls, up into the night sky. We stood together, arm in arm, his wife and his 'kid sister', and gazed into the darkness until long after they had disappeared into the void. Then the winds changed direction and started blowing straight at us, so we turned and went back into the house.

Next morning, I woke early. All was quiet. The storm had passed and Joan was still asleep. Overcome with grief, I went out for a solitary walk around the garden in the sunshine. At first, deep in my own thoughts, I didn't really take in my surroundings . . . until I turned the corner of the house. There, in front of me, were George's balloons, all of them, their ribbons tangled round a shrub under his bedroom window; the bedroom where he had passed away just a few hours before. I bent down to pick them up, pulled the ribbons apart, walked onto the open lawn and let the balloons go again. I can't describe the lurch inside me when they hovered in front of my face, motionless. I pushed them away. Still they did not move.

I felt a tug on my arm and looked down. The ribbons had wrapped themselves several times around my forearm. It felt as if he was holding on. Then I saw that there was a plastic clip that held them together. Why hadn't I noticed this before? I loosened the clip and said, 'You have to go now, George. We are all OK.'

Was it my imagination? As I let them go they seemed to bob in the air as if nodding a goodbye to me. Slowly, silently, the balloons drifted away, one by one, into the wide blue sky. I watched until the last one disappeared from sight. My brother was gone.

I still have the clip that held those balloons. I shall never part with it.

When I went back into the house, Joan was just getting up. I turned the clip over and over in my hands.

'What's that?' she asked.

I told her what had happened. 'This is the clip that was holding the balloons. It stopped them from flying free.'

'There was something between you and George,' she said, giving me a quizzical look. 'Something that neither Simon nor I can penetrate. You two were *so* close.' She paused, tears running down her cheeks. 'You know, he was always protective of you. I think he came back for you. To check you would be all right.'

We wept together.

*

As I returned home to England and slipped back into my life with Simon, there was an empty space in my heart. George and I had, for much of our lives, lived on different continents, but he'd always been there for me and his love had always comforted me. Now I had no sisters or brothers to share my triumphs or my troubles with. My mother was a permanent fixture in the midst of my marriage and, despite having my family around me, I felt more alone than ever.

Forced to retire from my job with serious back problems, I was often at home now, but my mother still came every day and sat around in our living room, a cuckoo in our nest. No amount of hinting sank in. She chose not to hear. We were so oppressed by her perpetual presence that we often had to resort to our timeworn method and get in the car and go out for a drive, just to get away from her. When we arrived home again some hours later, she was always still there.

The damage was insidious over many years. The children grew up and left home, each to places of their own. By this time, Simon and I were like two old friends – a pair of worn-out slippers, faded and frayed. I was wrung out. There was nothing left any more. We just padded along, day after day.

With the children gone, we both began to realize we had been unhappy for a very long time. And once the realization hit, there didn't seem any point in pretending.

One evening I said, 'We can't continue like this. We're not doing each other any good.'

And that was the way it happened – a mutual decision. There was a lot of sadness and turmoil for both of us. Deep down, I was very emotional about it all, but I'd spent so many years not showing my emotions that I kept a calm front, as usual. I feel that maybe Simon was more reluctant than I was. I think it's sometimes more difficult for a man in his early fifties to start again. Women are more independent in that way. For him, it was a bit of a culture shock having to start looking after himself, but he didn't resist the split. And I knew it was the right thing to do.

After thirty-two years of marriage, we went through an amicable divorce. It is a wonder to me that we survived under such extreme pressures for so long. Scott and Donna were stunned. They were both unhappy about it, but by now Scott was thirty-one and Donna was twenty-eight – they had left home and had their own lives, which lessened the hurt. When I told my mother we were going to be divorced, however, she didn't take it well.

'How could you do this to me?' she ranted. 'You've brought shame on me.'

I could not speak to her for quite some time after that.

We put our house up for sale and began to plan our separate lives, uncertain what lay ahead.

CHAPTER 30

Jenny

The Illegal Immigrant

Just as everything settled down into a comfortable routine, with the children thriving, us newly married and our house fitted out, Sam began to feel restless. I understood how he felt. Here we were, blessed with our lovely home and family, while there were so many in less fortunate circumstances. Sam had a yearning to do something, to redress that balance. We talked about it, of course, and agreed that he should look around for a project to take on.

By chance, he met my gynaecologist. Sam knew that he had some charity involvement in Romania, teaching young doctors over there, so he broached the subject with him.

'I'd like to do some charity work, or help with a building project. Any ideas?'

'Sam, I've got just the thing for you.' He knew Sam had a construction company. 'I'm off to Romania next week. If you like, I'll put you in touch with some of the guys out there. Maybe you could refurbish a hospital or something like that.'

It was all agreed, and Sam went over to Romania to see what was needed. A charity worker picked him up from the airport and took him to a town called Brasov, where there was a dilapidated building with barred windows, crumbling plaster and virtually no plumbing. This place had been ignored by the authorities for longer than anyone knew. It was in fact an institution for the incarceration of innocent children who had been abandoned there, often with a minor illness, and forgotten. They were living out their childhoods in the most appalling conditions. Most of the staff were unskilled locals, on minimal wages, often not paid at all.

Sam phoned me that first evening in tears. I'd never seen him cry, and to hear him sob as he spoke, unable to hug him, was heart-wrenching. He tried to tell me about what he had seen in the hospital.

'It's unbelievable,' he began. 'As parents of young children . . . just to see these kids, you can't believe how upsetting it is. They have nothing. No medicines, no toys, no attention, no facilities, no hope. They are all in an awful state.

'They are two or three to an iron cot, up to three years old. Not walking or standing, just rocking backwards and forwards, all day long.' He paused. 'I've got to help them. We could do so much here. Renovate the building, do the place up, put in hot water and everything. We could beg toys and games, clothes and furnishings to take over . . .'

By now, tears were falling down my cheeks, tears of sorrow and tears of guilt. Our beloved children had everything, and the children at Brasov had nothing. Above all, it seemed they had no love.

'When I get back home,' he continued, ' I'll ring round all my suppliers and get them to donate the things we need – the paints, shower-trays, plumbing, electric cables, light-fittings, tools, everything. We'll have to try and get hold of the right medicines too.'

And that's what he did. When he told the story of what he had seen, everyone wanted to help. He filled the first lorry with £100,000 worth of donated goods and equipment and drove it over there, at our expense. Even our own daughter, Katie, donated her tricycle to give to a child in the Brasov hospital. We helped her to load it onto the lorry herself, along with other toys donated by friends.

Of course I wanted to go with Sam this time; I needed to support him and to see for myself, so I arranged care for the children and we flew out together. A charity worker met us at the airport and drove us to Brasov just in time to see our lorry arrive.

There were several more trips over the following months, but this was the visit that changed our lives.

When we arrived, Sam took me straight into the hospital. My eyes took a moment to adjust from the sudden contrast of the bright April sunlight to the dark interior, but then I began to notice the condensation running down the walls and the worst stench you can imagine. I shuddered. I can still smell it now – it will never leave me when I think of that place. I fought to control the nausea that welled up inside.

As my eyes accustomed to the gloom, I began to see the squalor all around. Even though I knew from Sam what to expect, I could not have been prepared for this – the echoing wails of neglected babies, the filth and degradation everywhere. Cockroaches ran across the floor, around our feet, in the babies' cots, crowding the kitchens and bathrooms. There were five hundred patients in the hospital, but only six bathrooms and six toilets. All of these were beyond cleaning.

As I went into the rooms where the youngest children were kept, I could see their stained faces, hollow from lack of nourishment, their legs skinny from lack of muscle. As Sam had described, their eyes were empty. A rare carer sped in and out again as quickly as possible, with no eye contact, not showing any care or compassion. Certainly no love. The toddlers, who had no stimulation and were unable to bond with an adult, swayed rhythmically in a trance, just as Sam had described.

I looked at these destitute infants and thought of my own two healthy children at home. Suddenly overcome with it all, I ran through the hallway and out into the clean air and sunshine, where I sat on the kerb and sobbed. I couldn't stop. I couldn't speak – just cried and cried. It was all so unfair, so unthinkable that children should be left to suffer like this, day after day, year after year. I was overwhelmed with the knowledge that whatever we did, we couldn't help them all. This was just one place. There must be loads of others like it.

Sam came out to find me. 'What is it?' he asked, stating the obvious. 'Are you upset?'

'Yes, I am. I just can't handle it. I think of Katie and Ben at home and everything they have, a comfortable home, the love of two parents, warmth and food, toys, everything.'

I walked around outside for a while to try and compose myself in the fresh air.

Finally, I went back to the hospital entrance. Sam wanted me to come and be with him because he'd been so upset himself the first time he came. I had to steel myself to go back inside. When I found him he was talking with a young doctor, who spoke good English.

'Look, Sam,' the doctor said. 'You've got children of your own. Maybe you could help us. We have a baby here who has just been left with us, abandoned in the hospital. He's a healthy baby, tiny but perfect.' He studied Sam's face, turned to look at me, then back at Sam. 'If he stays here, you know how it will be for him. He needs a good home. Can you help?'

Shocked, we looked at each other. We had gone on this trip to bring them some of the things they needed, to plan the renovation of the building for them. Suddenly we were faced with the impossible challenge of rescuing a baby and taking him back to England. How difficult would that be, and were we up to it? What about our own children – how would they react? We weren't sure it would even be legal. So many thoughts crowded into our minds at the same time. We should have told them we needed time to consider the situation, but before we knew it, a nurse brought this tiny baby into the doctor's room, wrapped only in a bit of grey rag, with no nappy. She put him down on a table in front of us and opened out the rag so that we could see him in his nakedness. I was afraid for him, stunned, unsure how we were supposed to react. Then of course it struck me that they wanted us to see he was a perfect baby. Instinctively I nodded, at which point the nurse lifted up his bits, as if to say 'he's all there'. She looked from Sam to me and back to Sam with a questioning look, and I could almost hear her pleading prayer for us to rescue this innocent baby from his hopeless fate.

The baby was only a few days old, with dark blond hair and a thin, wrinkled body. Goodness knows what they were feeding him, but it didn't seem to be doing him much good. As I looked down at his pinched little face, he lay quite still with a steadfast gaze, his eyes fixed on mine. At first I did not dare lose that precious eye contact with him, perhaps the first he'd had with anyone, but after several seconds I couldn't hold it any longer as my eyes welled up. I turned to Sam and he put his arm round me, barely holding back the tears himself.

'Well, do you want him?' asked the doctor.

The tears were now running down my cheeks.

Sam looked at me. He paused for a minute or two, perhaps not even that long. Then I heard him speak. 'Don't worry. We'll get him back to England somehow.'

Sam, always the optimist, could not refuse. I wasn't sure whether he was speaking to the doctor or to me, but I nodded. I knew he was going to say yes. I wanted him to say yes. It was a joint decision. Sam's positive attitude to getting things done in any situation was one of the things that had first attracted me to him He was right about one thing –we could give this baby a wonderful life. But even in that moment I knew it was going to be a desperately difficult task to get him out of the country, across Europe and back home with us. Was it even possible?

Later that day, Sam phoned a British immigration lawyer. She advised us to drug the newborn baby and bundle him into the boot of a car to smuggle him out of the country. We were horrified by that idea and immediately said no. There must be a better way.

That was the start of the process. We didn't have any idea how complex it would be to foster and adopt a Romanian child in England.

The next day, the baby's mother suddenly reappeared, together with her mother and uncle. We assumed the doctor had traced her to her poor, rural home many kilometres away. Perhaps he'd arranged transport for her to come back and sign the papers. We met her and the doctor translated for us as we heard some of her story. She was nineteen and had been sent away from home to have the baby. Her brother had been stoned in their village because of the disgrace she had brought on the family. Villagers told her parents that she would be killed if she returned with the baby.

I was shocked and devastated hearing all this. It seemed such a primitive reaction from her neighbours – a terrible situation for her and her family. She had no option but to give her baby away and signed to say she wanted us to adopt him. The doctor had told her the baby would have a good life with us, but she seemed devoid of emotion as she signed the papers. I was stunned that she was signing away the life of her child yet showing no sadness or regret, though of course I could not imagine what she was really feeling. It was only when she left that she turned to give us a slight smile.

I thought then of my own adoption and how my mother must have felt. Was it a similar situation, being forced to give me away, and had Mercia hidden her feelings too? Would I ever know?

When we got home, Sam and I agreed that I should call Kent Social Services to start the process of getting our baby over to England legally.

They said very clearly that they could not help us because we did not meet their requirements as adoptive parents.

'We have three initial requirements, Mrs Lucas, and I'm afraid you fail to meet any of them. You have not been married long enough, you are too old and you already have two children of your own.'

Well, that was that. I told Sam what she had said.

'Right.' He refused to be put off. 'Then we'll have to do this another way.'

Sam rang up a friend in Bucharest who worked for a charity out there and had some experience of this sort of situation. She said the only way would be if the baby's mother brought him into the country herself and handed him over to us personally.

'Could you go ahead and organize that?' asked Sam.

'Yes, I think so,' she said. 'And I'll bring them over myself, so that I can explain things to the mother and do any necessary translating.'

So she got visas, booked flight tickets and made all the arrangements for the trip.

In July, ten weeks later, we went to Stansted airport, hoping to collect our Romanian baby. We'd kept it quiet and not told anyone, even the family, in case there was a hitch, which seemed quite likely.

We had arranged to meet in the airport car park, so we arrived early and waited anxiously as the minutes crept by. Just as we began to think they wouldn't be allowed through immigration, or there would be some other problem, our faces lit up as we saw them appear – our baby's birth mother, Gabriela, holding him in her arms and walking towards us, accompanied by the charity worker. To our great relief, it had all gone as planned. They had come through immigration with no questions asked.

As they walked towards us, I looked at Gabriela and was disturbed to see the complete lack of expression in her face, her eyes blank and her mouth set straight. Perhaps this journey, with the child she was giving up, had left her numb with pain. As I looked into her glazed eyes my thoughts once again leapt back to the day that Mercia handed me over for adoption. Did she have the same empty gaze, the same disinterested demeanour? Did she care as little as this woman seemed to do? How could anyone manage not to show emotion on what must be the most heart-rending day of their life?

As they were turning to go, I stopped them.

'Would you like us to send photos of him on birthdays and Christmases?'

The charity worked smiled and translated.

'No,' said Gabriela in English. But she did not thank me for thinking of it, and there were still no tears, no smile, no anything. She just turned her back and walked away. I felt dreadful for her. Surely she must be hurting so much inside.

Once we had recovered from the anxiety of waiting and not knowing whether he would be there, which was quickly followed by the euphoria of having our baby in our arms at last, our overwhelming concern was that the flight hadn't upset him and he would be able to adjust to his new surroundings. I couldn't wait to get him home, to be the best mother I could be to this little waif and surround him with all the love he needed.

That day, when Josh joined our family, we were all elated. When we got him back home that evening, the thing he needed most was a nappy-change. It was late at night, ten-thirty, when I unwrapped the little bundle and took off that first, awful nappy that he'd worn all day on the journey.

As I ran water into the baby bath, I heard footsteps along the landing. Katie, now three and a half, had woken up and heard the sounds, so came to investigate. We had told her about Josh coming to join us one day soon and she had been thrilled, but she had no idea it was going to be that night. She came into the bathroom and her bleary face immediately lit up when she saw him.

'My *own* baby!' she exclaimed. 'Mummy. He can be my own baby. I can look after him myself.'

'Not quite yourself,' I smiled. 'He will be our baby, your baby brother, and you can help me look after him.'

Katie doted on Josh from that first night on. We bathed him together, washing him all over at least three times to rid him of the smells and grime from that place. Then we laid him on the floor, covered him with sweet-smelling talc and wrapped him in our fluffiest towel for hugs. Now Josh was ours. A member of the Lucas family. We bonded immediately. For some reason I had a ready affinity with him, perhaps because I'd been adopted as a baby, just like him. I was determined to make sure he would always know his background and what happened.

'This child is going to grow up knowing he's adopted, and where he came from,' I said to Sam.

From that moment onwards, I started to compile a book for Josh. The story of his life. It would be his book, starting with a photo of his mother we'd taken when we met her at Brasov, then pictures of him at various stages throughout his childhood, right up to now. He looks at the book from time to time and shows it to his friends. I'm so glad we did it.

Sam continued to make regular trips to renovate the hospital in Romania, one week every month for the next year or so. It was hard on me with three children under five to look after, but it was much more difficult for Sam. He worked hard and provided so much for that hospital. It was depressing for him to find each time he returned that the low-paid staff had spirited away most of the toys for their own children and sold the drugs and electronic equipment to fill their food cupboards. We couldn't blame them. They had to live with poverty every day of their lives, struggling to feed their children and survive somehow.

About six months after Josh joined us, there was thick snow on the ground. Sam's children from his previous marriage were with us and were having a great time in the garden helping Katie and Ben to build a giant snowman. I put Josh in his bouncer in the kitchen doorway. Sam watched him as I went upstairs to get something and I heard the doorbell. Moments later Sam shouted up to me.

'Come on down, Jenny. There are some people in the kitchen I want you to meet.'

I went down to find two strangers in our kitchen with Sam. There was an air of menace about their visit.

'This gentleman is a senior Kent police officer, and this lady here is from Social Services.'

'Hello,' I said, shaking their hands in great trepidation. 'Can we help you?'

'Oh yes,' nodded the Social Services lady. 'We believe that you have an illegal immigrant living in this house.'

'Really?' I said, trying to keep my voice light, but I was quaking inside, petrified. It was all such a complicated process, and it still wasn't complete – I knew we had to register Josh with the courts and we hadn't done that yet. What if they had come to take him away from us? I looked at Sam, who must have been thinking the same as me, but he hid it well.

'Yes.' Sam smiled. I knew it was a nervous smile, but they couldn't have realized. 'That's him over there!' He pointed at ten-month-old Josh, bouncing with glee in the doorway.

I watched, anxious to see their response, but I began to relax as I saw their expressions change from officious to confused to embarrassed. It had been a tense few minutes, but by this time Sam didn't look worried at all. He was trying to keep his face straight. We explained Josh's circumstances. Our visitors made their hurried excuses and apologies, then left. What a relief! We laughed for a good ten minutes after they'd gone.

'How did they know?' I wondered aloud. 'Somebody must have told them about Josh, but who?'

'I think I know,' said Sam. 'I had to sack one of the men last week for stealing. He might have phoned up the council to get his own back on me.'

'Well, thankfully it misfired.'

We told Josh, years later, that when he was a baby he had nearly been arrested as an 'illegal immigrant'.

At this stage, we still had little idea of the mass of work we would have to do with Social Services, the Health Service and immigration, not to mention the various legal stages, culminating in the High Court. But finally, after three years, everything had been done and the High Court Judge agreed the adoption, so he became legally ours at last, though from day one he had been at the heart of our family and brought joy to us all.

*

In these glorious years with the children, my days were full and I had little time to think of anything else. But that visit to Mercia's sister, and the phone call, sat heavily at the back of my mind and in my heart. Now that I had adopted an abandoned child myself, I had experience from both sides.

Distressing as it had been to be rejected a second time by my birth mother, I was desperate to know more. And what about my half-siblings? Could I try and trace them? I went over and over it, but my mother Connie was still alive and I didn't want to hurt her. She had been over the moon when we'd told her about the new addition to the family and when Josh was about three-and-a-half she came to live with us in Kent so she could be with the family. She had her own little annexe, but always ate her meals with us. She and Sam got on like old friends, continually bantering about the merits of their favourite football clubs or the escapades of their players. Connie loved him like her own son.

As she aged, Connie became increasingly frail and began to have memory problems, though she still knew me and remembered much from my childhood and her early life. Her deterioration was very gradual. As the three children were young and lively, they took up nearly all my time, so I knew my birth-family research would have to wait a little longer. I would return to it as soon as I could, determined to follow it through and try to find my half-sister and half-brother, wherever they were.

CHAPTER 31

Jenny

Finding Mercia

For some time we had been planning a family move to Florida, so we all went over with Connie for three months one winter and tried it out. We had a great time and loved the lifestyle, which convinced us to make the move over there for a couple of years. So we signed the contract to rent out our home, booked our flights and began making all the arrangements for our move nine months later.

During this time, Connie had a series of mini-strokes. It all happened very quickly and her health deteriorated so fast that it became clear she needed full-time care. With three young children, the school runs and everything else, I just couldn't look after her round the clock, as she needed, so when the doctor offered respite care for her, we accepted it.

Ill though she was, my mother was still aware enough to hate losing her independence, and I didn't blame her for being crotchety about it. Sadly, the strokes increased in both frequency and severity. Meanwhile, our Florida plans were finalized for December that year, 1998. We had planned to take Connie with us, but of course now we couldn't.

I tried to visit her every day, but soon she no longer recognized me. Every visit was heart-rending. My occasional tears of frustration, and I suppose grief for the person she had been, confused her even more.

Her care home was in Surrey, a long drive away from Edenbridge, but it was the best place we could find. When they took her in, they said she could last two years, or three weeks. The weekend before we left, Connie had a massive stroke.

'I'm afraid your mother may not last the weekend,' said the matron in a gentle voice that Saturday morning.

'Oh no. We're due to move to Florida on the Monday flight,' I gulped. 'She was meant to be coming with us, but now of course . . .' A tear ran down my cheek as I tried to come to terms with this awful situation.

'Your mother is in and out of consciousness, so I don't think she will be aware of anything much now. But she is comfortable, and not in any pain.' I realized the matron was trying to be kind, but I was in a turmoil with so much to think about combined with the guilt that my mother was so ill and I wasn't there with her the whole time, and the added thought that I might have to leave her like this.

Sam went straight up to see her that afternoon.

'I sat with her, Jen. She was asleep most of the time and looked very peaceful. She did wake for a few moments, but didn't seem to be aware who I was,' he said. 'I think you need to go and see her yourself. She might recognize you.'

So we went up together the next day, the day before our flight. I knew it would be the last time I saw my mother. She was semi-conscious, but she didn't seem to know who I was. I held her hand and kissed her. I didn't want to leave her, but I knew I had to go, for the children and for Sam. I cried all the long drive home.

The next day, I wept all the way to Florida. My mother died just six days later. The dreadful thing was that I couldn't even go back to England to arrange the funeral as the US passport office were updating our visas. I didn't get my passport back till January.

Thankfully, my dear cousin Wendy organized it all for me. All except the flowers, which Sam ordered from Florida while I was on my way back to the UK. On the day of the funeral, I was in quite a state, but I tried hard not to show it; to be positive about celebrating her life. That was what she would have wanted. Of course, I would have loved Sam and the children to be there with me, but it wasn't possible.

Wendy, her husband Edd and I took our places at the crematorium with relatives and friends. The music started as the coffin came in with our flowers on top. There were three arrangements, one each from me and the children, and a ridiculous big thing, like a football, made of red and white flowers. Well of course I knew straightaway what that was about. I smiled through my tears. Sunderland, Sam's team, wore red and white, whereas Mam's team Newcastle was black and white. I knew that if Mum was looking over us, she would really appreciate that, because Sam had had the last laugh.

I called Sam that evening to tell him about the funeral.

'Did the flowers arrive OK?' he asked.

'They certainly did. I wish Mam could have seen them herself. But you wait – I'll have the last laugh on you when you go!'

It was the end of an era with both my parents gone. A

time of vivid memories and sad tears, thinking back over all those happy childhood years and all the love they had poured onto me, all the opportunities they had provided, marred only by the chance discovery of my adoption dropping like a stone into my teenage years – a revelation that affected my life more than my mother could ever have realized. I've never held grudges, but I had not yet erased my resentment of my parents' secrecy and the way I found out. Now, at last, I could stop pretending. I could come out with my need to uncover the truth. This was my time to start the search in earnest for my birth family.

Sam and the children were glad to have me back after the funeral and I soon picked up all the usual routines – the school runs, walking the dogs, games of golf, time out on the boat. My visa didn't allow me to teach golf, but I could play it as much as I liked. We lived next door but one to Monica Seles and became good friends. This was when she was still playing major tournaments all over the world and still winning the occasional trophy, though her best years as a singles champion and world number one had been curtailed when she was stabbed on court by a deranged spectator during a match in 1993. Monica's mother and I sometimes used to walk our dogs together and chatted a lot.

Our lives in Florida were full of sunshine and fun. We went for two years and we stayed for seven. Sam built some beautiful houses out there, and the children soon settled into their schools, made good friends and enjoyed the many outdoor activities. Sam flew back and forth to make sure the business was going well back in England, and often timed his visits to watch Sunderland play.

I kept in touch with my cousin Wendy with visits each

way and frequent phone calls. Sometimes we talked about the way Mercia had rejected me when I went looking for her, and the two siblings whose names I didn't know. At that distance, it seemed difficult for me to do much in the way of research. I tried to find Mercia's address on the internet, but with no luck.

'Look,' Wendy suggested on the phone one day. 'If you really want to give it another try, would you like me to see if I can find anything out for you? There's a new adoption charity in the city, mind. They might have some useful suggestions.'

'Could you? That would be great.'

I didn't expect to hear anything further about it for a while, but she rang up again the next day.

'I called them first thing this morning and they suggested I put an ad in the paper, in the *Evening Chronicle*. I emailed it in to them today.'

'What did it say?'

'"Trying to find the family of Mercia Dick" and my phone number.'

A few days later I could wait no longer so I called Wendy. 'Did you have any replies?'

'None at all, I'm afraid.'

'Really? I wonder why not.' The disappointment was like a punch to my stomach.

'Perhaps she has remarried.'

Of course, we later found out that that was true when Wendy went to look through the births, marriages and deaths at Newcastle Civic Centre. After a long search, she found Mercia's marriage in 1951 to Aaron Thomas Lumsden.

'So she's been known as Mercia Lumsden ever since

then. No wonder we didn't get anywhere looking for Mercia Dick.'

A few days later, with lots of encouragement from me, Wendy went back to check the electoral rolls for Mercia Lumsden. She called me that evening.

'I've found Mercia's address in Whitley Bay,' she said. 'I'll email it to you.'

I pondered over this for a couple of days. Finally I decided to write to her. I wrote what I thought was a sensitive letter, telling her I had a great life and a lovely family. I wrote it out a couple of times to get it just right. Then I mailed it and waited to hear from her. Weeks went by. No reply came. So I wrote another friendly letter, quite brief, to follow the first.

This time I did receive a letter back from her. I didn't recognize the writing, of course, but the fact that it was post-marked Whitley Bay told me it must come from her. I held it in my hands for a few seconds and studied the handwritten address, looking for clues. Would this be the letter I had so long yearned for? I tore open the envelope and found one single folded sheet of thin paper. Before I even unfolded it I could see there were only a few short lines of writing on it and my optimism fell away.

I don't have that letter any more. But I remember the words, brief and to the point:

'Stop bothering an old lady in ill health. Just get on with your life.'

I shed a few tears that day; tears initially of frustration more than anything, then shock and anger. This was my third rejection. Wendy and Edd were staying with us in Florida the day Mercia's letter arrived, and I remember crying on Wendy's shoulder as she hugged and consoled me.

'How can she do this to me?' I sobbed. 'What have I ever done to her?'

'Nothing,' she said, holding me. 'Nothing that you could help, anyway. She must be a very mixed-up old lady. Maybe she still feels too hurt by her own past to come to terms with it.' Wendy always knew the right thing to say. But just now I felt too hurt myself to think about Mercia's feelings.

I don't know why I'd set myself up for this. I didn't want anything from her, but had hoped she would show me a little compassion. Instead her letter was cold and hurtful. I'd gone through so much, and rejection wasn't any easier the third time round. I'd tried hard to find her, to follow her trail, and now that I'd tracked her down at last, it didn't seem fair. I was indignant, not just for me but also because my children were her grandchildren and she didn't want to know. I was drained and totally crushed.

A couple of years later, in 2003, Wendy and Edd's daughter was about to get married, and of course we were all invited to the wedding. Sam had the trip organized like a route march. We had a few days in Kent to see all the southern family, then we shot up north to have Katie's bridesmaid dress fitted. While this was going on, we spent a few relaxing days in Bamburgh and Embleton near the coast.

I felt so refreshed, coming from Florida's suffocating humidity to stand in the bracing North Sea breeze as we walked over the sand dunes and across my beloved third green to the bungalow, which we still owned, then down to the beach. We paddled across the ebbing stream, splashing each other and laughing, to stand on the Emblestones as I had done all those decades before. This was my place, my heaven. I thought of my dad, those little golf clubs he'd made me and our companionable days together on the course. I remembered my mam and how hard she had worked for us to keep the bungalow all those years after Dad died. I had been well blessed in my childhood and I silently thanked them both as I watched my own children, young teenagers now, breathe in that salty sea air, serenaded by the seagulls as they soared overhead.

I had a plan in my mind to visit Mercia. I had her address. I knew she had made it clear in her letter that she wanted no further contact with me, and I should have respected that, but I couldn't. It was an urge almost beyond my control. I've always been annoyingly optimistic and determined. This time it wasn't to win a trophy – it was much more important than that. I needed to find peace of mind. When I told Sam my idea, he agreed.

'But I'm not sure what we should do when we get there,' I said. 'I'd like her to see the children and for them to see her. After all, she's their true grandmother. Surely she won't be able to turn her grandchildren away?'

'Don't worry. We're going to do something about it, even if I get the door shut in my face!'

I felt wary but hopeful. Sam can sell a fridge to an Eskimo. I was confident we were not going to have the door shut in our faces. I was adamant that I would succeed this time.

Friday 1 August 2003 will stick in my mind for ever. It was the day before the wedding and the sun shone down on us as we five stood outside her house, Sam in the front, me crouched behind him and the children in line behind us. We must have looked ridiculous!

Sam strode over and knocked on the front door. Three sharp knocks. I felt apprehensive, almost a sense of foreboding, as I steeled myself for a fourth rejection. And more importantly, a potential rejection for the children. It was a risky strategy. But I had faith in Sam.

The moments slowed into a freeze-frame as I waited an age to see what would happen next. I wanted to speak to this person I had so many questions for. I didn't feel anger at that moment. She was my mother and I wanted to be re-united with her at last.

I observed a lot in those few frozen seconds before she answered the door. Mercia lived in what looked like an assisted-living flat, with a front door onto the street. It was in a red-brick building, newer than the terraced houses that surrounded it, in quite an old-fashioned area.

I clicked back into normal time as the door began to edge open.

Sam put out his hand. 'Hello, Mercia. I haven't seen you for a long time.'

'Really?' she said, and shook his hand. This little old lady, with a quizzical look, stood in her doorway, plumpish, in a white top and a patterned skirt, with grey hair and glasses. She was a little stooped but moved easily as she stepped forward to take a good look at Sam. She was obviously perplexed, uncertain, but not unwelcoming. I don't know if she was what I expected her to be, and of course she was so much older than her photo.

'Yes, it's been ages, hasn't it?' continued Sam. He has a

way of keeping situations like this going. It was interesting to watch.

'Aye, I suppose so,' she agreed, still uncertain.

I breathed a sigh of relief that at least she hadn't slammed the door in his face, but of course she didn't know who we were yet.

'There is someone here who wants to meet you.' Sam turned and beckoned me forward. 'Jennifer.'

It was like a shutter on a camera. Suddenly she was all smiles, her arms outstretched. She knew who I was. That was the moment I knew it was going to be fine.

She took me in her arms, hugged me and kissed me.

'Ee, I'm sorry,' she said. 'I'm so sorry. So sorry I gave you away.' She kept repeating it. 'You must understand how hard it was. You have to forgive me.'

I was astonished at this reception after those previous rejections, but I didn't dwell on that, just took her at face value now. She accepted me that day. It was all that mattered.

'There's no need for an apology,' I said.

'But I am so sorry.'

'Please don't keep saying sorry. And you don't have to ask for forgiveness. I understand. It's all right. I've had a happy life – great parents, a lovely marriage and three wonderful children.'

As she gave me another warm hug, the relief and joy after all those years flooded through me. I was stunned by the turnaround.

'Well, come in,' she said, with a furtive look around to see if anyone was watching. 'Come inside.' She almost pulled us in and hugged us all in turn, then back to me again. It was as if she couldn't quite believe I was there, and I felt the same. After fifty-five years, we were finally reunited and I couldn't believe it was real.

I was on a roller coaster that afternoon – my emotions were up and down all over the place. We couldn't stop looking at each other, Mercia and I. How strange to write that phrase, Mercia and I. And I shed a lot of tears, but there wasn't a single tear from Mercia, and although she was welcoming, she seemed very apprehensive about something and kept looking at her watch.

There were so many questions, so much I wanted to find out, but when I began to ask, she was reticent to give anything away. 'There's something I really want to know,' I started.

'You can't stay long,' she interrupted with an anxious look. 'But here, sit down and look at these photos.' She got down all the family photos on display and told me who they were. 'This is ma husband, Tommy, who died in South Africa. And this photo is of my two bairns when they were young and we lived in Seghill.'

'I was born before you married Tommy, wasn't I?'

'Aye, that's right.' She looked uncomfortable that I had raised this subject and wary of what else I might say. I noticed that her hands were fidgeting together.

'So who—'

'Shhh.' She stood up and listened, then sat down again. 'I thought that was someone at the door.'

I wanted so much to know who my father was, but I realized she didn't want to tell me. She seemed almost scared. I couldn't press it, as I was afraid of turning her against me once more. I sensed the whole scenario was fragile, so I trod carefully.

Mercia's television had been on when we arrived and of

course she'd switched it off, so I asked her what she liked to watch.

'Ee, there's not much on in the day, unless there's some tennis or golf. I like watching the golf – that's my favourite.'

'Did you know that Jenny was a champion golfer?' asked Sam.

'No . . .' She looked perplexed.

'Yes, you've probably seen her on the TV, a few years ago. She played at all the major championships, mostly in America.'

'Did she now?' Her expression changed to one akin to pride. 'Well, I probably might have seen her then.'

Sam kept the conversation going with his bright banter as she showed us photos of her two grandchildren, my children's cousins. She gave no names and I wanted to ask more, but I didn't dare. Sam kept things light-hearted with his jokes, so I was crying and laughing by turns, and Mercia enjoyed the banter too, but I sensed her increasing uneasiness. She was on edge about something, and soon we discovered what it was.

'My daughter Helen is staying here at the moment. She's a nurse at the Nuffield hospital. She may come home at any moment. Please don't say who you are,' Mercia pleaded. 'She doesn't know anything about you.'

'No,' I promised. 'We won't say anything.'

It was a strange meeting, and a situation that seemed almost unreal. At times I felt somehow detached from it all, as if looking down from above. Here was the woman who had given birth to me, and probably held me in those first precious moments of my life, yet I didn't know her. I felt dizzy with all the new names I'd heard, and the photo faces seemed to blur together as Mercia talked on about all these people who were my relations that I didn't have a clue about.

She looked happy to meet her grandchildren, and we took photos of all of us with her. I still have those photos. A couple of years later, I learned that the jeans draped to dry over Mercia's radiator in the background of one of the photos were Helen's jeans.

'Helen will be on her way home. Please go before she comes,' she told us three or four times, very restless. We kept trying to reassure her, but eventually we felt she'd had enough and it was time to go. So one last hug and I walked away from my birth mother with very few answers, but at least we had met and made up, I thought.

We left with no sign of Helen, but her name was engraved on my brain. I should have been elated, but instead I felt drained, with a distinct sense that I'd been short-changed and that Mercia had got the better of me.

'What did you think of her?' I asked Sam as we were driving away from Mercia's house. He always tries to lighten any emotional situation by making a joke of some kind, so I should have known not to bother asking him for a serious answer.

Sam turned to me with his head to one side. 'Now I know what you'll look like when you're eighty-four!'

When I got back home, I remembered what Mercia had said about Helen being a theatre nurse at the Nuffield and I rang them to help me trace her, but of course they couldn't, because the name I gave was Helen Lumsden. I knew nothing about Helen. She had probably married, and, if so, I didn't know her full name. I'd had several operations at the Nuffield myself over the years, so it was quite a coincidence and I wondered if perhaps we'd met, though when I thought a bit more about it I realized there must have been hundreds of nurses working there, so it would have been a real long shot. I had to accept I'd hit a dead-end.

CHAPTER 32

Helen

The Time Machine

After the divorce, it took me some time to adjust. I had never lived alone before and, at the age of fifty-two I felt a strange mixture of apprehension and anticipation. I was excited to be mistress of my own destiny, but where did I go from here? What would my future hold?

Simon and I sold our family home, and I took a flat high up in a Victorian building on the seafront at Tynemouth with a wonderful seascape view. I loved my new flat and my freedom there. I ate my breakfast by the bay window, with its wide, open outlook, and as I watched the early sun cast its light across the bay, it filled me with optimism for my new life.

Forced to give up nursing because of my back, I had trained and qualified as a hypnotherapist and psychotherapist. As part of the training, I had to be counselled myself, which I felt very wary of. I didn't know how I would take it, with my background, since I usually preferred not to mull over the past.

Throughout the sessions I was told I seemed a pretty capable person who coped very well with things. In one way

I was surprised – but I was also relieved. I knew my determination and positive attitude had always helped me through, and I was well aware that everyone has issues in their life, so I knew I wasn't the only one in the world with problems. I found it difficult at first to talk about the things that had happened, but it felt easier, somehow, with a stranger. I've never talked about my childhood much with my children. That's different, isn't it? I wouldn't want to upset them.

I took up my new career as a therapist over the next two years and found it very rewarding to see people getting better when I helped them to recognize their psychological difficulties.

After George died, his widow Joan was so lonely that she went to live in Fort Worth, Texas to be near her children and their families. We had always been close, and we were especially so now. I went over to visit her whenever I could.

On one visit to see Joan, I met Dennis. He was a Vietnam war veteran, badly affected both physically and mentally by his experiences in Vietnam, and he'd been awarded an honourable discharge. Once he was a civilian again, he spent twenty years working as an educational diagnostician with special needs children, during which time he continued to battle with his own post-traumatic stress disorder. He had finally come out of that tunnel just before we met. We got to know one another and our friendship quickly developed into a relationship, which over the course of a few months blossomed into marriage. We didn't see the point in waiting around for life to pass us by.

While preparing to go and live in America, I talked with

the children quite a lot. I think the idea of my moving over there was hard for them at first, although they were very supportive at the time. I felt guilty that first their parents had divorced, and now their mam was going to live in a different country. It was a difficult thing to do, to leave them behind like that, but I knew they were both secure in their own lives, in their relationships and their own homes.

I said to them both, 'Pick up the phone and I'll be back on the next flight.'

Scott nodded and Donna, being very stubborn at the time, said, 'Well, I can't imagine anything that we would need you for!'

Finally I broke the news to my mother, prepared to counter her pleading and recriminations. But her response was very strange and against all my expectations.

'How exciting,' she smiled. 'That will be a lovely move for you. Just what you need – a new start. When are you going? I bet you can't wait.'

This knocked me off balance. I didn't know how to take it. I found myself almost resentful, wondering if she actually wanted me out of the way for some reason. I couldn't believe it would be this easy, but it was.

So it was all arranged. This was my break. Here, finally, was the opportunity to have a new life of my own, unsullied by my mother's presence.

I moved over to Texas, where we built a beautiful house on a golf course and I opened an antique shop, a growing interest of ours. I enjoyed my work and had a happy marriage. This was a good life.

By now my mother had been moved into a purpose-built ground-floor flat in a modern building in Whitley Bay, with her own front door opening onto the street. I remember her amusement when she first realized she now lived on the site where the laundry had been, where she had injured her leg all those years before.

I think she felt more independent than in her previous place. She didn't go out much, but she did make a few friends amongst her neighbours. Both Scott and Donna visited their grandma regularly and made sure she was all right. I travelled back several times to see them all. I always stayed at my mother's flat, where I slept on her sofa.

I remember arriving home one day, late in the afternoon, to find her rather more pleased than usual to see me. I noticed she'd had the photographs out. She seemed nervous, on edge, and I thought this was curious.

'Are you all right?' I asked her. 'Did you have a good day?'

'So-so,' was all she said.

I did my usual thing of falling asleep on the sofa as I watched TV that evening. When I awoke, my mother was standing next to me. She was looking intently at my face, staring, as if searching for something in my features or expression. She was startled when I opened my eyes and caught her gaze. It seems odd to say it, but I felt as if she had drained me of something. I was unnerved. She recovered her detached expression and went out to the kitchen. I puzzled over this for a while, but couldn't think of any reason for her strange behaviour. She never did explain.

Sometimes Dennis came back with me to visit my family. Of course I'd told him about my mother and what she had been like with me as a child, but he took her as he saw her, 'a nice old lady' who brought him cups of tea and biscuits.

He used to tease her a lot, and she always enjoyed being the centre of attention, so she liked him. Sometimes he really took the mickey out of her and she loved that.

In between my visits back to see her, I called her regularly, though our conversations were often hard work.

'Hello, it's me. How are you getting on?'

'I'm all right.' Silence.

She never initiated any part of the dialogue, so talking to her felt like pushing a car stuck in mud.

In the summer of 2004 I came back to England for my daughter Donna's wedding. As usual, I slept on my mother's sofa. I stayed for a few weeks to keep her company and catch up with friends.

A few days after I'd returned to Texas, Mercia came down with pneumonia. She didn't see a doctor when she was first unwell, so by the time she was admitted to hospital she was seriously ill. If I had stayed longer, I'd have noticed and called the doctor straightaway, so I felt it was my fault because I hadn't been there. I hadn't been there when my father died, and now I was guilty of not being with my mother when she needed me. I was a trained nurse, so I knew what pneumonia could mean at her age.

Scott and Donna updated me daily.

'We visited her today. She was sitting up and pleased to see us.'

'Did she ask for me?'

'No.'

'She's probably cross with me.'

'The nurse said she's doing well.'

'OK. Let me know if there's any change. If she's recovering well, I'll wait to come over when she comes out of hospital so I can nurse her. If she gets any worse, let me know and I'll catch the next flight.'

Suddenly, her condition deteriorated. I left Houston at seven in the evening on a plane that was due to arrive in London at seven-thirty the next morning, and for the duration of the flight I could neither settle nor sleep, unable to shake off the melancholy that embraced me.

When the crew opened the blinds early that morning, I gazed out to see a blood-red sky. On all the long-distance flights I had made between various continents I had never seen this before. The tears coursed down my face and I knew at that moment that she was gone. I looked at my watch. It was six o'clock.

At Heathrow, I had a long wait for my connection to Newcastle, so I bought a cup of coffee and sat down. Just then, my phone rang and I was surprised to see it was Ian, my son-in-law.

'Donna and Scott have both gone to the hospital.' He tried to sound upbeat and I could tell he was being careful not to tell me anything more . . . but I knew.

When I walked out of arrivals at Newcastle, the faces of my precious children confirmed my instincts.

'What time did she die?' I asked.

'Six o'clock this morning,' said Scott.

They drove me to the hospital. I don't know how I managed to place one foot in front of the other as we approached the chapel of rest.

When we went in, she was lying on her back, covered by a flowered quilt. Somebody had combed her hair. I stood beside her body, with the children on either side of me. I said a silent prayer as I looked at her face, grey and hollow, but at peace.

As the tears came, I heard a voice say, 'I'm sorry, Mam. I'm so sorry.' It was my voice. Was it the little girl in my head, or did I say it out loud?

These were the words that swept me into the time-machine – the machine that took me back to the years when I felt I had to apologize, to say 'sorry' when my parents argued, when there was violence, when I was ill, when she was ill. It was 'sorry' for my whole life, apologizing and feeling guilty for almost every occasion in the family, as I'd been repeatedly told, 'If it hadn't been for you, everything would be all right.'

'The hospital asked me to register her death,' said Donna as we drove back that evening. 'I had to put my name on it as the informant.'

'Of course.' I nodded. 'That's fine.'

I stayed at my mother's flat while we organized the funeral and placed an announcement in the local paper. I agreed to read a short eulogy at her funeral, as well as a poem we had chosen, so I sat down the night before in turmoil, trying to write some brief words.

The day of her funeral was grey and misty as the family gathered. Dennis couldn't be there, so my dear cousin Malcolm, or Mac as we called him, arrived to follow the hearse with me. He was a tower of strength that day.

As we pulled away from her building, Mercia's neighbours were lined up to see her go and I noticed that a close friend of hers, an elderly man, was standing at his gate. I had spoken to him at length the day before.

'She was never the same after you left,' he said. 'After you went back to America, she never got over it.'

I thought: There you go, my fault again. I don't suppose he meant it that way.

'I hope you're coming to her funeral tomorrow,' I said. 'I know she would have wanted you to be there.'

'No,' He was emphatic. 'I can't go. I want to remember her as she was.'

'Well, if you change your mind . . .'

As we left for her funeral the next day, there he was, standing at his gate, head bowed, wearing the sweater my mother had knitted for him.

When the time came during the service, I walked slowly to the front, put my papers on the lectern and looked up. The attention of my mother's friends, our many relatives and the stricken faces of my children was focused on me, and all I wanted to do at that moment was to make them feel better. In my clearest voice, I recited the beautiful poem we had chosen for her. Then I paused, looked up and spoke the words I had prepared for my children's benefit.

My Mam did not believe in death. She believed in God. She believed in life ever after and the sanctity of the family, the flowers in her garden and all creatures great and small. Her greatest joy was the company of young people and the love and pride she had for her grandchildren. These words are for them.

I stepped down, with her coffin at my right. I could not physically turn my back on her, so I turned my back on the congregation, bowed my head and said once more, 'I'm sorry, Mam. I'm so sorry. Goodnight and God bless.'

I walked back to my seat and Malcolm took my hand.

'You were magnificent, Helen,' he whispered. 'I don't know how you did that.'

I stayed on after the funeral to sort out my mother's things. I expected to find her marriage certificate, the one she didn't know I'd found, when I was twelve – I wanted to look at it again, the proof of my illegitimacy – but it was missing. She must have destroyed the evidence so that I wouldn't find it. I sent for another copy. I don't know why I hadn't thought of it before.

I sold all her furniture and effects and gave the money to Scott and Donna. I didn't wish to have anything from her, but wanted my children to have everything I had never had. I hope to continue doing that for a long time.

I always knew I wasn't wanted. The guilt of that had been a weight on my shoulders down all the years, and was now compounded by the guilt of not being there for her when she was ill, when she needed me most. Grief overwhelmed me as I sorted out my mother's affairs.

But on the day I left, the grief fell away. I suddenly realized I wasn't ashamed of being me any more. I shut the door of her flat and walked away.

It was over, finally over.

Back in Texas, I learned that George's widow Joan was unwell. She had never got over his death, haunted by all their memories, and she passed away in hospital a few weeks later.

It was a sad time. I felt drained, exhausted, after these poignant partings. It was hard enough to say farewell to one beloved family member, but three so close together – that was tragic. Dennis was my rock. He helped me through it all while I began to regain my balance and adjust to a life beyond my past.

Then, late one night, came the bombshell that changed everything.

CHAPTER 33

Jenny
Revelations

'Are you sitting down?' Wendy asked on the phone in the autumn of 2004. I wasn't, but I plonked myself down in a chair. I knew it was some sort of news, and I was alone in our Florida house. She didn't sound upset, so I didn't think it could be anybody close.

'I've got some sad news to tell you,' she said.

'What is it?'

'Mercia's death was in the paper tonight.'

I don't know what I felt. Perhaps a kind of numbness tinged with relief that I'd finally met her before she died.

She read me the death notice and we chatted about it all for a while.

'Well,' I said. 'That was just fate that I had to go and see her.'

That night, I told Sam and the children.

'Mum,' said Katie. 'Are you upset?' She put her arms around me.

'Not really,' I replied. 'I can't get upset about somebody I only met once.'

Katie nodded in sympathy.

'I know she was my birth mother, but I didn't really know her.'

But yes, of course I felt upset in a way, though it was not so much about her death as about not having had the chance to get to know her properly. It was a tragedy really that we finally met so late in her life. I would like to have spent more time with her, had more time to ask the questions I still needed answered, but I don't think she would have wanted that. In fact, I'm sure she wouldn't. Especially when Helen was staying there.

In 2005, after seven years in Florida, we arrived back in England for good. Sarasota was a distant dream. Tenterden was our new home. The move from Florida's humid heat to Kent's fresh warmth was a welcome change for us all. We spent the summer fitting out our new house and moving in, making new friends and over the next couple of years set up a happy life for ourselves.

I woke up one morning with the name Helen carved in my brain. A hail of questions sprang out at me. What is she like? Is she married? Does she have a family and where does she live? It seemed crazy to have a half-sister and know nothing about her.

It was time I started a search. I could hardly believe we'd been back in England for two years and I'd done nothing about it. When I mentioned to Sam later that day that I was going to try to find Helen, I almost heard him groan.

'How can you do that when you don't know her surname?'

'I'll just have to find out.'

To be honest, I didn't have a clue how, but I just knew I had to find a way.

Then Sam had a brilliant idea. 'Why don't we send for a copy of Mercia's death certificate? You know when she died and where, so it should be easy to order it. Death certificates are usually signed by the person's next of kin. That's Helen, isn't it?'

'Yes, or her brother – Mercia's son on that photo. Either way that will help.'

We sent off for the death certificate and it arrived a few days later. Excited, I tore it open and looked at the name of the informant of Mercia's death. It was somebody called Donna. That was a surprise. Who was Donna? Not a sister, I'm pretty sure. After all, the aunt I visited that day gave me the photo and said, 'You have a sister and a brother.' So it was definitely only one sister, or half-sister, I reasoned. And that must be Helen, as Mercia herself said her daughter's name was Helen. So who was Donna? Another brick wall. This was not proving to be an easy quest, but I've always liked a challenge.

Several days went by as I searched various family history websites trying to find any clue that might help me. Nothing. It was a very frustrating time, but I refused to let it defeat me. I had heard about a website that can unite lost relations, Genes Reunited, so I Googled it and found the site. I looked at different things on there, then left a simple message of my own – *Looking for the family of Mercia Dick/Lumsden* – with her birth and death dates.

I gave my email address, just in case somebody who knew the family should see it. I didn't have great hopes, as I knew these things can take ages to be noticed, if at all. It was a remote chance.

So I was astonished to receive an email response the following morning from someone called Melanie, who wrote:

I am your cousin. You had a brother George who died. You have two sisters, Patricia and Helen. They know nothing about you.

I was stunned. *Two* sisters! How could that be? Melanie gave me Helen's email address and told me she was living in Texas. Wow!

I sat and read the brief message again – only a few words that opened a new world. I couldn't believe it. After all this time of getting nowhere, suddenly here was a means of contacting Helen direct.

So I sat down that night and began to write the hardest email I had ever written. How do you broach something like that? There is no easy way to tell anyone you are their long-lost sister, and it seemed to take for ever as I can only type with two fingers. I did a lot of thinking about it – different ways to say it. In the end, I made it short and to the point. I think I read it through about twenty times before I could send it, then finally I pressed the send button and off it went. I heaved a sigh of relief.

As I lay in bed that night, sleepless with apprehension, I wondered what Helen would make of it. Would she write back? Oh, please let her write back. What would she say? I hoped so hard that it hurt – willing her not to reject me like Mercia did. I tried to stop worrying, determined to be positive. Surely she would want to respond?

Tomorrow could be a momentous day – both an end and a beginning – the end of my long search to fill the void since

I'd discovered I was adopted, and a new start, to reclaim something precious that was stolen from us both at birth. I just hoped she would answer; would want to know me; that she would want a sister as much as I did.

CHAPTER 34

Helen & Jenny

Exploding the Past

Helen

Late one night, as I was checking my emails, a bomb detonated and blew my past into confusion. It tore into shreds all the certainties I'd grown up with. The bomb was an email from someone called Jenny who claimed to be my half-sister.

She mentioned a visit to Mercia, my mother, whom she had traced, but how could that be? I was staying there at the time, but I must have been out that afternoon. I could have walked in on their meeting at any moment. I wish I had. Why didn't my mother mention Jenny's visit to me? I never suspected anything. Did she deliberately conceal it from me? Were there other things she didn't tell me? I felt shocked and confused. Betrayed . . . and yet desperately sad.

'I believe you are my half-sister,' said the email. A sister – I'd always wanted a sister. Why didn't I know about her?

The tremors started again. I couldn't keep my hands still. I knew I was in shock. A cup of tea, that's what I needed. A cup of tea is the answer to everything, isn't it? As I tried to fill the kettle, my hand shook wildly, so I gave up and went into the bedroom.

'Dennis,' I shouted. 'Wake up, I need to tell you something.'

He groaned in his sleep.

I shook him awake. 'I've had an email from my half-sister.'

He turned over towards me. 'You haven't got a sister.'

I got him out of bed to look at the email and we stayed up talking till dawn. Finally Dennis could stay awake no longer, so I watched the sunrise alone, as I mentally wrote this astonishing new reality into the story of my life. I kept repeating to myself the key question: Why did I never know until now that I had a sister, something I always yearned for? And yet, wherever she had been all these years, she had somehow found out about me, tracked me down and told me herself.

Yes, this email was a shock, but it was a wonderful shock. The kind I'd never dreamed of, yet it felt right from that very first day. Wow! I had always sensed there was something or someone missing.

As I sat down to write my reply, the sky cleared and I recognized what I had known all my life. As a child I had always felt incomplete. I couldn't quite reach that missing part of me, so I had invented my imaginary sister to tell my troubles to. My secret sister.

Now she was real and I could talk to her properly at last. I wrote my reply and sent it.

From: helen
To: jenlucas
Sent: Thursday 12 April 2007, 5:37
Subject: Mercia Lumsden

Dear Jenny,

Your email came as a complete shock to me. I have not yet stopped shaking. I knew nothing about this. My head is spinning with questions, so far unanswered.

May I ask where you got my email address from and how you found me? Please tell me what information you have acquired from your investigations, and I will try to fill in the blanks. I just feel so very sad that I have never known you.

To discover, after all these years, that I may have a sister is overwhelming. That my mother had never told me of this is beyond belief.

Please write soon and hopefully by then I will have recovered a little and will be able to call you.

Helen

Jenny

As I logged on, I smiled, with relief . . . delight. Here was Helen's reply. I noticed how early in the morning she'd sent it. I was amazed – just amazed. She must be keen . . . or was it a 'don't contact me again' sort of reply, like Mercia's letter had been? My shoulders were tense as I sat down and opened it. Phew! I relaxed as soon as I start to read it through. She was obviously shaken by the situation, but it was a positive reply.

Helen told me recently that she kept that first email from me and her reply. I was shocked . . . and touched.

After all these years, the door was now open and I started to write back again straightaway. First of all I answered Helen's questions about how I found out about her and how I later came by her email address. To protect Melanie, I had to tell Helen a bit of a fib, saying that Sam had got it from a private detective. I hoped she'd understand. (Actually we did get some help from a detective guy that Sam knows, so it wasn't far from the truth.) In the rest of the email I told Helen about myself and my life, especially my childhood. I didn't want her to think I felt hard done by, or that I envied her the childhood she spent with our mother. None of that mattered now. I just wanted this to be the new start I'd been yearning for since I was fourteen, to build a relationship with one of my own birth family at last. I wondered what she was like, and hoped we'd get along with each other.

From: jenlucas
To: helen
Sent: Thursday 12 April 2007, 11:59 +0100
Subject: Mercia Lumsden

Dear Helen

I know all this must have come as a great shock and can understand how you are feeling. It seemed like every avenue I tried, I hit a brick wall. All the adoption lines, etc. I started going on the internet, every site

imaginable. Nothing came back at all. Finally my
husband sent for Mercia's death certificate, and of
course I found that her maiden name was Bradshaw.

When we met Mercia, she mentioned her daughter
Helen. She told me you were a nurse and that you had
worked at the Nuffield hospital in Newcastle. I have
had your name fixed in my brain ever since.

I was brought up as an only child, always wishing
for brothers and sisters. I found out at 14 that I was
adopted and since that point have had this empty void
in my life. Don't get me wrong. I have had a very
happy life. But it's hard to explain. I have never felt
I belonged anywhere. I had a fantastic childhood with
really good parents. Later on I bought a house in
Cramlington, only two miles from Seghill, where I was
born. (I didn't know this at the time.) I played golf for
my living as Jenny Lee Smith (mainly in America, on
the LPGA tour).

My dad died when I was 12. I was very close to my
mum and out of respect to her did not want to start
searching seriously until she passed away. My adoption
was a taboo subject in the family and was never spoken
about. A great shame really. Mercia gave me my name,
Jennifer, and my parents kept it.

Getting back to how I found you, my husband Sam
spoke to a private detective and he found out all the
rest (including your email address – don't ask me how!)

Like you, I feel very strange to find my family after all
this time. But I would love to talk to you and maybe

*we can catch up on some of the lost time. I hope you
are not in too much turmoil – I certainly am.*

Jenny

Helen

It was wonderful receiving this second email so soon, and I
was very glad to learn that Jenny had had a happy childhood. But what should I tell her about mine? It wouldn't be
fair to burden her with my experiences straightaway, not until
we knew each other better. We had so much to learn and to
share – I didn't want to scare her off before we began. The
time would come to talk about our mother. But not yet. I
still hadn't got used to the fact that Mercia was mother to
both of us – perhaps a better mother to Jenny, in giving her
away, than to me.

Why didn't she tell me about Jenny? Did she think
I'd never find out? How could she have done that to me?
Mercia denied me this knowledge; denied us both. Why didn't
Grandma tell me? Why didn't any of my aunts, uncles or
older cousins say anything about it? They must have known.
Did she persuade them to conspire with her in keeping such
a huge secret from me? And what other secrets might there
be?

This revelation of finding my half-sister and learning about
her happy childhood brought back all the painful memories
of my past. Things I hadn't thought about for years. Memories
I preferred to erase . . .

Over the next few days, emails flew to and fro between

us, adding more and more details of our lives and families. It was a glorious awakening, like opening the curtains on a sunny morning, but better still. Out of the darkness came light.

Jenny told me about her search for her birth mother, our mother, and how she had found out about me. She told me she had had her children late because she had been a professional golfer. It was obvious that she had enjoyed a highly successful career in golf, though she was characteristically modest about it. Only when I looked her up on the internet did I discover she'd won all these prestigious championships. Mercia had always loved watching golf on the TV. I wondered if she ever knew.

But there was one big thing I kept to myself in those first few weeks: I didn't tell Jenny about my upbringing. I needed to get to know her better before I could confront her with all that.

Jenny

We exchanged phone numbers, but I don't remember if it was that day or the next that we first spoke to each other. We both recognized the enormity of the occasion, the importance of finding each other at last. An ending and a beginning. We were keen to catch up on lost time, To continue together the search for those missing pieces of our story, the hidden truths.

It was a special moment, hearing my half-sister's voice at last. Though a little shaky at first, Helen's voice sounded wonderfully warm and caring, and I was surprised by the calming effect it had on me. I could detect my own accent in her voice, unaffected by the years she had lived in Texas. Hearing this familiar Geordie twang really put me at my ease, but my excitement bubbled up again as I fired myriad questions at her and she asked me as many back, if not more. Within minutes we were both in full flow and laughing easily together. It felt amazing – what a thrill! Helen was definitely more matter-of-fact than I was that day, but I suppose she was still trying to work things out as we spoke. After all, I'd had years to prepare for this conversation, but she must have been still in shock.

She wanted to know more about my visit to Mercia that day with Sam and the children, so I explained about her welcome, her apologies, how she had talked us through the various photos on display and her concern that Helen might come home early.

'She was so worried that you would come back and find us there. We had to promise not to let on who we were.'

'If I had come back and seen you there with Mercia, I would have known,' said Helen. 'I'm sure I would have known. In the photos you emailed me, you look so like her.'

'Mercia said you were working at the Nuffield Hospital and would be back any minute.'

'But I wasn't working there any more. I was just on a quick visit to the north-east from Texas and had gone out that afternoon. I wonder why she lied to you? But it's true I could have come back at any moment. I wish I had.'

We exchanged information about our lives, our husbands, our children, even our dogs. We discovered we were both mad keen on dogs, and even had pets of the same breed.

I finally found out the identity of the mystery name

on Mercia's death certificate: 'So the Donna who registered Mercia's death was your daughter?'

'Yes,' explained Helen. 'Because I was on the way back from Texas when Mercia died.'

'If it had been your name, I'd probably have found you even sooner,' I said.

Helen

The first time I heard Jenny's voice was eerie. She sounded just like my mother – it was my mother's voice. We were both a bit tongue-tied to start with. All those years . . . where do you begin? But we soon got talking, and we haven't stopped since! One of the things we discussed was Jenny's research to find me. She told me about the Genes Reunited message that she received from Melanie.

'So what did Melanie actually say?'

'She told me that she was my cousin, our cousin, of course. And she said that I also had a brother called George and another sister called Patricia.'

'Another sister?' I gasped.

'Yes. I assumed you knew about her.'

'No. I had no idea. No idea at all. Who is she? Do you know anything about her?'

'Only that her father was an American airman.' She told me Patricia's surname.

'What?' I couldn't believe it. It was as if something had my stomach in a grip. I felt clammy and sick. This Patricia had been brought up as a distant cousin, a few years older than me. We grew up together. She was often there at family gatherings, but we were usually kept apart. I never thought it strange at the time, but now I realized why.

Once I'd recovered from this startling news, I couldn't wait to find out more. From my home in Texas I started on some internet research of my own. It took me ages, but eventually I managed to track Patricia down through her marriages and the electoral roll. Nobody in the family seemed to know her address, but one cousin had a vague idea she was still in the north-east. That was enough for me to be fairly sure I had located the right person.

'I've found Patricia,' I told Jenny on the phone.

'What are you going to do?'

'I'm all packed up to fly to Northumberland tomorrow anyway – I'm moving back – so I'll go to the address and see her as soon as I can.'

'Have you called her to check it's OK?'

'No. I don't have her phone number – just an address.'

A couple of days after I arrived, I got in the car and drove to the address on the electoral roll. I turned up without any warning, so I was apprehensive about how she would react. I hadn't seen her in years.

She answered the door and looked blankly at me. 'Yes?'

'Hello, Patricia,' I said. 'I'm Helen.'

She stepped forward and flung her arms around me. We both cried.

'Come in.'

She made some tea and we talked – pleasantries at first.

Then I told her about Jenny, how she had searched for me and the first email.

'I was so shocked,' I said. 'But it was a good shock.'

Then, when she seemed relaxed, I brought up the subject of how we were related. 'I've known about this for five years,' she said.

'Really?' I was astonished. 'How did you find out?'

'It was when I was looking into my adoption information. I wanted to know who my birth mother was, so I went to see the counsellor. She gave me my original birth certificate and there was Auntie Mercia's name on it, Mercia Dick.'

'Why didn't you tell me this before?'

'I didn't want to hurt you. I didn't know if you knew about it, so I thought it would be best to leave it where it was. I just continued with my life and went on as before.'

'So Mercia was your birth mother, I'm your half-sister and George was your brother. Is that all you know?'

'My half-brother, I think. And what you've just told me about Jenny. Yes, that's all.'

'So your father wasn't Mercia's husband?'

'No, George Dick was a prisoner of war in Germany. I have no idea who my father was.'

'Well, would you like me to tell you?' I asked her.

'Do you know?'

'Yes, Melanie told Jenny. He was an American airman billeted in Seghill during the war.'

She was shocked, just as I had been when I had first heard from Jenny. It was one of those struck-dumb moments.

Now that I knew where Patricia lived and she gave me her phone number, I could put her in touch with other cousins she hadn't seen for twenty years or more.

I rang Jenny that afternoon and told her all about my meeting with Patricia.

'Was she pleased to see you?'

'Yes. She seemed to be. She was all hugs and smiles.'

'So do you think she'd be happy to meet me too?'

'Yes, I told her about you; how you tracked me down and everything.'

'What's she like?'

'Wait and see!' I smiled. 'You'll have to come up and meet all the family.'

Soon after that, I called Melanie. She answered the phone and immediately started to cry.

'What are you crying for?' I asked her gently.

'I feel terrible. I've done . . . all this . . . and I shouldn't have . . . I'm sorry, I know I've made trouble . . . it was a secret . . . I thought you knew . . .'

'Don't be silly,' I said, trying to calm her down. 'You haven't done anything wrong.'

She carried on sobbing.

'Melanie! Listen. I'm not crying. I might do in a few days, but I'm not crying now.'

She calmed down and we talked a little more. Then I texted another cousin, Mac, who I'd always been close to: *I need to talk to you Mac. When can I call?*

The reply came back immediately: *Now!*

So I picked up the phone and called him. When I explained the discovery about Patricia, he didn't sound surprised.

'I've known that all my life, about you and Patricia.'

'Really? Why didn't you tell me?'

'My mother told me. But you know what, Helen? I'm just a guy. I was very young when I heard about it. It's family stuff and it didn't really mean anything to me. In fact, to be honest, I'd forgotten about it. But I've always known.'

I took this in with a sense of alarm. Everyone in the extended family seemed to know, except for Patricia and me, and even when she had found out she hadn't got in touch with me to tell me. They also knew about Jenny's birth and adoption out of the family. All these relatives had taken away from me the pleasure and support of having a sister. Now, suddenly, I had two.

When I spoke to George's son a few days later, it was a similar story. George had apparently known about these two sisters who were adopted out, but he'd never thought to mention it to me. His son said that George had been forbidden to say anything. I felt overwhelmed by the regret and sadness that we'd missed out on so much, Patricia, Jenny and I. Indignation, too, that everyone knew my business except me. I was denied that right.

I was now determined to discover how it had all happened, and why. Bizarrely, my mind began to dredge up small details from my childhood. For example, I knew that George used to get into fights at school. I think I overheard someone say once that the other kids teased my brother George about his illegitimate sister. Of course, that was before I was born. I think when I heard this story I just dismissed it as a ridiculous rumour.

Once I started thinking about it, I recalled snatches of other whispered conversations, things I wasn't supposed to hear. As a small child I had never understood them. Now I wished I could remember them better.

Then there was the way I was always blamed for everything: 'It's all your fault.' Perhaps I was being blamed for being the one Mercia kept. There had always been something wrong. Why had I not noticed this? I was angry with myself.

I discussed everything with Dennis, of course.

'This family secrecy has been an abscess for decades,' I said. 'And like all abscesses, it grew bigger and more poisonous until eventually it just had to burst.'

'Oh, not another one of your metaphors!' he groaned.

When I spoke to another cousin, Alice, a few days later, I asked her why nobody had told me, even after my mother had died and it didn't matter any more.

'Why did everyone continue to keep it all secret?'

'We didn't want to. We thought you had a right to know,' she explained. 'And we told Mercia, "Helen has a right to know she has a sister. We think you should let her know. You can't leave her living her whole life and never knowing." Mercia said, "I forbid you to say one word to Helen. I absolutely forbid it." And she said it in such a way,' said Alice, 'that I thought I'd be murdered if I said anything at all.'

So that was it. Fear of my mother had been the power that blocked the truth. Nobody dared to betray her. But surely it was me they betrayed by not telling? To be fair, I don't suppose it ever occurred to them. But I resented their silence all the same. How would it be when we all met up?

CHAPTER 35

Helen & Jenny

Reunion

Jenny

When Helen returned to England, we agreed that once she had found somewhere to live and had settled in, we should meet as soon as possible. I couldn't wait to see her. I knew she needed time, but we'd waited so long and now I didn't want to wait any longer.

'Look,' said Sam. 'We're going to go up there and I'm going to organize a dinner.'

We drove up and stayed at the Holiday Inn hotel. That's where I met my half-sister, Helen, for the very first time.

'Jenny,' she said with a broad smile as if she knew me, had always known me. Her voice was so calm and serene – how did she manage that?

'Helen.' It felt good to say her name face to face. 'Oh, Helen.'

We hugged each other for what seemed like an age. It had taken so long to find her, I didn't want to let her go. I can't describe how I felt. It was spooky, like snapping your fingers, the bond we had – it happened just like that. We both felt it immediately. We kept looking at each other, beaming. It was incredible. We were like that all afternoon. Here we were, aged fifty-seven and fifty-nine, sitting together after all these years. Helen looked so happy to see me, and I couldn't stop smiling at her either.

I don't think either of us had known what to expect. I didn't know whether she was angry or bitter at the way her mother had kept everything secret from her, but if she was, she didn't show it. She was openly accepting of me. It was a great relief. But it must have been traumatic for her.

Helen

It was such a coincidence that when I first heard from Jenny I'd already booked my flight back to England. I had packing cases all around me as we had planned to move back to live in the north-east where my children and their partners lived. I went first. Dennis was about to retire and he would follow me out a few weeks later.

When I got back to Northumberland, Sam arranged to have this big family reunion at the Grand Hotel in Tynemouth. Before that we were going to have a barbecue at my cousin Mac's house. The first time I met Jenny, I didn't want it to be when we were surrounded by other people, all looking at us, so I asked her if I could come to the hotel where she was staying and meet her there. We agreed that it would just be her and me, and her children, as mine would be at work.

I drove to the hotel. I arrived first in the reception area, so I called Jenny on my mobile.

'I'll be straight down.'

As I sat and waited, I was in complete turmoil inside. This was such an important meeting. I watched as the lift descended and the door opened. When I saw her come out of it, I knew it had to be my sister. Straightaway, it was as if she was the missing part of me finally restored. We fell into each other's arms. I can't remember what we said. We just hugged each other and cried. I noticed straightaway that she was the double of Mercia. The image of her. It was eerie to see that resemblance.

On the day of the barbecue at Mac's house, it was just Jenny, Katie and Josh. Sam and Ben were going to come up north later and join us, so they weren't at Mac's that day. Donna and Scott couldn't be there either. We met up with Patricia and her partner, so the three of us, Patricia, Jenny and I, got together for the first time that afternoon. Patricia seemed a little more detached and reserved, whereas Jenny and I felt very close and completely open with each other. We all marched in with our bundles of photographs, passing them round to share over our drinks. 'That's George, and this is . . .' We explained everyone to each other.

Seeing all the photos started a conversation about resemblances.

'I can't get over how alike you two are,' commented Mac to Jenny and me. 'And what's so amazing is Jenny's resemblance to Mercia. It's uncanny.'

Mac's girlfriend Debbie turned to Patricia. 'You don't look much like Helen and Jenny,' she said, 'so I suppose you must look like your father.'

Patricia looked uncomfortable. 'Maybe,' she said. 'But I've no idea what he looked like.'

'Well, he must have been good-looking,' said Mac with a smile.

As the afternoon went on, the conversation focused by turns on our families, on what we were all doing, and finally, amid much laughter, to reminiscences of family gatherings when we had been children, all except Jenny, of course, who was keen to learn more about the different family members.

It was as good a first meeting as it possibly could have been – light and easygoing, warm-hearted and fun. Fortunately, all our children were happy for us too. I remember a conversation I had with Donna at around this time, discussing Mercia's secrecy.

'Why didn't she tell us?' asked Donna. 'You know the number of times you sit with the family and you watch a programme about adoption, or about a woman who is having an unexpected baby? That would have been an obvious opportunity to have those sorts of discussions. She could so easily have slipped it into the conversation, but she never did.'

'Yes, you're right. She must have had to work hard not to mention it at times like that.'

'I could strangle Grandma! What must she have put herself through, living with that secret all of her life?'

'Well, the family used to call her "the ostrich",' I said, 'because she wouldn't face things, and that was the ultimate example. These days we'd call it the elephant in the room.'

The main reunion event was the dinner at the Grand Hotel. As we walked in and I introduced Scott and Donna to Jenny, Donna just took one look at her and burst into tears. That was rather disconcerting, especially for Jenny.

'I haven't seen my gran for three years,' Donna said, 'but I've just seen her again now.'

Despite the more formal surroundings of the hotel, the whole evening was an absolute riot. Jenny had all her family there, and I had my children and their partners with me. What a lovely night that was. So much laughter, and quite a few tears as well. Right from the start, we all felt we were just one big family.

During the evening, I noticed Patricia leaving the room, so I followed her outside. She was crying; just leaning on the balcony with tears coursing down her cheeks. I put my hand on her shoulder and said, 'It's OK, Patricia. We've got each other now.'

She turned round and hugged me, and I started crying too. Then Jenny came out and joined us, and she started crying as well! So there we were, three sisters, all blubbing together.

We went back inside, just in time for Sam's speech.

'It's so good to see the whole family together at last. There are twenty-four of you here tonight. When I first met Jenny, we had our family reunions in a telephone box. Now we've got a whole hotel! I think we should drink a toast to the three graces – sisters at last – Helen, Patricia and Jenny.'

We all joined in with gusto. For some reason, I suddenly felt a rush of emotion. Without thinking, I stood up and added, 'I'd like to make an additional toast to the one person who's responsible for us all being here tonight. To Mercia.'

Everyone repeated 'Mercia'.

I don't know why I did that. What was I thinking of? Yes, she had been our birth mother, but we hardly owed her a thank you for bringing us together when she had done every-thing in her power to keep us apart and ignorant of our sisterhood. If it hadn't been for her, we wouldn't have needed a reunion, would we?

Jenny

What a night the dinner was! We all had a great time, meeting so many unknown relatives and getting to know each other on neutral ground.

I was a bit concerned, though, at one point, when Patricia was upset, but that wasn't surprising. I think we were all emotional. But I wondered if there was a sense of uncertainty in her reaction.

I felt uncomfortable about that, as it was me who had spilled the beans to Helen about Patricia being another half-sister. Was she cross with me? Perhaps she didn't tell Helen herself because she wasn't sure in her own mind how she felt about it? It had been an epic shock for Helen, who'd grown up thinking that Patrica was a distant cousin, so it must have felt awkward for them both.

I find all that really odd – the way the family guarded Mercia's secrets, almost as strongly as she kept them herself. Mercia must have been quite something, quite a manipulator. I mean, you've got to be pretty cool, haven't you, to do things like that? Is it hard? I wondered. I just can't imagine giving away your own child. There was so much to learn about this woman who was my mother, and the things she'd done, and who my father was, too, but now at last I had an ally in Helen and we could try to find out more together.

CHAPTER 36

Helen & Jenny

Too Many Coincidences

Helen

I began to piece together the facts. My mother was married in 1939, at the age of twenty, to George Dick. My brother George was born the following year. George Dick had gone to war by this time and was captured by the Germans. He was a prisoner throughout the rest of the war. During 1943, my mother had a relationship with an American airman, from which she had a baby girl. This was Patricia. Apparently, when she discovered she was expecting, she concealed the pregnancy by wearing tight corsets. No one knew until the local midwife stopped my grandma in the street.

'You'd better get home quick. Your Mercia's just had a baby!'

When I told Jenny this, she was amazed. 'What kind of corsets?' she asked.

'I've no idea. Why do you want to know that?'

'My mother used to sell Pul-front corsets in Seghill from the beginning of the war to earn some extra money, so perhaps she sold a corset to Mercia.'

I was stunned.

'Wouldn't that be an amazing coincidence?' continued Jenny.

I tried to picture these two women together, perhaps in my Grandma's house, five years before Connie unknowingly adopted Mercia's next baby.

Baby Patricia was hastily handed over to relatives, who had just suffered a miscarriage. It would have been shameful in those days for anyone outside the family to know Mercia had given birth to a baby while her husband was a prisoner of war. I suppose this must have seemed like the perfect solution. Nobody gave any thought to what might be best for the baby, though I think Patricia had a happy upbringing; a great deal better than mine, at any rate.

Patricia's health visitor was a great friend of Jenny's adoptive mother and became Jenny's godmother five years later.

In the meantime, Mercia's first husband, George Dick, my half-brother George's father, came back from the war with a German girlfriend and eventually divorced Mercia in June 1950.

Jenny was born in 1948 from a different relationship. Neither Jenny nor I had any idea who her father was. This was something we would need to try and extricate from the family's vault of secrets, if it wasn't too late. All Mercia's siblings had already gone to their graves, and none of the cousins would tell us when we asked. They just gave out euphemisms like, 'Oh, that was a long time ago,' or 'It's water under the bridge.'

I was born in April 1950. I remember discovering from those papers I found in my mother's bureau when I was about twelve that I was born before Mercia and Tommy were married, which horrified me. It was still quite a stigma to be illegitimate in those post-war years.

Our initial hypothesis was that we three girls and George were all from different fathers. This said a lot about Mercia, of course.

Patricia lived a lot closer to me than Jenny did, with me in Northumberland and Jenny in Kent. I met up with Patricia every now and then at first, and we got on well, so I was surprised when she suddenly stopped calling me and didn't answer the phone any more. When I spoke to Jenny, she said she hadn't heard from Patricia either, until she received one short letter from her.

Jenny

Quite out of the blue one day, I opened our mailbox to find an unfamiliar handwritten envelope. I set the bills aside and opened it. Inside was a letter from Patricia, a few brief sentences, in which she explained that she was beset by anger about the family's deceits over the circumstances of her birth. She wrote that she would prefer to have her life back 'as it was', before she found out about being Mercia's child. There was to be no more contact between us.

I called Helen straightaway and read it out to her.

'That's very sad, isn't it?' said Helen.

'I don't know what she means about having her life back as it was.'

'Well, I suppose she wants to pretend it didn't happen.'

'But she can't just put it all back in a box and shut the lid.'

'No. Once you know something like this, you can't go back.'

'It's a shame we can't talk that through with her.'

'I know, but it sounds like she doesn't even want to think about it.'

'It's sad that she has cut herself off from us.'

'Yes, it's a loss to all of us, especially to her.'

'I'm so glad you didn't reject me like that when I first wrote to you,' I said. 'I feared you would.'

'It never occurred to me – you are the sister I've always wanted,' said Helen.

'Me too.'

'We have such a strong bond now. I could never go back on that. I wouldn't want to. Maybe Patricia will change her mind one day.'

'Yes. She knows where we are.'

I tucked the letter away with a photo we had taken of the three of us together. It was an important link in our story. Patricia would always be our half-sister.

Helen

I was deeply upset by Patricia's letter, but I understood her reasons for feeling the way she did. She had to make the decision that felt best for her. We agreed not to try and make her change her mind.

Jenny and I continued to keep in touch regularly. By now, this was more or less daily and sometimes more than once a day. The more we talked, the more we came to realize how alike we are. Not just in appearance, but in our likes and dislikes, hobbies and interests, and, of course, our love of animals, especially dogs.

All of this would be joy enough, but when we started to compare notes about our health, we discovered we also shared a number of physical conditions. We both sleepwalked as children, we are both allergic to wool, we have both had serious back problems, we both suffer from chronic sinusitis and chest infections, we both have arthritis in our hands and both have crooked right index fingers, Reynaud's syndrome and cramps in our legs. That's not all. When we were little we were both investigated as a child at the Newcastle Royal Victoria Infirmary at about the same time for the same peculiar symptoms of fainting and blacking out. Jenny had a suspected heart problem, whilst I had a suspected brain tumour. Happily, both conditions were ruled out fairly quickly.

If we'd been the same age, we would have suspected we could be twins. It was strange how alike we were when we'd never even heard of each other over all those years.

The more information we shared with each other, the greater the coincidences became. There were circumstantial similarities too. One of these was Embleton. Jenny had virtually lived there throughout her childhood, whereas I had often visited the beach on summer weekend days when my parents met up with Uncle James and we all drove to the coast. In fact, when I showed Jenny my photos, they included one of me sitting in the shallow water on the beach at Embleton. I remember that day quite clearly, as Tommy was trying to coax my mother to come into the picture with me. She agreed with great reluctance and refused to come any closer to me than she had to. This was nothing unusual, so I don't know why I remember it, except that it was such a beautiful day. As I played happily in the water, I noticed a group of children at the top of the bank, where there were some wooden bungalows. There was one girl standing near the edge and looking down at me. I thought she looked about the same age as me, or not much older.

Jenny gasped when she saw that photo. It seemed to bring back a memory of her own. She looked at it very intently.

'That's Mercia, isn't it?'

'Yes. My father insisted she come into the photo, but she didn't really want to.'

'I remember watching you that day. I was standing at the top, looking down onto the beach.'

'I saw some children there. I think I saw you. Were you standing near the edge, and then you ran away?'

'Yes. Isn't that amazing?'

There were other coincidences in where we'd lived and places we'd been. Our brother George lived in Cramlington at the same time as Jenny. When I used to visit George in Florida, he lived very close to where Jenny lived with her family at that time. If only we'd known about each other then!

The most remarkable link of all was that we had actually met and had probably spoken to one another without realizing it. Jenny had a series of surgical operations on her back following a golfing injury. Rather than have those operations in America, she had come home to Northumberland to consult David Stainsby, the renowned orthopaedic surgeon with whom I'd worked as theatre nurse.

I assisted in hundreds of his operations over the period when I worked at the Newcastle Nuffield Hospital, where

Jenny had her operations during that time. We are both certain that I was present in at least one of Jenny's operations, and possibly all of them. Sometimes I used to be scrub nurse in the operation itself, whilst other days I would talk to the patient in the anteroom to the operating theatre, calming them and inserting their cannula to begin the anaesthetic procedure, or in recovery as they came out of the anaesthetic. It is very likely that I was in all of those roles for Jenny over the different operations she had. And we had no idea at the time, of course. Indeed, if we'd known then that we were sisters, I wouldn't have been allowed to assist in her operations.

Our many physical coincidences in particular began to make us wonder. Then we worked out that there were only seven months between Jenny's birth and my conception. This seemed almost too close. I looked out the box of papers I had kept when I cleared out my mother's house and extricated the document I was looking for, along with a couple of others. As I read, my eyes opened wider and wider. Why hadn't I noticed this before?

I got straight on the phone to Jenny.

'I've just been looking at three documents I found. I only discovered the main one after my mother died, when I cleared her house. There was so much to do that I only gave it a cursory glance. I read it properly today for the first time, and the obvious stared me in the face!'

'What do you mean?'

'OK. The first document is my birth certificate. It says my name and birth date and Tommy's name is written in the "father" column. The address is in Newcastle. I went there one day to see what it was like. They lived there in that period when Mercia went missing. Her mystery year, the family called it. She only turned up in Seghill again a year later.'

'Maybe she went there because they didn't approve of Tommy,' suggested Jenny.

'They didn't know Tommy until he came back with Mercia and me. Anyway, the next document is their marriage certificate.'

'So they definitely were married.'

'Yes, but rather late. In fact they were married a whole year after I was born.'

'Wow. That was unusual in those days.'

'Yes. I discovered this document when I was about twelve, when I was alone in the house and rifled through my mother's bureau to see what she hid in there. I remember being appalled when I noticed the discrepancy in the dates. Even at that age, I knew what that meant.'

'You said there were three documents?'

'Yes. The third one is the one I had never seen before until I found it in Mum's flat when I was clearing it out. It's Mercia's divorce decree from her first husband, George Dick. That was George's father, the one who was a prisoner of war for years.'

'Well, you knew about that, didn't you?'

'I knew they were divorced. But I didn't know when. It was in June 1950, two months after I was born, ten months before Mercia and Tommy were married.'

'So do you think maybe this George Dick was really your father?'

'I hadn't even thought of that. But I'm pretty sure not. From what my cousins told me, she had nothing to do with him when he came back after the war. No, the really interesting thing on this divorce decree is that it gives the name of a co-respondent.'

'What's his name?'

'Wilfred Harrison.'

'So what does that mean?'

'It means that her first husband knew Mercia was having a relationship with Wilfred Harrison in the period leading up to the divorce.' I paused for Jenny to take that in. 'I'm wondering whether this Wilfred Harrison could have been your father, since you were born only sixteen months before me and eighteen months before the divorce decree. That means that she must have been going out with him before Tommy.'

Jenny was silent at the other end of the phone. I guessed it was quite a shock for her to hear a possible name at last. Now that I came to think about it, I remembered that name.

'When my mother was elderly, I used to take her out for drives sometimes on Sunday afternoons,' I said. 'She usually wanted to go to this one place, The Avenue, a straight, tree-lined road that used to be the driveway to Seaton Delaval Hall. As we drove down it, she always told me the same story. "This is where I used to go for walks with Wilfie Harrison, when we were courting. He was a handsome man."'

'Wow!'

'It sounds as if she went out with him for quite a long while. She always sounded quite smitten with him. At the time I didn't take much notice, but now it all fits into place, doesn't it?'

'That's spooky! You didn't realize it, but you had the one document that could be the answer to my main question – who was my father? That's amazing!'

'I don't know why I never thought of it before.'

'Never mind. This is my best lead yet. Now we're on a roll.'

'Maybe we should do some research into this Wilfred Harrison,' I suggested. 'It seems unlikely, but it's just possible that he might still be alive.'

'No, he's not,' sighed Jenny.

'How do you know?'

'Because when I went to speak to Mercia's sister Dorrie that day, she told me quite clearly that my birth father was dead. She said he was a bad bugger and that he was long gone, six foot under.'

'Really?' I paused.

'You've got me wondering now,' said Jenny. 'Do you think maybe she wasn't telling the truth, to put me off the scent?'

'Well, after finally finding out all the lies I've been told, I'm questioning everything now!'

'I just assumed all these years that I'd never find him, never even find out who he was. Now I have a name, on top of which there's a chance he's still alive after all!'

I could almost hear Jenny smile, but my thoughts were already racing on. 'I've just thought of something else. We know there were only seven months between your birth and when Mercia became pregnant with me.'

'And if Wilfred Harrison was my father,' continued Jenny, 'and your mother's family didn't know anything about Tommy until after Mercia reappeared in 1951 . . .'

'Hold on a minute. Tommy was on my birth certificate, so Mercia must have been with him then.'

'Yes, but maybe he knew you weren't his?'

I couldn't speak for a few seconds and Jenny waited to let me take in this new possibility.

'Well that's a revelation! Why has it never occurred to me before?' I said. 'If that were true, it would explain a lot, like why she often said, "She's mine" when they argued about me. It could be why he always told me everything was my fault. He would think that if I wasn't his daughter and I was in the way of his relationship with Mercia. Or maybe it was the reason why he felt he couldn't leave us, or something. Or maybe he even knew this Wilfred Harrison, saw him around in Seghill every day and resented what he knew, resented him . . .' I could hardly believe it. 'But that could mean . . .'

'So you're thinking what I'm thinking?' asked Jenny.

'Yes!'

We both paused. Then a great idea flashed into my head. 'Would you do a sibling test?'

'DNA?'

'Yes. That's the only way to find out for certain.'

'Let's do it!'

So we both did the saliva tests and sent them off to the DNA lab. Now we would have to wait the longest weeks of our lives to find out the result.

CHAPTER 37

Helen

Making Memories

Dennis retired, sorted out his affairs and moved over to join me in our new home in Northumberland. The first time he met Jenny and Sam was when Sam got some theatre tickets. He took the phone from Jenny and said to me, 'Will you and Dennis come down and see *Oliver* with us?

'Oh, absolutely!' I knew Dennis would enjoy that.

We thought it was a great idea. I found out later that it was almost impossible to get those tickets, so I don't know how Sam managed it. Dennis had been in Texas when we'd had all the reunion festivities, so he'd missed out on meeting the new branch of the family. I was glad there was an opportunity now for him to meet Jenny and Sam and for us all to enjoy some time together.

We took the train down and stayed in a hotel. Jenny, Sam and the kids came up from Kent to meet us and we all had a lovely evening. We had front-row seats, the best in the theatre, then went out for a meal afterwards. It didn't take long before the men were doing their own version of bonding. You know what it is with these guys and their drinks? From the beginning they got on like two buddies, and of course they're brothers-in-law, aren't they? Isn't that strange?

Dennis being an American, I think the fact that Jenny and Sam had lived in Florida for a few years helped him to feel comfortable with them straightaway They and the children stayed at the same hotel as us and we all had breakfast together in the morning. The whole trip was a lot of fun. Jenny's like that anyway, and Sam's very funny – he kept us all laughing.

When the DNA test results finally came back, Dennis was away in Texas visiting his daughter Amy, so I was at home on my own. In fact, we'd just finished speaking on the phone. I made myself a cup of coffee and started to check my emails.

There it was: 'DNA test result.'

Suddenly, I was in quicksand. I started shaking before I even opened it. Of course I wanted to see what it said, but I was apprehensive in case it wasn't what we thought. Mind you, by then I think we were both sure it would be. When I clicked on the header, the email opened. It didn't say anything. Then I realized there was an attachment. It took ages to open. It seemed like ages, anyway.

Finally, there it was. A kind of certificate, all written in gobbledygook! I stared at it, trying to make out what it said, but I couldn't understand a word of it. All I could see was this figure: 99.97%. What did that mean? Then I noticed a bit that said something about 96%. I thought, wait a minute, there are two readings here. Which one is it?

I looked down the page and there was a chart listing 'first sibling', 'second sibling' and lots more figures. The more I looked at it, the more I felt like I was about to have a car-crash. You know – that feeling when you get an acid taste in your mouth? I suppose it's a kind of shock reaction. The figures on the chart were virtually perfect matches all the way down. I read it again and again. I still couldn't take it in fully. The more I tried, the less I understood and the more anxious I felt.

Finally I just rang up the number of the laboratory.

'I'm sorry to bother you on the phone, but I've received the results of our DNA test and I don't understand all these figures. Can you please explain them to me?'

'Yes, of course.' She sounded sympathetic. Tell me what % it says at the top of the page.'

'99.97%. What does that mean?'

'Well, it means that you and the other person you were tested with are 99.97% full relatives. Of course we can't usually give absolute guarantees, but in your case, no question! You share the same parents.'

'Really?' I gasped in a strangled sort of voice. 'Both parents? You're kidding?'

'No, I'm not kidding, Mrs Edwards.'

'Well, what does it mean underneath that, the bit about 96% for half-sibship?'

'Well, that's just a baseline test. We do that one first. That proves you are at least half-sisters. But in your case that is irrelevant, as the top figure proves you are full sisters.'

'Wow! You've made my day!'

I called Jenny straightaway. I had hardly taken it in myself yet, but I was desperate to share it with her.

She picked up the phone. 'J-j-jenny . . .'

'What is it? Have you heard anything yet?'

Yes. Yes, I have.'

'Well, what does it say?'

I tried, but I couldn't get the words out, I was so excited.

'You're upset, aren't you?'

'Not upset. Shocked!' I paused, trying to calm down enough to tell her. 'We're full sisters!'

'That's wonderful.' I could imagine her beaming face. 'I'm so thrilled.'

'Me too.'

'It's nothing we didn't already know. This just proves it, doesn't it?'

We talked on for a while as I related to her what the chart showed and what the woman at the laboratory had said. We were both so excited, we cried and laughed all at once. But Jenny was right. In our hearts, we'd felt it all along. We weren't just half-sisters any more. We were full sisters.

I was non-stop on the phone that morning. After I'd finished speaking with Jenny, I dialled Dennis's number in Texas. It rang and rang. I thought I must have missed him and was about to put the phone down when he answered.

'I've got the DNA results.'

'Really? What do they say?'

'We're full sisters.'

He was happy for me of course. Then he said, 'I can't believe that your own mother would do that to you.'

'But don't you realize? The first thing it says to me is that my father is not my father any more!'

'You mean you went through all that for nothing?'

I heard myself laugh a brittle, high-pitched peal. It was a kind of relief, I suppose. Yes, he had been a terrible father, but now that I knew he wasn't my father at all, that explained everything. Why hadn't I realized before? I felt stupid not to have questioned it when I was younger. It just didn't occur to me.

As I put the phone down, suddenly the shock hit me. Total shock. I went into the bathroom and stared at my face in the mirror. I studied every feature and line of it. I didn't know who this person was who was looking back at me. Who was I? Who did I look like?

Suddenly, in front of that mirror, waves of grief washed over me. It was grief for the man I had always thought was my dad, who had died when I was twenty-one years old. I thought back to the day we had left South Africa, Simon, Scott and I. As we went through into departures, I had turned to say goodbye to my parents. I remember Tommy warded me off and shook my hand.

'Goodbye,' he'd said in a cold voice. 'Have a good flight.'

It was this coldness from both my parents that had made it easy for me to leave them behind. I never saw him again. In the years since then I suppose I had tried to remember only the good things and forget the bad. Perhaps I'd mellowed and buried all that misery where it belonged, in my past. But now it had all jumped out at me again.

With the knowledge that Tommy was not my father came a clarity I'd never known before. As a little girl I had always wanted him to love me, but as I grew older I think I sensed that he never really did, or at least was incapable of showing any love towards me. I could remember very few happy moments in his company, except when I was very young and going on those trips in his lorry with him. But something changed at some point, I'm sure of that. Perhaps something revealed during one of their flaming rows, or maybe an unexpected meeting. What effect would that have had on Tommy?

From then on I would have been a continuous irritant, eating away at him. I can see now that they were struggling to deal with their demons every day and I was in the way, making it worse.

I wanted to call Jenny again, but I was now beset with a gnawing anger, having just been so elated. I had to sit down and sort out some of the confusion in my mind.

There had been so many lies and deceptions. They had even lied on my birth certificate, to hide the truth. Why had I always believed everything I was told? This was one more proof of betrayal. They had all betrayed me . . . and they had betrayed Jenny too.

But who was my father, our father? Was it Wilfred Harrison? We felt we knew, ourselves, that he was, but we couldn't prove it. That was our next challenge, to try and find out for certain . . . if we could. I began to feel more positive again with a quest to undertake.

I spent the next few days trying to think of some way to confirm whether Wilfred Harrison was our father or not. Suddenly it came to me. I went to see Alice, one of my oldest cousins.

'Come in, sit down,' she said. 'How are you? Would you like a cup of tea? Have some cake.'

I told her about the DNA test.

'You know that means that Jenny and I are full sisters?'

'Yes.' She nodded and smiled a Cheshire cat smile.

'Well,' I continued, as calmly as possible. (I needed to make sure this didn't sound like a question.) 'We now know that Wilfred Harrison was our father.' I held my breath.

'Yes. He knew about you both.'

That was it – the proof! I felt like getting hold of Alice

round the throat and strangling her for never telling me. But I held my composure – I think she meant to be kind.

'I'm really glad that you're not Tommy's daughter. Nobody liked him. He was a bad man. We could all see that.' She paused. 'You're Wilf's daughter. And Jenny is Wilf's daughter too. You came from a good, upright family. They were lovely people.'

I did some research locally, which confirmed quite quickly that Wilfred Harrison had died twenty-five years before. I checked the date with Jenny. We were both appalled to realize that when Jenny had first gone looking for Mercia and was told that her birth father was 'long gone', Wilfred was actually still alive. If she'd only known, she might have been able to trace him then and see for herself the kind of man he was.

I was relieved when I managed to track down Wilfred's brother, John. I called straightaway and arranged to visit him and his wife.

'I'll be proud to meet you, Helen,' he said. 'I'll ask my older sister to come and join us as well. I think she remembers your mother.'

The next day I went to their house. John hugged me straightaway. 'I'm so happy that you found us.'

It was a delight to meet them – such lovely people. They welcomed me with open arms and hearts. I explained the background as far as I knew it, and they confirmed what we had thought, and what our cousin had finally told me. Wilfred Harrison was our father. Indeed, when they showed me photos of him, I instantly saw a likeness in both Jenny and me.

Wilfred's sister remembered Mercia and Wilfred going out together for quite a long time, during and after the war.

'She was beautiful, you know. She used to do my hair. I

used to say, "Mercia, will you do my hair, just like yours?" She usually did.'

'Wilfred was a sweet man,' said his sister-in-law. 'Everybody loved him.'

I loved what I was hearing about the man who was my father. What a contrast with Tommy. They went on to tell me that Wilfred had six children. He was a wonderful father, and the other main thing in his life was his love of animals, especially dogs. So that was how Jenny and I gained our love of dogs. He worked in the mine at Seghill. He was there throughout the war; as mining was a reserved occupation he wasn't allowed to join up. He joined the Home Guard instead. Apparently, one day he went home to show his mother his training routine.

'There he was, in full uniform in their kitchen, coming to attention,' said his brother, 'when up went his bayonet – straight through the ceiling!'

'They walked out together for ages, you know, and Wilfred doted on Mercia,' said his sister. 'His eyes used to follow her around the room. Then, all of a sudden, they weren't going out together any more. I don't know what happened. Your mother went away and we didn't see her for a long time, not till she came back with you.'

'Yes,' added her brother. 'I always thought there was a skeleton in the closet, you know. Something going on. It was such a close-knit community in those days. Everyone knew who was walking out with who.'

'Why did they not just get married?' said his wife. 'What happened? It can't have been that bad. What a tragedy.'

'We'll probably never know,' I sighed. What else could I say? My life could have been so different.

As I looked at the photo of Wilfred smiling warmly into the camera, I almost felt he was smiling at me. He was standing with his beloved dog. I could see the kindness in his eyes and a deep well of sadness opened up inside me. My whole life had been tangled up in the lives and selfish whims of my parents. I had had such a miserable childhood in so many ways. I wonder sometimes how I survived that degree of abuse, the psychological abuse in particular, and still managed to grow up relatively sane!

My anger had turned into a kind of grief for the father I never met, for my lost childhood, the sisters I never knew till now. Most of all I grieved for my true father, Wilfred Harrison, who had lived in the same village, yet was completely unknown to me. He could have been one of those black-faced miners on their way home from the pit and waving at me, a little girl sitting in the window, as they went by. Why did I never know? It seems he did.

Jenny and I are both in our sixties now. The time for making allowances and excuses for my mother's behaviour is long past. No child should have to grow up with that legacy from their own mother, should they?

These kindly people, my unknown uncle and aunts, had given me their morning and I knew that Wilfred's brother was particularly keen to watch the golf that afternoon, so I left them reluctantly. I told them about Jenny and her golfing career. I said I'd bring her with me to see them next time she was up.

'Yes, please. We'd love to meet her too.'

As I related all this to Jenny when I got home, we realized that we now had six more half-siblings that we hadn't known about. Our family had grown so fast.

'From being an only child, I now have one full sister and eight half-siblings!'

She couldn't quite believe it. 'I just feel robbed that I never met my father. I could have done. But it was taken away from me by all the deceit that Mercia perpetrated.'

Soon after that, Jenny contacted one of Wilfred's daughters, but they hadn't known about us, so it was a shock for them. She said they needed time. Frustrating as it is, we shall just have to wait and see if they want to meet one day. Or perhaps, like Patricia, they'd prefer to pretend this didn't happen. We have to respect their feelings. It all just brings Jenny and me even closer together.

Now I knew who my real father was, and I had a full sister, I felt as if I could at last lay the past to rest. But it wasn't going to be quite as simple as that.

CHAPTER 38

Helen

New Challenges

The revelations about my mother's secrets and lies, and the family's concealment of the truth over all these years, began to eat away at me. I've had to learn from my earliest childhood that the only way for me to survive harm is to be strong, like an iceberg, with most of my emotion buried beneath the surface, internalized. Through all the years, each blow, physical or verbal, left a mark for ever, but I learned not to let them see how much they hurt me. It was safest that way. I got used to crying alone.

I had grown up feeling my mother owned me – that I was merely a piece of property. I was the baby she kept, but I paid the price for that. She expected me to be eternally grateful to her. I cared for her when she was ill, but who cares for the carers? Blame and disdain were her only responses.

Now I realized I had been betrayed by Mercia, and by all her family. My whole life was based on a lie. I was devastated, seared to the core, angry with everyone who had lied and kept my own story from me and kept my sister and me apart. I was even angry with George for a while. We were so close, and yet he kept the truth from me. I realize now that he didn't dare say anything, like everyone else. But I could no longer stop my emotions from rising to the surface and impacting on everyone around me. Gradually I filled up with all that anger knotted up inside me, until one day I could hold it in no longer and it poured out over my family – all those I loved. Now I was clawing my way up a mountain, unaware that I was pushing my companions aside, but the summit rose further out of reach with every move I made.

The kids noticed it. 'You need to move on, Mum,' said Donna. 'Try and put it all behind you and not dwell on it.'

'I'm not dwelling on it,' I said, indignant. 'There's a difference between dwelling on it and getting stuck in it, unable to escape.'

They were both impatient with me at that time. They didn't seem to be able to understand how I'd become caught in this mire of anger and couldn't find my way out. But then they didn't know most of the worst things that had happened to me, or just how manipulative my mother had been. After all, she had looked after them daily as children far better than she had me, all positive and loving towards them, in contrast to her psychological manipulation of me as a child. Mercia was their grandma, and they didn't deserve to have me mar their memories of her, so it wasn't surprising that they felt I should buck up and get on with my life. I don't blame them for that.

I was seriously floundering under the weight of all these revelations, though, and I knew it. But I couldn't climb above this as I'd always managed to in the past. My mind was in turmoil and I felt I was beginning to drown.

I must have been impossible to live with. Dennis, who knew everything I had been through, was tremendously patient

and supportive. It wasn't easy for him. We had both had difficult issues to deal with on a daily basis even before all this
came along, but in some ways that helped us to help each
other. He has always been a great support to me and tried
his best to help me through. Sam was great as well. Two
fantastic guys.

But still I couldn't break through this wall of resentment.
What did I do to deserve it? What did Jenny do? She had
come face to face with her demons as well, about her adoption. That was also my mother's doing. Why had everything
always been my fault? Perhaps it was. The guilt loaded onto
me as a child was still there, but now it was finally wreaking
its revenge, not on Mercia, but on me.

I withdrew into a bitter cloud, cut off from everyone. I
wept for no apparent reason. I couldn't sleep for long, always
pacing around in the middle of the night. And when I did
sleep, I had nightmares most nights. I was imprisoned in my
own anger. It felt evil and destructive, but I couldn't shed it.
I couldn't move on. I couldn't get myself out of that ravenous
fury, silently raging at my mother. It changed me. I became
almost malicious towards them all – Mercia and her family.
In my confusion I developed a hatred for them and what
they had done.

I know I'm not a person who hates others no matter what.
Now, looking back, I can see that this hatred was really about
the dysfunctional childhood I had had, and not being loved
or protected by them. It was about my lost childhood, and
having to grow up too fast and deal with their issues. It was
a mixture of hatred and fury that besieged me. I was usually
such a calm person – self-controlled, laid back even. That
was the usual me, not the monster I was turning into. As a

trained therapist, I recognized what was happening and rang the doctor, who referred me to a counsellor.

It was quite funny the first time I went to see him. He's a bit of a character, and I love eccentric people, so from the very beginning I couldn't help smiling, which relaxed me, of course. He stood up to greet me, his trousers turned halfway up his legs and his socks rolled like sausages round his ankles. His cardigan was done up wrongly and he had a big cowlick in his hair. I thought: I really like you! I felt this was going to be all right.

He started by encouraging me to talk, about my childhood and the years since. About my family, finding Jenny and my hopes for the future. Gradually the rancour poured out, the rage that had recently enveloped me. I had so much to be glad about and to look forward to, so why could I not shed this terrible inner fury?

'You're justified in your anger,' he said. 'You're feeling guilty because you're angry, but you're justified in that. You're right. You *have* been betrayed and you *have* been lied to. It's true. You *have* had a lousy childhood. It's not you; it's what happened to you.'

He affirmed my resentment as understandable. I felt encouraged that someone objective should see it like that. The greater the mandate he gave me for being angry, the more that inner rage ebbed away.

'It seems to me that you've come out of it with remarkable strength of character,' he continued. 'Indeed, it was your strength that got you through it all. If you hadn't been as strong a person as you are, if you'd been someone who buckled under at times of emotional stress, you may well not have survived. And I'm serious about that.'

The more I told him about the past, and about Jenny and me discovering each other, the more impressed he seemed to be.

'You know, I hear a lot of people's stories in this job. But I really think that your story, the story of you and Jenny, is an exceptional one.'

He gave me some relaxation techniques, which of course I knew from my own therapist training, but it helped me to focus on them. He also taught me various strategies for coping day by day. Walking the dogs was one of them – that's a pleasure of course, and it worked. Gradually, almost imperceptibly, I became calmer again and life slipped back into its usual rhythms.

After six weeks, he said to me, 'I don't really think there is anything more I can do for you. You're doing very well. So I'm going to discharge you. But if you need to come back, just give me a call.'

He was right, of course. I realized as he said it that in that short period I really had turned round. I had got myself out of that cloud of rancour, with his help, and now I was ready to shed my past and move forward.

On an early spring day recently, Dennis and I drove to Embleton to the beach Jenny and I both played on as children, and the golf course where Jenny grew up, where she first learned to play golf. We drove down the stone-walled country lanes, through tunnels of cherry blossom, past fields of shaggy sheep with their lambs and occasional swathes of daffodils on the grass banks. I was travelling the roads of my childhood again, the only really happy times, when we used to meet Uncle James, Auntie Gladys and my cousin

Malcolm and go off for days out to the coast in our rickety old cars that as often as not broke down on the way.

Dennis and I arrived outside the Dunstanburgh Castle golf clubhouse at Embleton and parked the car just as a haar came in from the North Sea, sweeping its mist like a rolling carpet across the dune grasses towards us. We went inside to have a drink and let the mist disperse. I didn't need to speak to anyone. I knew what I was looking for.

There was a glass cabinet in the bar full of grand silver cups, and a whole room decked out with trophies and plaques. I scanned them all, one by one, and blazed with pride every time I saw my sister's name engraved or painted in gold. She had been part of this place, just as it was part of her. Now it was part of my story too.

The mist dispersed and the weak sun came out as we walked the path Jenny had walked so often before across the tufted dunes until we came to a primitive wooden bridge. No handrail; just wooden sleepers, blanched by the years of north-eastern weather, laid parallel across a meander of the stream. As I crossed the bridge, I felt like I was walking back in time across the links and down to the golden sands of our childhood. To the far right, on its headland, the ruins of Dunstanburgh Castle rose eerily above the last vestiges of mist that wreathed its foundations. To the left were the Emblestones and the bank with the bungalows strewn across the top like jacks in the children's game.

How many times did Jenny play with her friends nearby while I built my sandcastles? How often did I walk past her practising golf on the green outside her door? We'll never know. But Jenny does remember one time, and recognized the photo I showed her as the image in her memory of me that day. We were both oblivious of our circumstances then, so close to each other without realizing. We each walked that path across the dunes separately before, but now we no longer need to walk separate paths. Our paths are no longer parallels, never to meet. Now they are linked together and we have built our own bridges to join them.

It would have been so much easier, of course, if someone had given us the information we needed from the start, or at least earlier, as we made our separate journeys. Mercia could have given us the keys. She had them in her hand, but she made the deliberate choice of concealing them, holding them out of our reach. Our families knew where the keys were, but she forbade them to tell us. Mercia was the keeper of the keys, the one person who had locked every possible access to our story.

Even without those keys, Jenny and I have eventually broken through and found each other. It has been a wonderful journey, our new life as sisters. We're still learning about each other and making new memories together.

But like that rickety old wooden bridge with no handrails, there were still additional details to find to complete our narrative, and an important visit we needed to make.

CHAPTER 39

Helen & Jenny

One Regret

Helen

One evening, sitting at home with Dennis, I took out my mother's 'treasure box' – a shoebox, full of old birthday cards, letters and other things she kept. I've been through it a million times since she died. As I picked my way through the box I came across an old black and white photo. I took it out and looked at it. I thought I recognized the child as another distant cousin. She has lived abroad for many years but we talk occasionally.

I turned the photo over to make sure, but all that was written on the back was the date – 1937. There was nothing to say if that was the date of the photograph or the date of the child's birth. Knowing how much older than me she is, I worked out that her year of birth probably was 1937. I looked more closely at the child's features. I felt sure it was her, but at that moment I was suddenly struck by her resemblance to my mother. Well of course, she is related, so it was not surprising that there should be a family likeness. But strange, I thought, that this cousin's photo should be in

Mercia's treasure-box when she had so few photos in there.

I handed the photo across to Dennis. 'Who do you think that is?'

His answer was immediate. 'It's your mother when she was young.'

'No, it's my cousin in America.'

'Diana?'

'Yes, Cousin Diana.'

He looked at the back of the photo. 'How old was your mother in 1937?'

'She was seventeen.'

He gave me a long look. I could tell he was thinking the same as me. In fact, I think he was ahead of me.

The next morning I told Jenny about this and she was almost speechless. Then I called Diana. She answered the phone and we talked about family things for a while. Finally I plucked up courage to say why I had really called her. I explained about finding her photo, the date on the back and some of my conversation with Dennis.

'I'm not sure which photo it was,' she said, 'but my parents doted on me so much that they took a lot of photos of me. So it's not really surprising that Mercia had one of them in her box.'

'Well, it's the only photo she had that wasn't immediate family.'

She paused. 'So what are you saying?'

'Do you realize how much you look like my mother?'

'It's a family likeness.'

'I think it might be closer than that. You know about Jenny

and Patricia – do you think you could have been Mercia's daughter, given to your parents to adopt?'

'No, of course not. No way. That's a crazy idea. In any case, I'm sure my parents would have told me if I was adopted. They never told lies. I completely believe everything they told me about my birth.'

She was indignant that I should even have thought such a thing. 'In fact,' she continued, 'I'm so sure about this that I think we should have a DNA test to prove it.'

'Really?' I could hardly believe she had suggested the one thing I didn't dare ask her, assuming she would refuse. 'That's a good idea. I could get it organized through the same people Jenny and I used, if you like.'

'Yes, that would be fine. You organize it and I'll do my bit. You'll see. I'm sure it will prove you wrong.'

We all did the tests, Diana, Jenny and me. Weeks later, the results came back positive. Diana was definitely our half-sister, another half-sibling! I emailed the results page to Diana and to Jenny. Immediately I received a brief reply from Diana, convinced that the test was wrong.

'I'm definitely not Mercia's daughter,' she insisted. 'But don't let that worry you. We're all of us sisters in the end.'

I called Jenny and told her what Diana had said.

'Isn't it strange?' Jenny, always so straightforward herself, was perplexed by Diana's response. 'She insisted she wanted proof, and now she says the proof is wrong.'

'I think she wants it to be wrong,' I suggested. 'She has very firm ideas about things, and she seems to have convinced herself they made a mistake.'

'I suppose she doesn't want to disbelieve her parents.'

'Well, we could all say that, couldn't we? But look how wrong we would have been!'

'Yes, we would never have found each other for a start.'

'She did say that it didn't matter because we were all sisters in a way.'

'Well, just when we thought we'd got all our mother's children sorted out,' said Jenny, 'here comes another one, the very first of her babies, and she was given away too. That was obviously where all the lies began!'

'But isn't it amazing? Do you realize we each now have one full sister and nine half-siblings!'

'Don't blame your mother for all this, Helen,' said one of my other cousins recently. 'Don't blame her. What you need to remember is that Auntie Mercia was a beautiful woman. She was this tall, Titian-haired, glamorous woman with movie-star looks. She turned heads wherever she went.'

'That's what caused all this trouble,' I cut in. 'She turned too many heads! This is my mother you're speaking about – the woman who had all these illegitimate children.'

'Yes, but you're remembering your mother, and I'm remembering the beautiful woman she was when she was young.'

'Hmm!'

'I remember when Wilf, your and Jenny's father, used to come round to Grandma's house with her. He adored her. He absolutely adored her. His eyes would never leave her as she walked around the room.'

'Yes, his sister said that.'

'He watched her every movement. It was a great love story.'

'So why did it end?'

'That was the mystery. Nobody knew what happened. She

just disappeared without him. He waited for her. He adored her. It was only much later, after she came back to Seghill with Tommy and you, that she told Grandma you were Wilf's baby.'

'Did Wilfred know what happened, do you think?'

'I think he must have done. He married only two or three months after Mercia came back with you and Tommy. I'm sure he must have realized, and perhaps married on the rebound.'

'Did Wilfred know about Tommy?'

'Yes, I'm sure he did. Seghill was a small place.'

'That would explain a lot.'

'Yes.'

'And Wilfred must have seen me around the village. Perhaps he even spoke to me and I never knew.'

'Maybe.'

'Why didn't you tell me all this before?'

'It was Mercia. She swore us all to secrecy. And Tommy threatened any of us who told you. He was a forceful man.'

'Yes. I certainly knew that, every day of my childhood.' I couldn't suppress a slight shudder at the memory.

Then she told me something else I didn't know.

'Mercia went away to have Jennifer at a home for unmarried mothers in Stannington.'

'But . . . that's near where I live now.'

'Yes, I know.'

'What was this place called?'

'They didn't tell me that, and I didn't find out till much later.'

'I must tell Jenny. I wonder whether the building is still there. I shall have to try and find out. I could go and see it. Jenny could come with me to see it next time she comes up.'

I called Jenny, but she was out, so I sat and pondered about my mother's babies. Diana, born illegitimate when my mother was only seventeen, was given away to a childless relative. George, her only legitimate child, was born in 1940, when his father was away at war, so Mercia was alone with her young baby. Then there was the war effort, and women doing the men's jobs. At some stage she had to go and work in the ship yards, building tanks and machine-guns. Twelve-hour shifts at night. Of course the bombers used to come up the Tyne especially to bomb the ship yards, usually in the early hours. They were a prime target and there were bomb-raids most nights. She was just a young woman from a small village. It must have been terrifying for her. I think she did what she had to do to survive, to have some sort of a life, as so many of them did during the war. 'Live for the day,' as they used to say. I can't blame her for that. There were so many women like her.

Patricia was born in 1943 and again was given away to relatives, Jenny in 1948 and adopted out. Then I came along in 1950. Why did she keep me, I wonder? I suppose it was because she hooked up with Tommy and could pass me off as his. But I never looked like him. Why didn't I question that? And I suppose I should really have been named Helen Dick, because that was still my mother's surname when I was born, but of course, that never occurred to me either. My birth certificate was a big lie – two lies really – Mercia's surname and Tommy being my father. But I didn't realize the second of those till recently. Why wasn't I even suspicious? I must have been wearing blinkers all those years – quite oblivious. I can't believe I missed so many clues along the way.

If she was so beautiful, I wonder how many other boyfriends Mercia had? All the adulation definitely turned her head. She was full of life and laughter when she was the centre of attention in a family gathering, as long as Tommy wasn't there. He always soured those occasions.

She demanded that adulation from him at home too, but she didn't often get it. I think that was why she continually goaded him into some kind of reaction. Good or bad, at least it was some kind of recognition, though she suffered from his temper as much as I did.

Mercia could have been anything – a glamorous model perhaps – but she ended up as my mother. For someone whose essential nutrient was attention, this was a considerable blow. When she wasn't noticed, as a housewife, for example, she was miserable. She craved admiration. Even to the extent of competing with her own daughter. Being a child, I sapped her glory. No wonder I had such a hard time with her.

Many years later, when I trained to be a nurse, I read about narcissistic personality syndrome. It was a revelation. I was reading about my mother. She was a classic case.

I could never do anything right for Mercia. I was always in the wrong and always to blame. That was me as a child. My parents convinced me in the end. The damage was done. All through my life, I continued to apologize. I think that's part of the reason I felt so confused about it all after Jenny found me and the family started to reveal some of Mercia's secrets. Even then, as always, I assumed my confusion and my anger were my fault too. Talking it through with the counsellor made me realize that and come to terms with it at last. Now I know I don't have to say 'sorry' any more.

Walking the dogs one day, Dennis and I were chatting as usual and somehow came round to the subject of Mercia again. Following all the revelations of her lies and deceits, and since the counselling sessions, I felt I could stand back and take a more dispassionate look at my strained relationship with her throughout our lives together.

'I still can't help wondering why I always went along with it all,' I said. 'Why did I let her dominate our lives and insidiously destroy our relationships?'

Dennis gave me a look. 'Why do *you* think it was?'

'Well, I think the main reason was the conditioning I'd had from a very young age. I was conditioned that Mercia came first and that I was there for her needs, not the other way round. I felt that she owned me.'

'Really?'

'Yes. It was easier to go along with it all, rather than causing any rows or fights. She was so dominant and controlling when she lived with Simon, me and the children, and we had both been so conditioned by then that it was the easiest option to go along with her wishes. Anything for the sake of peace, I suppose.'

'Hmm. Was that the only reason, do you think?' Dennis prodded further.

I thought for a moment, then continued. 'She was so dependent on us that we didn't know how she could get on without us, and I was always anxious about that. But of course, I didn't know then all the manipulative things she had done from the very beginning. If I had, things would have been different. But Simon felt it was easier to blow in the wind than stand against it, and I agreed with that.' I paused to think. 'Of course there was one other big reason – just before Tommy died, Mercia had asked him what she should do if she was left alone, and he said, "Go to Helen. She will look after you." This felt like an order, and I had always had to jump to his orders, so this one also had to be obeyed.'

Dennis had listened patiently as I'd waffled through all this. Now he gave me a quizzical look that unnerved me.

'Do you know what I think?' he said.

'No?' I'd never asked him.

'You just adored your mother and you always felt guilty to leave her. You were totally blind to that. After all, she was abused, just as you were. You were together in that.'

I was stunned, speechless.

'A child can ignore so much and refuse to believe anything uncomfortable. You saw her then in the same position as you – you were both the abused. So you always felt protective towards her, regardless of how she was with you. Remember, you had no awareness of all the betrayals she perpetrated on you. So it was about solidarity, and maybe always the hope that she would show her love for you, just as much as you loved her.'

I tried to take all this in. It turned me cold. I'd never considered my relationship with Mercia from this angle before.

'Do you think I'm right?

Slowly I emerged from the fog of my confusion and nodded. 'Yes . . . I think you are right. I think that's exactly how it was. Why did I never see it for myself?'

'Maybe because you were too close to it and too wearied

by everything at the time,' said Dennis. 'The shadow of Mercia has hung over you all your life, and perhaps it always will.'

This conversation has stayed with me. Dennis was absolutely right. Now at last I understand.

Finding Jenny has helped me to put the past where it belongs and move forward. There is so much joy in having a sister after so many solitary years. We laugh a lot together – that's a great healer. Both of us have a deep well of inner strength, germinated in our past. It has made us the two people we are today – survivors.

Jenny

I've said to Helen that I feel guilty because I had the life. Not a lot of money, not a lot of glamour or possessions, but unstinting love. I couldn't have had two better parents, who cared for me and look after me brilliantly.

It was a great shock for me to learn that I was the more fortunate one. I escaped when I was six weeks old. Helen is really only escaping now.

Looking back on all those years of searching and finally finding Helen, it's been a big thing in both our lives. It's not that I feel any different. I still live the same life. But I now have my sister to fill the void I always had. Helen is that something that I always knew was missing – a sister of my own. We speak to each other all the time, but we live three hundred and fifty miles apart, so we don't get to meet up much. The last time Helen came down here, we had a great time together.

'It would be so good to have you living just round the corner,' I said.

'Do you know what? I love it here.' She smiled. 'It's great!'

I know it isn't likely to happen, though. Her children are up there and ours are down here and the family business is down here too. At least we can talk as often as we like, and we do chat for ages once we start! Phone calls often last for an hour or two, most days, and texts on top of that. Well, we have to make up for lost time.

I know we'll always be close now, and I hope our relationship continues to develop. Every time we talk we find out something new about each other. That's how we discovered so many similarities and coincidences. It was quite spooky to find we had so much in common.

I would strongly recommend anyone to go ahead and track down their missing relatives. You might well get knocked back along the way, like I was, but stick at it if you can. The outcome is fantastic. I'd say, 'Go for it! And don't take no for an answer.'

We have a lot to look forward to, most of all to be a greater part of each other's lives, doing things together. When Helen was here last it was absolutely brilliant. We just wandered along the high street laughing and talking all the time. These are the simple, special times we've missed, so it's important that we do things and go places together now. That's what families do, isn't it? Share their lives with each other.

Helen

'Nothing surprises me after all this,' I said to Jenny. 'The sky could fall in and I wouldn't flinch. And if, somehow, some revelation came out that we were actually twins, I wouldn't be surprised.'

Our relationship is very strong and we are so alike, not just physically, but in the way we think. Sometimes I decide I'll just call Jenny, and the phone will go and it's her. Occasionally I'll send her a card to say, 'Hi, how are you?', and she'll post me one on the same day. It seems almost telepathic. I always knew there was part of me missing, but now I feel more complete.

We're not together on a daily basis, Jenny and I, but we don't need to be. We each know the other is there. That's the main thing. We both really want this sister relationship. We need it. So we're determined that nobody is going to take it away from us again. This is ours. It's something we have waited a long time for.

We each feel that we have done things as sensitively as possible, because that's what we're both like. We've tried not to upset or hurt anyone. We only wanted to find out what should have been our right to know from the beginning. But the penny has dropped. All this happened because the adults in our lives were not being considerate or thoughtful towards us, keeping secrets and refusing to answer simple but crucial questions. I wouldn't change anything about the way we acted on this journey, except for one thing. We should have done it years ago!

On a search like ours, people have to be prepared for some

pain along the way. There was a lot of pain in our story. A lot of rejection and opposition. As adults, we all need to reflect on the choices we make and understand the potential consequences of our actions. The decisions we make as parents can affect a child for the rest of their life. Such a decision needs to be the best one; not necessarily for the adult, but best for the child. We all have the right to know our own stories, and nobody should deprive a child of that.

Jenny and Sam adopted Josh and they told him right from the start. Jenny made a book for him all about it. It's his book. They are planning to take him over to see his birth country. That's a healthy approach to adoption.

For us, Jenny and me, finding each other has been very healing, cathartic. Before Jenny found me, there was something wrong in my life, something bad. I always knew it was bad, and I thought it was me, because that's what I was always told, and I came to believe it. But it wasn't me, and I know that now. All that poisonous influence has finally gone. I don't mean life is all chocolate boxes and fairies, but it is positive now, and so am I.

The joy of Jenny and me is in the fact that we have found each other, that we wanted to be found. It might be late, but it's not too late. We're like kids together, catching up on lost time, and it's a joyful feeling just having each other at last.

Jenny and I now focus on today and tomorrow, not the woes of yesterday. But there is one regret that lingers in both our hearts – the longing, the most natural longing, of a child to know her father. A longing denied us by the family's deceptions. That regret will be with us for ever.

On the anniversary of Wilfred's death, we made a special journey together. We found out that there is a memorial to him at the crematorium, so we went there. We found his name in gold letters in the book of remembrance, and we found his memorial plaque. We stood quietly together and cried as we thought about all the good things we had learned about him.

We left a big bouquet of spring flowers for him. We had intended to leave a card anonymously so as not to upset anyone who might see it after we'd gone. But at the last minute, I changed my mind.

'Dammit, he's our father – no more secrets.'

So we wrote our card and left it on show with the flowers:

Wilfred Harrison, Our Dad, with love always,
Helen and Jenny xxxx

EPILOGUE

After we had finished writing this book, we discovered a new and unexpected trail of clues, which we followed to unearth the most exciting secret of all.

Jenny

We both thought we had found out everything there was to be found out, with only a few loose ends left to tie up. But one day I was sifting through some photos and documents when I picked up my original birth certificate and looked again at my place of birth – the Mona Taylor Maternity Home, Stannington. I knew Stannington was near Morpeth where Helen lives, so I called her.

'I know Stannington,' she said. 'But I've never heard of the Mona Taylor Maternity Home. I can ask around. If it's still there, I could go and have a look and maybe take some photos.'

'That would be great. I'd really like to try and find out what it was like there and what happened to me in those six weeks between my birth and my adoption.'

'And I'd like to know about my missing year,' added Helen. 'But I don't know if I'll ever be able to do that.' She paused. 'Have you tried looking up the Mona Taylor place online?'

'Yes, but I didn't find out much, except one important thing. The National Archives site says there are some patient records from the Mona Taylor that can be seen at Northumberland Archives.'

'Would they cover your birth date?'

'Yes, they're from 1948 to 1951, so they must include my birth in December 1948.'

'Would you like me to go down there and look at them for you? If you like, I could call them to see when they're open.'

Helen

I phoned the Northumberland Archives and spoke to their senior researcher.

'I'm afraid these files are closed for a hundred years,' he said. 'So you will need to apply for permission from the guardians for me to search them on your behalf.'

I called Jenny to tell her.

'I filled in the form, and he said he would do what he could, but we might have to wait for a while.'

'Well, I did some phoning round too,' said Jenny. 'And I spoke to somebody at the Family Placement and Adoption Team. Strangely enough, they're based in Morpeth. Anyway, the lady there couldn't tell me much about the Mona Taylor Maternity Home, but she did say something else that stunned me.'

'What was that?'

'Apparently the law changed in 1981, allowing adopted children to request to see their original adoption files. That was news to me. I've filled in the forms and she's sending them off for me, so now we've both got something to wait for.'

'Do you know what your file will contain?'

'No, but it might have all sorts of information I don't know about.'

These two new lines of enquiry were the start of a long haul of research to see if we could find out anything more about Jenny's birth and the six weeks before her adoption.

The Mona Taylor boxes were searched, but many of the records were missing and the rest were severely damaged by water, so there was nothing there. However, the archivist did find the admissions register, which listed Mercia Dick, admitted on 1 December 1948 and discharged on 11 December, and her address was given as Bowmer Bank, Morpeth. This was a new trail to follow.

Sadly, when it came, Jenny's adoption file contained nothing new, so that was a great disappointment. But one by one, we found other avenues to explore. We visited various archives, sent emails, made phone calls to others and spent many long hours on the internet. The clues were few and the waits for information endless. We were in the hands of the paper-shufflers. At every turn we came up against new brick walls and at times we felt it was hopeless, but there was something that kept us going when most people would probably have given up. I can't explain it. We both felt strongly that it wasn't over yet.

We were continuously amazed at the coincidences that tied us, even to the point that we often both attempted to call the other at the same time and got engaged signals. We joked about this. 'Do you think we could be twins?' Yet now, as the smallest of new clues began to come to light, this whim became less far-fetched and an increasingly serious possibility. But would we ever be able to find the answer?

One of the turning points in our quest was when I got out my own birth certificate again, the one I had found in my mother's desk as a child. I already knew that two important facts on this certificate were lies – my mother's surname, and Tommy being named as my father. I now began to wonder anew. I called Jenny.

'Supposing the date on my birth certificate is wrong?'

'What do you mean?' she asked.

'Well, you know we've always said we could be twins?' I took a deep breath. 'Maybe we could!'

'Because we're so alike?'

'Yes, but that's not all. Now that I think back to my childhood, why was I always the biggest in the class? And why did I do so well in lessons and in sports? That could have been because I was older than the others, couldn't it? And I remember distinctly a feeling of being different from my classmates when I was at secondary school. I used to think that was just my background, but now I'm not so sure.'

'That's spooky.'

'Yes, and even amongst my cousins, I seemed to fit in more easily with those older than me than the younger ones. I've never really thought about it before, but now I'm wondering . . .'

'So you think your birth certificate could be a fake?'

'It's possible, isn't it? They told two lies on it, so the whole thing could be a lie. I think I need to do some more research into this.'

'Well, we might find some clues in some of the other records we've requested.'

'Yes, and I think I'll go along tomorrow and see if I can find the registration of my baptism.'

'Hey, this is exciting!'

'I hope we can find out for sure, one way or the other,' I said. 'But yes, wouldn't it be great?'

The next day I went to the Civic Centre in Newcastle to look at the parish registers and found my baptism on 3 May 1950. At first I was disappointed it was 1950. But then I noticed that it gave my date of birth as 24 April 1950 – three weeks later than the date given on my birth certificate! What was going on here? Couldn't they even remember when my birthday was? My internal alarm bells were clanging wildly and I had to sit down quietly to calm down and think this through.

Over a period of five months, we must have spent a fortune between us on our researches, mostly to no avail. On many occasions we were frustrated by endless bureaucracy and legal issues. On one occasion we even had to invoke the Freedom of Information Act to access our own details.

Whilst there were many disappointments along the way, we did find out some startling things, and not all of them in the archives. My cousin Alice came up with a surprising comment.

'Mercia was still seeing Wilfred, you know, when she was

living with Tommy, while he was on driving jobs away from home,' said Alice. 'I think that went on for quit᠈ a while.'

'Really?' I was astonished at Mercia's audacity. 'That was a bit dangerous,'

'Yes, I suppose so. But Wilfred definitely knew about you both,' she said.

Thinking about this afterwards, I couldn't help wondering now how that could be if we were born separately and Jenny was adopted before Mercia went back to Seghill.

I discovered where the Mona Taylor Maternity Home had been and went to visit its empty building, disused now but in a reasonable state. First I took some photographs, then a woman came over and asked me if I'd like to go inside. She took me round and showed me the institutional passageway that led to the mother and baby rooms. I shuddered as I imagined Mercia entering that stark, cold corridor in labour.

'It was really weird,' I explained to Jenny after my visit. 'When I was standing in the reception area, I had the distinct sensation that I had been there before. I couldn't explain it, I just felt the hairs stand up on the back of my neck, and my whole body turned cold for a few seconds.'

'Well, maybe you have been there before.'

We requested a search of the Midwives' Files, and after the usual frustrating wait, we had an email that said there was 'an item of a sensitive nature' that would require more permissions and some counselling before I could see it. That sent my mind racing. What could it be? After several days of phone calls and emails to and fro, the authorities eventually relented and sent it to me. By this time I expected it to set out clear evidence that would end our search. But of course I was wrong, again. However, it was intriguing.

It was a handwritten letter from Mercia to Bowmer Bank, the hostel for unmarried mothers and babies, asking them to take her in for the four weeks leading up to the birth and afterwards. Why had she chosen to go there for this birth, when she'd had all her other babies at home in Seghill? Could it be because it was likely to be more complicated . . . or perhaps to conceal her actions?

I immediately forwarded this to Jenny and then phoned her to discuss it.

'She doesn't say anything about expecting twins.'

'No, but I don't think they often knew in those days,' I explained, drawing on my nurse's training. 'They were still using those old trumpet things to listen for a heartbeat. Once they'd found one, they didn't usually listen for another.'

'She sounds a bit desperate.'

'Well, it obviously worked. We've found out from the Mona Taylor admissions register that she was at Bowmer Bank before and after the birth.'

'And didn't Alice tell you that Mercia was there for about three months after my birth?' asked Jenny.

'Yes, that's right.'

'But I was adopted at six weeks old,' she paused. 'So why did she stay on after that?'

'Well, Alice was only a child then, so she might not have a very clear memory of it. Maybe I should give her a ring and ask her a bit more about that. But if Mercia did stay longer, there must have been a reason.'

I called Alice.

'We received a copy of a letter from Mercia to Bowmer Bank in 1948, just before Jenny's birth,' I told her. 'She had written to ask them to take her in.'

'Oh yes? What else did it say?' Alice sounded a bit guarded.

'Nothing we didn't already know, but she seemed rather desperate.'

'How did you find this letter?'

'Well, both Jenny and I are doing some new research into our births. I've found out I have two birth dates in 1950, and both of them look as if they could be wrong. It's made us think, and we're wondering now whether we could be twins, both born in December 1948. What do you think?'

'You couldn't possibly be twins,' Alice cut in very quickly. 'I remember my mam taking me to see you as a newborn baby in Newcastle in 1950,' she said. 'I told Jenny about this. Mercia was in the bed and you were in a crib alongside. Tommy was there, and so was his sister and her little girl.'

It was the first time I'd ever heard that. Alice would have been about ten if I was born in 1950, and I wondered if she had remembered it right.

'Are you sure?'

Later, as I thought it all through, I realized that Alice's memory of me must be mistaken, in part at least. Tommy's only sister was his half-sister, more than twenty years younger than him, and she would therefore only have been about ten years old in 1950, so she couldn't have had a little girl of her own.

And there was another thing . . . it was Alice who'd originally told me that nobody knew where Mercia and I were in the first year after my birth. Yet now she was saying she'd visited us in Newcastle. Knowing that Alice and all the rest of the family had been sworn to secrecy by Mercia and Tommy all those years ago, I assumed that would explain the disparity.

*

We both feared we'd never find out the truth. If it wasn't for Jenny, I think I would have given up. I'm sure she felt the same way, but together we kept going. Every now and then a small ray of hope glinted through and got us back on track.

One of these was the day I decided to contact Mercia's doctor's surgery to see if they still had her medical records. It was a long shot, I knew, but worth a try. I specifically asked them, 'If you do, could you please check for any references to her giving birth between 1948 and 1950.'

Knowing that Mercia had died eight years before, I didn't hold out much hope, so I was amazed when they rang back later to suggest I make an appointment to come and see her file.

'It was a discharge letter to Mercia's GP from the Mona Taylor Maternity Home,' I told Jenny on the phone that evening.

'Well, what did it say?'

I read out the exact wording to her. 'It was a kind of short form. It said at the top "Normal full-term delivery." Then underneath, where there was a large box headed "Suggestions", it just said one word.'

'What was that?'

'"COMPLICATED" in capital letters.'

'That's spooky. What do you think it could mean?'

'I don't know. But it made me wonder if this one word might hide a lot.'

'Mmm. So you think that, with it saying the delivery was normal, maybe the word "complicated" referred to Mercia's situation?'

'Exactly.'

We both paused to think that through. 'So,' Jenny continued.

'Perhaps it could have been a twin birth, but the doctor wasn't able to say? Maybe Mercia pleaded with him through her tears not to tell anyone she'd had twins.'

'That does seem possible, doesn't it?' I agreed. 'Especially knowing what we now know about some of the other facts she either hid or distorted.'

'Does it say anything else?'

I read her the rest: 'It says, "Infant breastfed. Weight satisfactory. Child to be adopted." And that's all.'

'So it was infant, not infants?'

'Yes. It does sound disappointing, doesn't it? But there was one other important thing I found out. I checked her medical record from 1948 to 1950, and there were no other births recorded!'

'Wow! So, that means the doctor had no record of your birth, other than if you were included on that form with me?'

'Yes, that's right,' I agreed. 'And when I asked them if I could have been born somewhere else without Mercia's GP knowing, they said. "Only if it was abroad."'

'What about the last bit, about the infant breastfed and the child to be adopted? Do you think it might be his way of covertly hinting that there were two babies?'

'I hadn't even thought of that!'

Apart from another adoption file that Jenny was still waiting for after more than two months, but which was unlikely to show anything new, we now felt we had exhausted every possibility. Mercia's GP's file was maybe the closest we were going to get, but not close enough. I was completely worn out with the search – really in the doldrums. But unknown to me, Jenny had suddenly come up with an idea. She called me to tell me about it.

'I'm in a bit of a dither now,' she said on the phone, her voice sounding breathy with excitement. 'I fished out the DNA results we had from our sibship test, and that 99.97% hit me in the face.'

'You mean because it's so high?'

'Exactly. So I looked up DNA labs near here and phoned two of them to ask what they thought. The man at the first one was flabbergasted by the extremely high sibling result of 99.97%. He said, "Sometimes in a sibship test we would get an average 70 to 80% positive result." He said we should take the twinship test. The other one said 99.97% is "a very strong result. You could well be fraternal twins." That's what he actually said!'

I was completely stunned. 'Why didn't we think of this before?'

'Isn't it amazing? We have known about this percentage for two years, and done all these months of research . . . Shall we take the test?'

'Yes, let's get on and do it straightaway. I'll call the Canadian lab we used originally and ask them to do it. They might still have our DNA on file, so that should make it quicker.'

'Great. Can you call them today?'

'Right now!'

Jenny

Helen phoned the lab and they confirmed they still had our samples and could do the twinship test straightaway and get back to us with the result within five working days. It was Thursday when we asked them to go ahead, so we would hear back by the following Thursday. We couldn't bear to wait. We were both so excited about this we could hardly think of anything else, knowing that in a week's time we might at last know for sure, one way or the other.

The next day was my husband Sam's birthday, and, following tradition, we had a big party late into the night. We all had quite a lot to drink, so it was a shock when the phone rang at seven on Saturday morning. I had just got up to feed the dogs, but I was a bit groggy and bleary-eyed. I shot across to pick up the phone before it woke Sam, who is never at his best till later in the day, especially after a party. As I picked it up I saw it was Helen and my heart immediately began to race.

'Well, the final result came through overnight,' she exclaimed, her voice rising. 'WE ARE TWINS!' she shrieked down the phone, her elation overflowing.

For an instant I was completely dumb. I couldn't say anything. The tears welled up and I started shaking with emotion. Then I heard my voice: 'Oh, I'm so happy! So very happy!' The tears were pouring down my face and I felt this enormous relief. It was an incredible feeling.

'I'm crying with excitement,' said Helen. 'Are you crying?'

'Yes, I'm crying too. I have hoped so much that we were twins, but it was almost too distant or ridiculous to hope for. I can hardly believe it!'

'Well, you can believe it. It's true. We *are* twins! Fraternal twins.'

I think I must have screamed at that point. Helen told me later that she heard me shrieking with joy as I rushed up the stairs, crying and laughing at the same time, to tell Sam.

He heard my scream and shot out of bed.

'WE ARE TWINS! WE ARE!' I shouted as I reached the bedroom.

'Bloody hell, Jenny,' he exclaimed. 'I thought somebody had died!'

I felt elated, deliriously happy and highly relieved, all at the same time. This had been a last dive into the unknown in our quest for the truth. Now our heads were reeling as we spent the next half hour going over all the connotations of how we had been separated.

'How do you choose, after giving birth to twins, which one to give away?'

'Or maybe she gave both of us away, but they didn't want me and gave me back,' suggested Helen. 'Or perhaps Tommy refused to keep us both, but I can't imagine how she could choose between us. It must have driven a wedge between them. That explains a lot.'

'All the lies and deceit, covering up our existence, concealing the truth.'

We talked and talked about Mercia, about Helen now having three birth dates, about the implications of her being older than she thought she was, about all sorts of things. There was so much more to say, but we would have to leave that till later.

My emotions bubbled up again. 'It's so exciting! I feel like dancing down the high street in my pyjamas and shouting it from the rooftops!'

Helen laughed. 'I'm just as excited and thrilled as you are,' said Helen. All I know is that I went to bed aged sixty-two and got up this morning aged sixty-three, going on sixty-four! And even worse, I thought I was an Aries all my life, and now I find I'm Sagittarius – I've been reading the wrong stars!'

I laughed as I said to her, 'Well, you've had one birthday present this year, so don't expect a second one in December!'

Helen

We've had many more long talks since then, realizing that we probably shared a cot for six weeks before Jenny was taken away from me and adopted, that we could have been breastfed together, that we were so close for all that time in the womb and afterwards. No wonder we always felt there was a void in our lives, a yearning for something we couldn't discern. We wondered again and again how Mercia could have chosen between us, how she could bring herself to give one of us away and keep the other.

We both feel that we have been in a wind tunnel and come out the other side. We are going to take a little while to recover, I think, but this feels so right. Jenny heard someone say on a TV programme recently, 'You will never be at peace until you have all the pieces.' It's true. It's been fulfilled for us. We both feel that we have found all the pieces, and that the jigsaw is complete.

What a joy that is.

ACKNOWLEDGEMENTS

We would both like to thank a number of people who have been instrumental in our finding each other and in the writing and publication of this book.

First we would like to acknowledge the great help and support of our families and friends.

Helen

I would like to thank my very dear husband Dennis Edwards, who has walked every step of this eventful journey with me and given me his unconditional support at every stage. Without him at my side I could not have written this book. I also thank my much loved son and daughter, for whom this has been a painful and unsettling time. They were there for the later part of my personal story, which was about my mother, but also their beloved Grandma. I dedicate the story of my life to them.

For my extended family and all of those who have known me all my life, thank you for your help, patience and understanding. Thank you also to all my family and friends in Texas, who always welcomed me with open arms and have shown great compassion during the unfolding of the story of Jenny and me.

To Wendy and Edd Ferguson, thank you. Without you, Jenny and I would not have found each other. You will always be my honorary cousins!

Finally, an enormous thank you to Jenny, my sister. Were it not for your determination and forbearance, we would not be together today. I bless the day that you found me.

Jenny

I would like to thank my dearest husband and the love of my life, Sam Lucas. Sam has supported me through this tumultuous quest for the truth. I shall be eternally grateful to him for his sincere love, guidance and strength, which has eased the pain and heartbreak along the way.

Thank you to my lovely daughter Katie and my sons Ben and Josh, all of whom have had to live with me through the highs and lows of this endless pursuit. I am sure at times they have found it difficult to understand the importance of my task, but I am positive they share the joy in my heart.

I want to thank my dearest cousin Wendy, her husband Edd, Simon and Louise, for all their continued love and support as they accompanied me on this momentous journey. Wendy, without your understanding and perseverance, I might never have found Helen and this book would not have been possible.

I thank my wonderful parents, Connie and Sid, who gave

me their endless love, fantastic opportunities and high expectations in life. It was drummed into me from an early age to do my best and never give up. I will always be grateful to them for their inspiration and direction.

Finally, to my dear sister Helen. Although it took nearly forty-four years to find you from when I first knew I was adopted, I am so very glad I didn't give up.

Together

We would like also to thank wholeheartedly Jacquie Buttriss, our ghostwriter, who has during the writing of this book become our dear friend, and who has shared our roller-coaster ride of overwhelming sadness and joy. She has guided and helped us to produce our story in this wonderful book for the world to read. We were extremely fortunate to find her.

Also, to Clare Hulton, our agent, and to Ingrid Connell of Macmillan, our publisher, who both believed in our story from the very first day, thank you.

A note from our ghostwriter, Jacquie Buttriss

Helen and Jenny have kindly, and most unusually, invited me to write a few words of my own to include in their book, a gesture which is characteristic of their openness and generosity of spirit.

This has been a harrowing and heart-warming story to tell, and I feel privileged to have been a partner in writing their book. They are both lovely people and deserve the great happiness they now share in each other as twins. They have been a dream to work with, and I shall treasure their friendship over the years to come.

Picture Acknowledgements

All photographs from the authors' own collections
apart from p. 4, bottom, © the *Newcastle Evening Chronicle*,
p. 8, main picture © Mike Sanders and the *Daily Mail*.

Every effort has been made to contact the copyright holders
of the material reproduced in this book. If any have been
inadvertently overlooked, the publisher will be pleased
to make restitution at the earliest opportunity.